THE BOX
WITH THE
SUNFLOWER
CLASP

THE BOX WITH THE SUNFLOWER CLASP

Uncovering a Jewish Family's Flight
to Wartime Shanghai

RACHEL MELLER

ICON

First published in the UK in 2023 by
Icon Books Ltd, Omnibus Business Centre,
39–41 North Road, London N7 9DP
email: info@iconbooks.com
www.iconbooks.com

This edition published 2024

ISBN: 978-178578-982-3
eBook: 978-178578-983-0

British Library Cataloguing in Publication Data.
A catalogue record for this book is available from the British Library.

Typeset by SJmagic DESIGN SERVICES, India.

Printed and bound in the UK

For Ilse and Lisbeth
And in memory of Claudia, 1947–2022

Contents

Abbreviated Family Trees

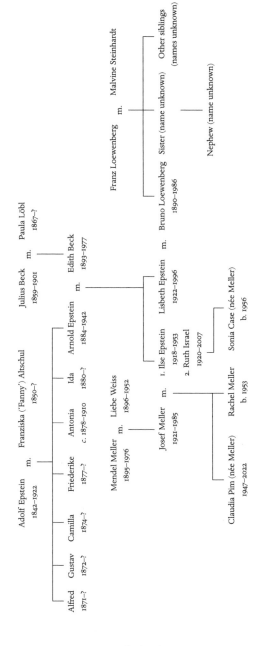

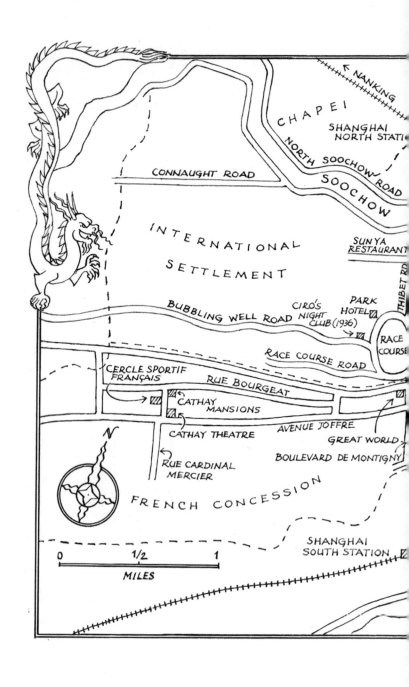

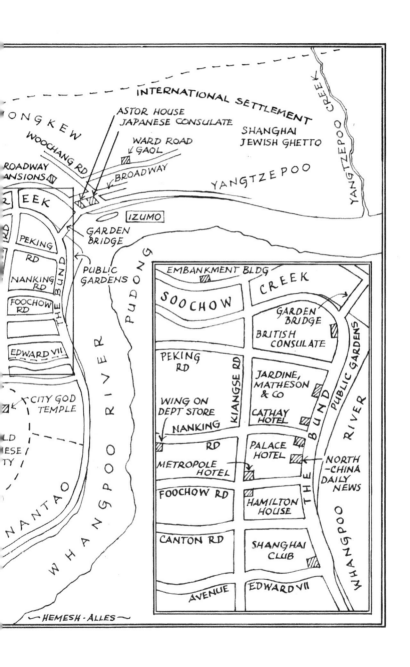

'Shanghai is like the emperor's ugly daughter; she never has to worry about finding suitors.'

– Popular Chinese saying

'This ugly daughter "revelled in her bastard status. Half Oriental, half Occidental; half land, half water; neither a colony nor wholly belonging to China; inhabited by every nation in the world but ruled by none, the emperor's ugly daughter was an anomaly among cities."'

– Stella Dong, Shanghai: The Rise and Fall of a Decadent City,
1842–1949

'I had no idea what Shanghai was. You could have told me I was going to Mars or Jupiter ...'

'We thought it was a desert. We didn't know anything. To get out of the country, that was all.'

– Jewish refugees describing their knowledge of the city
that was to become their haven during the Second World War.

Author's Note

Shanghai is a city whose character has been moulded by a succession of foreigners. Over the centuries, as traders and invaders made their mark on this vibrant metropolis, the names of her roads, districts and waterways have been changed repeatedly to reflect the language and interests of the then ruling powers. What was once Avenue Edward VII or Édouard VII became the Great Shanghai Road under Japanese occupation, and then – for a few years after the Second World War – Zhongzheng Road, after the Chinese name for Chiang Kai-shek. Bubbling Well Road became the more prosaic Nanjing Road (West), or Nanjing Lu, and Moulmein Road is now Maoming Road North.

In this account of life in Shanghai during the Second World War, I have used the names current at the time: that is, those on maps of the late 1930s and 1940s, before the Communist era.

Not every detail can ever be known about an individual's life, and my aunt was perhaps less knowable than many. I have occasionally had to guess how she may have acted or reacted to events happening around her. However, these speculations have always been based on extensive research of the experiences of other people at that time, and on the nature of the woman I knew. I have not invented any conversation between the characters, instead citing interviews published in Steve Hochstadt's book *Exodus to Shanghai* and elsewhere. I have tried to represent the facts of my aunt's life as accurately as possible. Ultimately, only she knew the truth behind them.

Prologue: Sisters and Silence

'What haunts are not the dead, but the gaps left within us by the secrets of others.'

          – Nicolas Abraham, 'Notes on the Phantom'

To my great sadness, I have no memory at all of my mother's voice. By the time I was three months old, Ilse had taken her own life.

At some level, my mother's death is always with me. Knowing so little about her means the least expected of triggers can conjure up tears. Like the moment a character in a soap opera heard a message that his dead mother recorded years earlier. It made me realise with a jolt that I have no idea of the sound of Ilse's laughter, or her weeping.

I was too young to remember anything of the events immediately after my mother's death in October 1953. I was born in Southwest London five weeks after the Coronation, and given the middle name of Elizabeth. Back then, the treatments for postnatal depression were electroconvulsive therapy and barbiturates. Years later I was shocked to learn that Ilse's hospital bed was surrounded by policemen, waiting to arrest her should she survive: until 1961 suicide was a criminal act. But the drugs she had been prescribed for this poorly understood condition proved effective when she made her fateful decision, and the need for her prosecution never arose. Meanwhile, my father Josef's loss was temporarily doubled; I was removed from what remained of the family and taken into care. In one blow, my father had lost not only his wife, but also his three-month-old baby. This was a sadness he and I would never discuss.

The state-run nursery to which I was taken was probably perfectly pleasant, but part of me imagines that I was incarcerated in a Dickensian orphanage. The fact I developed a chest infection there reinforces that fantasy. Despite this, my early experiences never crushed the optimistic side of my nature. Nor can I say that I grew up unhappy. Nearly all childhood photographs show me beaming – before the onset of the usual teenage moodiness. This was not so for my elder sister, who appeared serious, her brows furrowed. This is hardly surprising: Claudia was six years old when we lost our mother. After Ilse died, and my sister was left with just our father, she simply asked him: when would she get a new mother?

We were lucky: the answer turned out to be very soon. Josef could retrieve me from state care only if he found someone to help look after us. My father, a young refugee from Vienna's Nazis, was reeling, numb with grief and barely able to think. How could he get his family back, and continue his work as an architect for Hammersmith Council, when he could barely boil an egg? His father, *Opa*, as we called our grandfather, saw a small ad pinned up at the premises of a local Jewish organisation. It had been placed by a woman seeking a domestic position. He arranged a meeting between his son, a shell-shocked widower, and the prospective 'help', to see if she might assist him with cooking and childcare.

Ruth was a refugee from Saarbrücken in Germany, at 33 a year older than our father. She had been working as a maid in the home of a demanding family in Golders Green. Seeing the broodingly handsome man and his two dark-haired little daughters, she accepted the challenge of taking us on. Her role quickly changed. On New Year's Day 1954, little more than three months after Ilse's death, Ruth and Josef were married. In my judgemental youth, I viewed this as taking place with indecent haste; I am much wiser and more understanding now of my father's pragmatic decision to remarry so soon.

I knew no other mother but Ruth. With the arrival of this kind and practical woman, a new, more capable family unit was born. By 1956 so was my half-sister, Sonia. Ruth showed all her daughters equal love, concern and affection – a superhuman feat I would not appreciate until much later. She never merited that dark label of fairy tales, 'stepmother'.

But I always knew someone was missing. My 'real' mother, Ilse.

We all long to understand our roots, where we come from. How that which we inherit from our past – through both our genes and our environment – makes us the person we are. As we grow older, this desire seems to strengthen. But our ties to the past are easily snapped. Political persecution can uproot our ancestors, displacing them from their home and all that's familiar. The death of a parent – especially one whose life is never spoken of – steals at least half our connection to our roots. My mother's death was a tragedy that remained shrouded in silence, barely mentioned after I first learnt of it.

I was three years old when Ruth took me gently aside for a serious talk. She sat me on her lap and explained that she was not my 'real' mother. My father stood silently by, pipe in hand, leaning against the living room wall, while she imparted the unbelievable truth. I told her not to be silly; I refused to accept her ridiculous words. Of course I loved her not one jot less that day. Only as a teenager did I come to resent her existence and curse my luck at having a stepmother. I would storm away from each row to fling myself on my bed and shed hot tears in my candlewick bedspread. At night I would weep for my 'real' mother (who would have understood me *so much* better than this one). But once the turmoil brought on by surging hormones had passed, so did my unjust anger towards Ruth. In truth she understood me better than anyone ever has.

Although she never met her predecessor, Ruth must have talked to my father about Ilse. But it felt wrong to quiz her about the woman she had replaced, and so I almost never did. I deliberately avoided the subject with my father. My feelings towards him were simpler than those towards Ruth: I adored him. When I was little, he entertained me with funny faces and stories, and immortalised me in an affectionate nonsense rhyme that still gives me pleasure:

> *Rachel Elizabeth is a fine child*
> *Although there are times when she talks a bit wild –*
> *Ly-lora, ly-lora, this is a queer rhyme*
> *But still I do love her at any old time.*

I loved to curl up in my father's soft corduroy lap, inhaling the scent of Balkan Sobranie pipe tobacco and Brylcreem as I snuggled in close. Years later I learnt something that made me love him yet more. On Ilse's death, childless friends of the family, a genteel English couple named Lola and Jim, asked to adopt me. My father refused their kind offer. This revelation overwhelmed me with joy: he had wanted to keep me! I wish I could have thanked him, but by then he too was gone.

I could not mention Ilse's name to my father. The man was damaged, too fragile for such questions. A barrage of losses – of his homeland, his hoped-for career as a writer and his first love – took its toll. I was around ten when his first heart attack struck. From that day on, we had to tiptoe around him, avoiding any kind of upset. Doors must never be slammed; all conflict or argument was forbidden. So how could I ask him about Ilse? I dared not upset the man lying upstairs in bed, the invalid whose new-grown beard contained shocking streaks of pure white, despite being only in his forties. By then I had started experiencing tugs of guilt about being the cause of my mother's premature death. I could not risk triggering my father's as well.

That left Claudia. Some sisters have a bond closer than that of best friends. But for children, six years is a vast gap to bridge, and she and I would not connect until our twenties. Even then, Claudia offered few insights or memories of our mother, rarely mentioning her name. She had begun to shield herself from more damage by developing a tough skin. This appeared overlaid – on topics concerning her inner feelings – with a thick cloak of silence.

And that was how, oh so gradually, Ilse transformed into a mythical figure, a hazy idol wreathed in mystery. I would gaze at an album I had compiled of photos of her, memorising her gleaming hair and sparkling eyes, to try to keep her alive. I still glance every day at one I have framed, in which she's laughing and carefree, a vein standing out on her forehead. It proves my troubled birth mother had, at least once, experienced real joy.

But someone else was still alive who had been close to my mother, who had grown up alongside her for sixteen years. This was Ilse's younger sister, Lisbeth. Like my parents, Lisbeth had escaped Vienna and survived the

Ilse smiling, c. 1952.

Second World War. I knew little more than this of our aunt's story, apart from rumours of a mysterious accident – some said, self-inflicted – which occurred in her youth, and that she had spent the war years in China. She now lived in San Francisco. But this geographical separation proved less problematic than my inability to close the emotional distance between myself and my aunt. She was languid and slow, in both movement and speech; cool and inexpressive. On my visits over the years to her home, despite my efforts, I learnt nothing of her past, or of my mother. I suspected the two sisters had never been close.

Then Lisbeth's own death changed everything.

On one of my visits to her home, I admired a large cabinet of East Asian origin. It stood nearly five feet high, since it rested upon a carved wooden base with lion's paw feet. I knew the Chinese-style cupboard was no antique – Lisbeth told me she and her husband had bought it in California in the 1950s. Yet I loved its ebony lacquered wood, painted with swirling flowers and strange hornbills in thick layers of apricot, bronze, cream and duck-egg blue.

Lisbeth's Chinese cabinet.

My silent aunt must have listened to me more closely than I had realised, or than she had ever let on. For she bequeathed me the Chinese cabinet. And more than that.

When I opened its glossy twin doors, I found something deep inside. Pushed to the back of the top shelf was a rectangular package, wrapped in layers of dry, yellowing newspaper. I reached in and drew out the object, which was much heavier than I expected. Beneath the newspaper I found a dark-brown wooden box, etched with deep carvings. Men and women, their hair in topknots, were depicted within Chinese landscapes full of shell-like blossoms, bamboos and pagodas. The lid showed a man reading to two adults from a scroll, while two children clung to his robes, one looking away, more interested in the scenery than the scholar. Other figures around the side played among tall spiky plants with unfamiliar fruits. At the front, a round metal clasp, engraved with a large sunflower, had two loops for a pin to slide through. The closure had no pin. I gingerly opened the box.

Lisbeth's box

Inside was a set of envelopes and faux-leather wallets, filled with photographs, letters, and official-looking documents: marriage and death certificates, passports, and records of vaccinations and visas acquired. Picture postcards showed people and country scenes. Most of the items dated from the mid-1930s, with the last from the early 1950s. As Lisbeth had been born in 1922, the collection covered her early teens to her thirties.

Flimsy yellowing sheets bore Chinese characters handwritten in red pencil. A few sepia postcards looked much older than the rest. Could the date on that incredibly faint postmark over the Deutsches Reich stamp really be 1919?

Sifting through the box, I found a set of pale-blue airmail letters addressed to Lisbeth. All were sent from England to San Francisco in the early 1950s. Half a dozen were in a rounded, childlike hand, in distinctive green ink. As I recognised the writing, my throat tightened. These were letters from Ilse, my mother, to her sister. In the later ones she was no longer using German, but writing in imperfect English. I swallowed with difficulty as I read. My mother was giving Lisbeth news of Claudia, now six years old; then effusive thanks for the gifts of clothes her sister had sent to England. When I picked up the last letter, I stared at the date. The writing blurred after I made it out: May 1953. Two months before I was born, and five months before Ilse's death, at the age of just 35.

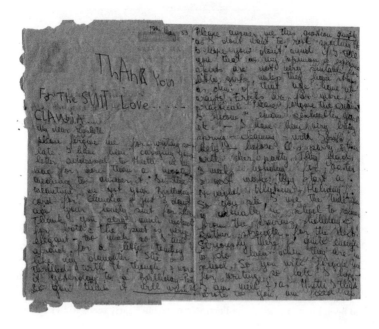

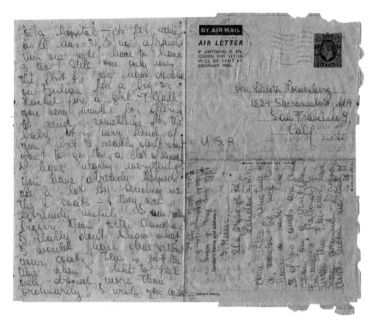

Above and opposite: Ilse's last letter to Lisbeth, May 1953.

As I refocused on the pale-blue paper, the box's significance dawned on me as if a blind had been snapped open to the sun. With neither notice nor explanation, my aunt had left me a collection of items she had treasured for decades. During her lifetime, this woman, the only close female relative in our small scattered family apart from her mother – our grandmother – was always reticent. An enigma, unwilling – or unable – to speak of her feelings, or her past. Her gift made me look at her anew. Were the contents of this box her way of telling me her story at last?

Lisbeth's box with the sunflower clasp would lie untouched in a corner for years, vanishing beneath the cloak of familiarity. The routine of everyday life took over, the focus on two adolescent sons and a challenging career taking priority over the past. Until one day I found myself drawn back to the box while I had been contemplating my Viennese roots. I lifted the clasp as if for the very first time, and looked at the contents anew. I resolved to study every single item inside, something I had never yet done. I would use them to reconnect with, and discover, my family's past. The voices of my mother and her sister had been silent for too long. The time had come to make them speak, and to listen to their story.

1

Vienna, June 1937: Thwarted Ambition

Lisbeth and Ilse grew up cocooned in middle-class ease, living with their parents, Arnold and Edith Epstein, in one of Vienna's elegant apartment buildings on a street named Am Tabor. This lay in Leopoldstadt, the city's second district, whose famous Ferris wheel still towers over the Austrian capital's amusement park, the Prater.

The girls drank *heisse Schokolade* at Kohlmarkt's Demel café, where my aunt developed her lifelong love of thickly whipped cream. Their vivacious and attractive mother was an excellent cook: her fruit-filled dumplings married sweetness and sharpness to perfection. In the summer the family stayed in a welcoming *Pension* outside the city.* The air was fragrant with the smell of hay, and filled with the sound of birdsong and clanking cowbells. Lisbeth loved the sweet yellow butter that accompanied their crisp breakfast rolls and jam.

The sisters lacked nothing, except perhaps closeness to one another. I had long ago picked up this sense of their separation, but have no knowledge of its source. What united them was their love for their parents, and a shared passion for dancing. As small girls, they were taken for portraits at studios run by Michael Sohn in Heinestrasse, and Weitzmann's in Praterstrasse. Ilse had been blessed with the family's good looks; by her side, Lisbeth appeared

---

* A small hotel or boarding house, often on a farm.

plain, with her heavy jaw and straight, severely cut dark hair. Perhaps the four-year age gap kept the girls distant, or was it their contrasting natures: the older, pretty one lively and impulsive, the younger more measured? I doubt they had many friends in common.

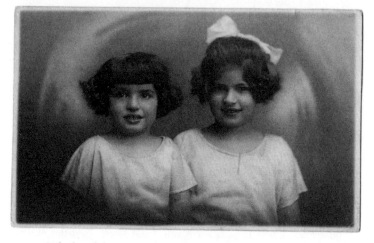

Lisbeth and Ilse in an early studio portrait taken at Michael Sohn
Photowerkstätte, c. 1925.

When I first looked at what lay in Lisbeth's box, I knew very little about Vienna. A visit there with my family when I was ten had left just one clear memory, more worldly than spiritual. It was of the melting flavours of chocolate, sharp cherries and whipped cream in my first slice of *Schwarzwälder Kirschtorte* – Black Forest gateau: a combination so wonderful that even my father's undisguised gloom at revisiting his birthplace could not ruin the moment. Nor did I know about the district where my aunt and mother had grown up. Their address – Wien II, Am Tabor 22 – came from a picture postcard sent to Lisbeth, kept safe all those years inside her wooden box. The date mark was illegible, but it was signed by a Judith Benedikt who was sending *beste grüsse** to my aunt. The picture on the front of the postcard showed a Gothic-looking guest house in the mountain resort of Spital am Semmering.

---

* Best wishes.

One morning as I sat at my desk, the sun shining in through the Velux attic window, the postcard with the Austrian guest house on seemed to demand my attention. The address on the front prompted me to type 'Am Tabor' and 'Vienna' into Google. Up popped a link to a documentary called *Vienna – City of Dreams*, presented by an American art historian named Joseph Leo Koerner. Like me, he was a Jew with Viennese roots.

The film confirmed what I knew of the stately capital, heavy with baroque eighteenth- and nineteenth-century buildings, and rich in composers, psychoanalysts and writers. But then, to my amazement, Koerner mentioned Am Tabor, where his parents had lived. At one end of the road was the great Nord Bahn,* significant as the arrival point of nineteenth-century migrants flocking to Vienna from all over Europe. Many were poorly-off Jews from Galicia, Bohemia and other parts of the Austro-Hungarian empire in search of work or a better life for their families. And many were fleeing antisemitism. They would stream down Am Tabor from the Nord Bahn to find lodgings. By settling here, in Vienna's second district, the immigrants transformed Leopoldstadt into the city's new Jewish quarter, the other side of the Donaukanal (Danube canal) from the medieval Judenplatz. That square had been purged of its Jewish residents by the bloody pogrom of the fifteenth century.

In my family's time, most of Austria's 200,000 Jews lived in the capital.[1] In the early 1920s, Leopoldstadt was almost 40 per cent Jewish; ringed by the Donaukanal, the district's nickname became *Mazzesinsel* – 'Matzo Island'.†[2] Years later, Leopoldstadt would be twinned with Brooklyn, and Tom Stoppard would write his searing play of that name. The Epsteins lived among a large community of assimilated and mostly secular Jews. Judaism meant little to them; synagogue was reserved for the highest of festivals. Lisbeth later wrote that the family 'were not religious at all. [Her] mother fasted on Yom Kippur and went to Kol Nidrei'.‡ Like other Jews

---

* North Railway Station.

† Matzo is the Jewish unleavened biscuit for Passover.

‡ Kol Nidrei is the evening service before Yom Kippur (the Day of Atonement), Judaism's holiest day of the year.

after the First World War, they felt tolerated, protected by their patriotism and loyalty to the vast Austro-Hungarian empire. Arnold had fought as an officer in the war, prepared to die for Franz Joseph, the benign emperor who had always supported the Jews. He and Edith saw themselves as Austrian citizens first, and Jews second. But their predominantly Catholic homeland disagreed.

Lisbeth was very young when she first experienced antisemitism, although she did not yet know the word itself. Despite both her mother and grandmother having been born in Vienna, she discovered that she would never be truly Austrian, not 'one of them'. She was aged eight or so, and on a spa holiday with her family, when she was told by her mother not to talk to a particular man at the resort. The reason was, Edith told her daughter, that the man was a Nazi. Lisbeth asked: 'What is a Nazi?' and her mother said: 'A person who hates Jews.' With a question that my aunt later feared 'brought the whole thing [the Holocaust] on', the little girl asked: 'How come he doesn't kill us?'[3] It was the start of the 1930s.

Antisemitism was never deep below Austria's surface, and Franz Joseph – for whom Arnold would have died – would not reign for ever. As a character in Joseph Roth's great political novel, *The Radetzky March*, mused after the funeral of the hero's father, neither the old man nor the Emperor Franz Joseph could have outlived the dying empire.[4]

My grandfather grew up in Bohemia, (part of Austro-Hungary, and known as Czechoslovakia after the First World War). In 1884, the year of his birth, the town's name was Saaz; today it is Žatec. It was famous for hops and beer production: his father, Adolf Epstein, traded hops.[5]

At 21 Arnold had come to Vienna to join the army as a reserve cadet. In his new city, he had lodgings in the four-storey red-brick barracks on the Obere Donaustrasse, overlooking the waters of the Donaukanal. Two years later, in 1907, he became a lieutenant officer of the reserve. By May 1918, aged 34, he would rise to the rank of *Rittmeister*, a commissioned cavalry officer. A photograph of my grandfather taken in March 1918 shows him in imperial uniform, his sleek dark hair immaculately cut above heavy-lidded eyes and a stylish moustache. Below his chiselled jaw, two silver stars adorn his high military collar.

Above left and above right: Arnold Epstein in uniform, 1918, and
Edith Beck as a young woman.

Edith Beck was a striking young woman. She lived with her parents,
Julius and Paula, at 11 Taborstrasse, also in Leopoldstadt but a more
prestigious street than Am Tabor. Julius Beck had done well as a professional photographer, and their apartment was in an elegant building. It was
less than twenty minutes' walk away from Arnold's red-brick barracks.

I shall never know how my grandparents first met. Edith may well
have caught her first sight of Arnold in his dashing military uniform. The
young cavalryman regularly paraded with his comrades on horseback by
the Donaukanal. Whether it was by the water, or at a Viennese ball, or
at a Jewish social event, I can only imagine. But on 26 April 1914, three
months before the start of the First World War, Arnold Epstein and Edith
Beck were married. The ceremony took place beneath the blue, star-
studded dome of Vienna's grandest synagogue, the Stadttempel, where the
wedding of Edith's parents had also been held. Members of both families
looked on as the couple exchanged rings, the women from their columned
gallery, kept apart from the men. Arnold had just turned 30; his bride was
ten years younger.

Paula and Julius Beck, and below with daughters, Edith and Alice (known as Lidzie); Arnold Epstein in his youth.

Within months of the wedding, Arnold was on active duty, fighting for his emperor. He took leave towards the end of 1917, coming home to Edith to celebrate the New Year. The couple's first daughter was born in late September 1918; they called her Ilse. Six weeks later, the Great War ended, and the Austro-Hungarian empire was no more. Out of its humiliating defeat was born the tiny Republic of Austria. Vienna was now the capital of a much reduced nation, in both status and size. The Allies' post-war treaty forbade the new republic from amassing an army of more than 30,000. It also granted minority rights to Austria's Jews, as it did to other religious, ethnic or linguistic minorities in the new states born from the empire's ashes.

Jews like the Epsteins and their neighbours felt safe, believing that the treaty's policies might protect them. Furthermore, their city was now known as Red Vienna, having elected its first Social Democrat mayor in 1919. The previous mayor, Karl Lueger, had been a notorious antisemite, whose election was repeatedly opposed by Franz Joseph.[6] The forward-looking capital attracted intellectuals, thinkers and left-wing sympathisers such as Freud, Schnitzler and Wittgenstein, as well as scientists and composers. Vienna seemingly tolerated its Jews; so much so that the writer Stefan Zweig declared it a place where Jews could be 'free' from all 'confinement and prejudice', a city where a Jew could live easily as a 'European'.[7]

So it was with optimism that Arnold began his new life in February 1919. He left the army and set up a wholesale business at 27 Volkertstrasse, in the heart of Leopoldstadt. Advertised as Arnold Epstein & Co., *Grosshandel mit Galanterie und Parfumeriewaren*, it supplied perfumery items, gifts and 'fancy goods' to retailers in the city. Delivery, his advert declared, was '*schnell*; *solid*; *billig*' – fast, reliable, cheap. By July 1921 the company sold directly to the public as well; that month he advertised for an assistant for his shop. The firm was registered in the name of Arnold and Edith Epstein, at their home on Am Tabor 22, Wien II. Full of hope for the future, the couple's family grew. On 4 January 1922, their second daughter, Lisbeth, was born.

Lisbeth idolised her father. She felt safe in his arms. He was the only person who ever called her by her middle name, Erica. It was always their little secret, a token of their particular closeness. When not at school, she would visit the shop, admiring the samples on display. She would hold the delicate soaps to her nose, and raise the crystal bottles of perfume to the sunlight to see the rainbows inside. It is easy to imagine her marvelling at the amber Meerschaum pipes, fine leather gloves and porcelain knick-knacks set out on the shelves. I can picture her stroking the fine-bristled clothes brushes with shiny wooden handles as her father looks on, his lit cigarette close by. And I like to imagine her heart swelling as she turns to smile back at the man she would always call 'Papa'.

The family *galanterie* business flourished. But things around them were changing. In 1933 Austria's new chancellor was a fascist named Dollfuss. Originally a member of the right-wing Christian Social Party, that year he created an even more nationalist new Catholic-based party, the Fatherland Front. Dollfuss crushed all opposition – that is, anyone not committed to his dream of Austrian independence. This included both right- and left-wing parties; both were violently suppressed. He banned the Nazi Party in June 1933 as they wished for a union between Austria and Hitler's Germany. Then, after a left-wing uprising in February 1934, he outlawed the Social Democrats.

The Nazis in Austria were not prepared to take this. In July 1934, a group of them entered the chancellery building and shot Dollfuss for opposing them. Half a million Austrians (out of a population of 6.5 million) attended the murdered Austrofascist leader's burial. Kurt Schuschnigg, another fervent nationalist and anti-Nazi, but weaker than Dollfuss, replaced him as chancellor.

The Epsteins sensed the change in atmosphere, as did others in liberal-minded Vienna. With the Jewish-based Social Democrat Party banned, antisemitic feeling was flourishing unchecked, encouraged by German Nazis just over the border. But for left-leaning people, as well as for Jews, the culture felt unpleasant rather than threatening.[8] And besides, around this time, the Epstein family was more concerned with a personal tragedy than with outside events.

In the summer of 1937, while still a schoolgirl, Lisbeth had the accident that almost killed her. I had grown up hearing rumours of a terrible fall that my aunt suffered as a teenaged girl. But like so much of Lisbeth's past, no word of the story was ever spoken aloud. I finally discovered much more of what happened from a small faded envelope inside her carved wooden box.

The envelope contained a dozen or so picture postcards. Some were unused, others written and addressed to my aunt. Four had been sent to her in July 1937, when she was fifteen and a half. They were all addressed to the same destination: Wien IX, Allgemeines Krankenhaus, Unfallstation I, Zimmer 81. Lisbeth had been a patient in room 81 of Vienna's general hospital, in the trauma surgery ward.

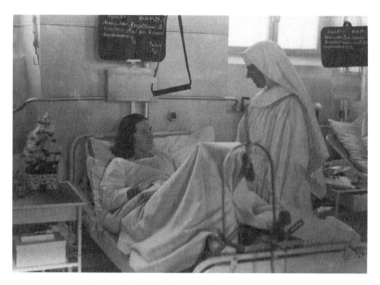

Postcard of Lisbeth's hospital in Vienna, 1930s.

Some unwritten cards showed the *Krankenhaus* itself. White-clad nuns are tending white-gowned, smiling patients in spacious open wards; above each door hangs a large crucifix. At that time, 1937, the Catholic hospital still had to treat Vienna's Jews, unlike such hospitals in neighbouring Germany. That country's Nuremberg Laws of 1935 prevented Jewish patients from being admitted to municipal hospitals. In another card, the hospital's Terrasse der Unfallstation has a row of patients lined up in beds in the fresh air of a balcony outside the ward. Overhead awnings protect the occupants from the elements, with a surprisingly low wall lined with potted plants separating them from the concrete three storeys below. Had my aunt convalesced on that terrace, I asked myself?

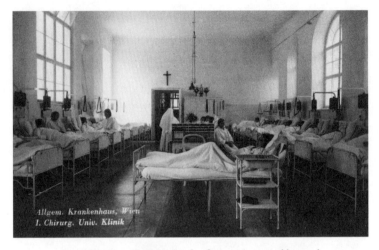

Above and below: More postcards of Vienna's general hospital.

The used postcards expressed the writers' wishes for Lisbeth's speedy recovery. Two came from people whose names I did not recognise. Another was from Lisbeth's grandfather, sent from a picturesque hunting lodge (Jagdhaus Reh-hof) in the forests of Upper Austria. *'Grossvater'* wrote warmly to his grand-daughter, telling her she would soon have her favourite raspberry roulade, and signing off with 'heartfelt greetings'. The other, a view of an upmarket resort, Feld am See in the Austrian province of Kärnten, came from Lisbeth's aunt Lidzie, Edith's only sibling. A steepled church was reflected in a lake, framed by branches of blossom, with white-topped mountains in the distance. In tiny handwriting, Lidzie also sent *'herzlichste Grüsse'*. She wrote of a great festival the following day, in which the whole town would dress up. But, she added, she would not be joining in.* Were Jews already not welcome? Below, a different hand had added a few words: I made out the name Herbert – Lidzie's husband.

Above and overleaf: Postcards sent to Lisbeth in hospital by her grandfather and her aunt Lidzie.

* Every summer, in the middle of July, the upmarket resort of Feld am See still holds a fish festival; this may have been the celebration that Lidzie mentioned in her postcard to Lisbeth.

Keen to find out more about my family's life in Vienna, I contacted a researcher based in that city, Kerstin Timmerman. To my astonishment, her reply came with an email attachment containing 24 pages of detailed information about the Epstein family. This had come from records at the offices of the Israelitische Kultusgemeinde Wien* (IKG), as well as other national archives and databases. Like me, Kerstin had held little hope of anything emerging about a teenaged girl in Vienna in the 1930s. She had been surprised to be proven wrong.

Entering Lisbeth's name into a news database revealed a report with a sensational headline. Although the article was printed in an indecipherable archaic Gothic font, I could see from Kerstin's highlighting that its subject was my aunt.

Eine lebensmüde Fünfzehnjährige.
Gestern hat sich die Am Tabor 22 wohnende 15jährige Mittelschülerin Lisbeth Epstein vom vierten Stocke des Hauses Kohlmarkt 10 in den Liftschacht hinuntergestürzt und erlitt lebensgefährliche Verletzungen. Der Beweggrund der Tat scheint noch ungeklärt, es wird aber vermutet, daß sich die Fünfzehnjährige, weil sie an einer im Hause stattfindenden Tanzveranstaltung nicht mitwirken durfte, dies so zu Herzen genommen hat, daß sie den Sturz ausführte.

Newspaper cutting mentioning Lisbeth Epstein (Source: Wiener Sporttagblatt, 2 June 1937, page 6, courtesy ANNO / Austrian National Library)

The report had appeared in Vienna's *Sporttagblatt*, the sports edition of one of the city's highest circulation dailies, the *Neue Wiener Tagblatt*. It was dated 2 June 1937. The story, in its Germanic dark typeface, was titled, '*Eine lebensmüde Fünfzehnjährige*'. Kerstin had translated this as: 'A suicidal fifteen-year-old'.[†] The words at last confirmed the whispers I had heard about my aunt's youthful trauma. In translation, the article read:

Yesterday the fifteen-year-old middle school student Lisbeth Epstein, who lives at Am Tabor 22, threw herself down the lift shaft from the fourth floor of the house at 10 Kohlmarkt and suffered life-threatening injuries. The reason for the fall remains unknown, but it

---

* Jewish Community of Vienna.
† A more literal rendition of *lebensmüde* would be 'tired of life'.

is believed that the fifteen-year-old, because she was not allowed to take part in a dance event in the house, took this so to heart that she decided to jump.

Seeing those words in print sent a cold shock through my body. How could a fifteen-year-old feel so desperate? Could the pain have stemmed simply from her exclusion from the event? Was that all that mattered in her life? Was nothing – or no one – worth living for? How different this passionate young girl seemed from the impassive woman I knew. My heart ached for the teenager, unable to manage her desperation. And yet I found it hard to believe that this single frustration could have driven her to attempt suicide; that being forbidden to dance could evoke such a violent response.

Much later in my research, when more papers had been scanned into the Vienna archives, Kerstin sent me two reports published in a different newspaper, *Die Stunde*,* which explained my aunt's actions more fully. The first, of 3 June, the day after her fall, gave more details:

During the night there has been no improvement in the state of health of the 15-year-old pupil Lisbeth Epstein who yesterday, due to thwarted ambition, jumped down an elevator shaft and received life-threatening injuries. The state of her health continues to be very serious.

In the meantime there have been investigations about the cause and the course of events of the tragic incident. Lisbeth Epstein, who is a pupil at the Realgymnasium in the Novaragasse, and in addition practises gymnastics and art dance with great ambition, was due tomorrow to participate in a dance performance, which had been planned by her dance teacher Frau Grete L in agreement with the director of the Realgymnasium. In the course of preparing this event, Lisbeth had been asked by the school director to request tickets from the dance teacher but it appears that she forgot to do so. In the

* *The Hour.*

[24]

Die Tragödie der Lisbeth Epstein

In dem Befinden der 15jährigen Schülerin Lisbeth Epstein, die gestern aus gekränktem Ehrgeiz in einen Aufzugsschacht gesprungen ist, und lebensgefährliche Verletzungen erlitten hat, ist im Laufe der Nacht keine wesentliche Besserung eingetreten. Ihr Zustand ist nach wie vor sehr ernst.

Inzwischen wurden auch noch ergänzende Erhebungen über die Ursache und den Hergang des tragischen Vorfalles durchgeführt. Lisbeth Epstein, die ein Realgymnasium in der Novaragasse besuchte, außerdem aber mit großem Ehrgeiz Gymnastik und künstlerischen Tanz betrieb, hätte morgen an einer Tanzaufführung teilnehmen sollen, die von ihrer Tanzlehrerin Grete L. im Einvernehmen mit der Leiterin des Realgymnasiums hätte veranstaltet werden sollen. Im Zuge der Vorbereitungen dieser Tanzvorführungen hätte Lisbeth von ihrer Schulleiterin eine Bestellung bei ihrer Tanzlehrerin gehabt, doch vergaß sie offenbar darauf. Inzwischen hatte sich jedoch die Schulleiterin mit Frau Grete L. in Verbindung gesetzt und zu ihrem Erstaunen erfahren, daß Lisbeth Epstein den ihr erteilten Auftrag nicht ausgeführt hat.

Die Tanzlehrerin stellte Lisbeth daraufhin gestern zur Rede, doch bekam sie auf die Frage, warum Lisbeth ihren Auftrag nicht ausgeführt hatte, keine Antwort. Darauf teilte ihr die Lehrerin mit, daß sie von der Tanzvorführung ausgeschlossen werde.

Bei der anschließenden Probe tanzte Frau Grete L. selbst den Part Lisbeth Epsteins.

Das Mädchen war durch diese Mitteilung sehr deprimiert, doch hoffte sie, daß Frau Grete L. ihre Verfügung doch zurückziehen werde. Als sie jedoch nach Schluß der Probe hören mußte, daß sie heute zur vorletzten Probe nicht mehr zu kommen brauchte, ließ sie auf den Gang, um dort in heftiges Weinen auszubrechen. Die Beamtin einer im gleichen Hause, I, Kohlmarkt 10, untergebrachten Firma, die das Weinen hörte, ging daraufhin auf den Gang und versuchte das Mädchen zu trösten; sie schwang sich jedoch im Augenblick, als es die Beamtin erblickte, über das Stiegengeländer. Wenige Augenblicke hielt sie sich noch an dem eisernen Gestänge fest, und zwei Herren, die eben im fünften Stockwerk über die Treppe gingen, riefen ihr zu: „Halten Sie sich noch einen Augenblick, wir ziehen Sie gleich zurück!"

Ehe die Helfer aber noch zur Stelle waren, ließ Lisbeth plötzlich mit beiden Händen los und stürzte zum Entsetzen der anwesenden Augenzeugen in die Tiefe. Ihr Körper durchschlug eine große Glasscheibe, zertrümmerte eine Wand des Aufzuges und verklemmte sich derart fest an der Rückwand des Schachtes, daß sie dann nur mit Mühe von der Feuerwehr geborgen werden konnte. Einen Schädelgrundbruch, mehrfache Knochenbrüche und zahlreiche Rißwunden mußte dann der Arzt der Rettungsgesellschaft feststellen.

Die Ärzte der Unfallstation bemühten sich, das Leben des unglücklichen jungen Mädchens zu erhalten.

The tragedy of Lisbeth Epstein (Source: *Die Stunde*, 3 June 1937, page 10, courtesy ANNO/Austrian National Library).

meantime, the school director had been in communication with the dance teacher and had realised with great surprise that Lisbeth had not asked for the tickets. The dance teacher subsequently asked Lisbeth why she had not done as she had been told but received no satisfactory answer. Subsequently, the dance teacher told Lisbeth that she was excluded from the performance. In the following rehearsal, the dance teacher performed the part which Lisbeth Epstein had been due to dance.

The article continued:

Due to these events, the girl was extremely depressed but she still hoped that Frau L would change her mind for the final performance. However, when Lisbeth heard after the rehearsal that her presence at the next rehearsal was no longer required, she rushed out into the corridor and burst into passionate tears. An employee in a business located in the same building I, Kohlmarkt 10, heard the sobbing and went out into the corridor where she tried to comfort the girl. However, the moment the girl saw this lady she hurled herself over the banister. For a few moments she clung on to an iron railing and two gentlemen who were just at this time on the fifth floor of the staircase called out to her saying 'hang on for a moment, we will be able to pull you up very shortly'.

However, before the helpers reached the girl she suddenly released both hands and to the dismay of all witnesses fell into the depths. Her body broke through a big pane of glass, shattered one wall of the lift and became lodged so awkwardly at the back of the lift that she had to be freed by the fire service. The attending medical doctor of the fire brigade had to diagnose a fractured skull, many broken bones and several lacerations. The medical doctors of the emergency services are trying to save the life of the unhappy young girl.

These graphic details left me sickened. No wonder no one had ever described them to me. I found myself catching my breath at the thought of the two men so nearly stopping my aunt's fall. Had she deliberately released her grip on the railing, or simply lost the strength to hold on?

My aunt's injuries were so severe they needed weeks of care in the trauma surgery ward. It was only thanks to Edith's pleading that the surgeons did not amputate her shattered leg straightaway. The following day *Die Stunde* explained:

As has been reported, the 15-year-old pupil Lisbeth Epstein was delivered to the emergency department. Due to thwarted ambition – she was not allowed to participate in a dance performance organised by a dance school in I, Kohlmarkt 10 – she had jumped into the lift shaft of the building. The girl, who had suffered a broken skull and

Die Tragödie der Lisbeth Epstein

Die 15jährige Schülerin Lisbeth E p s t e i n, die aus gekränktem Ehrgeiz — sie durfte nicht an den Tanzvorführungen einer Gymnastikschule im Hause I., Kohlmarkt 10, teilnehmen — in die Tiefe gesprungen ist, wurde, wie berichtet, auf die Unfallstation gebracht. Dort hat man das Mädchen, das einen schweren Schädelgrundbruch und Beinbrüche erlitten hat, operiert und die Bemühungen der Ärzte scheinen tatsächlich von Erfolg gewesen zu sein.

Nach den letzten Meldungen dürfte Lisbeth Epstein gerettet werden können

und auch das Bein, von dem man befürchtete, daß eine Amputation notwendig werden wird, kann voraussichtlich erhalten bleiben.

The tragedy of Lisbeth Epstein, (Source: *Die Stunde*, 4 June 1937, page 10, courtesy ANNO/Austrian National Library).

breaks to her legs, was operated on and it looks as if the attempts of doctors to save her life have been successful. According to the latest news, it looks as if Lisbeth's life might be saved. Also, the leg that was feared to require amputation can probably be preserved.

Lisbeth Epstein would never be able to forget her wilful act of self-destruction. From that day on, far from dancing again, even walking would prove difficult. Her left leg remained stiff and swollen throughout her life. Who knows how or when her psyche was broken? But her fall down the lift shaft marked one of a string of misfortunes, black as jet beads in a mourning necklace. That same autumn, another tragedy hit Lisbeth's family.

This was the only family story my aunt ever shared with me. I remembered her telling it on one of my visits to San Francisco, speaking in her usual flat voice as we sat at the kitchen table. Her aunt Lidzie had contracted tuberculosis as a girl, and knew that she could never have children. When a hotelier named Herbert Reisenfeld fell in love with her, she warned him that her life would likely be short. Nevertheless, they married, and lived in wonderful places: on the Riviera, and in Lisbon and Madeira. Herbert swore he could never live without his beautiful bride, and that he would kill himself if she died before him. Lidzie begged him, should that happen, to wait for a year, by which time he would have recovered and found a new love. When Lidzie died, in autumn 1937, she was aged only 39. Her husband kept his promise to her, and waited exactly one year. The following day, Lisbeth's uncle took his own life.

I felt icy fingers run over my skin as I recalled yet another thread of suicide running through our family tapestry. I shook my head to dispel the dark thought. All my life I had grown up wondering if I too had been affected in this way, a feeling that escalated to real dread as I approached the birth of my first son. Fortunately, his arrival seemed to cause me little more than the classic 'three-day baby blues'. But I have never totally dispelled the fear that a fragment of this self-destructive tendency may still lurk deep down within me, like the Snow Queen's splinter of ice.

The Epstein family could never have been the same after the fall that shattered Lisbeth's leg and fractured her skull. How hard her parents must have worked to rehabilitate their younger daughter, both physically and emotionally. I shall never know how far they succeeded in pulling the family back together after so many tragedies. But by now, a more serious danger was brewing beyond their home in Am Tabor. External events were about to take over, threatening the stability of not just their city, but the whole of Austria itself.

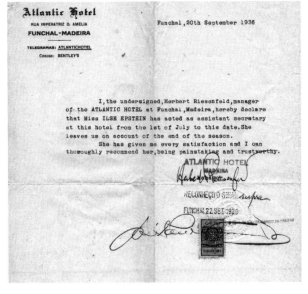

Ilse's visa to Portugal and reference letter from her uncle Herbert, hotelier at Atlantic Hotel in Madeira, September 1936. Herbert died the following year.

2

Vienna, March 1938: A World Falls Apart

In March 1938, Lisbeth's physical injuries were healing. But political events were about to turn her world upside down.

By the start of that year, relations between the Austrian and German chancellors were deteriorating. Austria's Schuschnigg was set on his country's independence from Germany, while Hitler's goal was its annexation: it was the land of his birth. In February 1938, Hitler summoned Schuschnigg for talks. Instead he delivered a threatening ultimatum. He would invade the tiny republic unless Schuschnigg rehabilitated Austria's Nazis and placed some in his cabinet. Schuschnigg agreed to Hitler's demands and left. According to a contemporary writer, Schuschnigg had been deprived of the cigarettes to which he was chronically addicted for the many hours of the meeting with Hitler, and left in a state of nervous collapse.[1] But on 9 March he declared a plebiscite in his country, to let the people decide if they wished to join Nazi Germany or not. The vote was to be held on 13 March.

Lisbeth's family saw signs appear on all the streets around Am Tabor that read '*SCHUSCHNIGG JA!*' or a big simple '*NEIN*'. The plebiscite's wording was strongly biased towards '*Ja*', Schuschnigg's desired outcome of staying a separate nation. It asked: 'Are you for a free, German, independent and social, Christian and united Austria, for peace and work, for the equality of all those who affirm themselves for the people and Fatherland?' Hitler was not prepared to wait for the result. He mobilised his army for invasion and demanded the referendum be scrapped. Schuschnigg gave in, and on 11 March he resigned. He handed power to a Nazi supporter, enabling Hitler's troops to march into Austria the next day.

How quickly public opinion changed! The Epsteins suddenly saw windows draped with swastika flags, and uniformed policemen openly displaying the banned swastika badge of the Nazis. Plebiscite posters were ripped down, replaced with new ones saying '*ANSCHLUSS Ja!*' Youths in knee-length white socks – the illegal sign of allegiance to Hitler – gathered brazenly on street corners. On 12 March, those who would have said '*Nein*' to Schuschnigg's vote now ecstatically cheered the German forces, who marched in unopposed.

By that afternoon, spurred on by Austria's enthusiastic reception, Hitler began his triumphant tour. Proudly wearing the brown uniform of his storm troopers, he stood ramrod-stiff in a shiny black car, saluting the crowds. They responded with extended right arms, fingers straight. Young girls in national dress flung flowers at the man they saw as their liberator; others wildly waved Nazi flags and yelled out '*Sieg Heil!*' Older people wept unrestrainedly with joy.[2] Mainly lower-middle-class Austrians, they welcomed their glorious future as part of a much richer nation, as the 'newest bastion of the German Reich'.

This was how Hitler described Austria in his rallying speech at his parade's climax in Vienna. In the Heldenplatz* on 14 March he declared: 'As leader and chancellor of the German nation and Reich, I announce to German history now the entry of my homeland into the German Reich.' Two hundred thousand Viennese applauded their new leader and the *Anschluss*. Lisbeth's family was not among them. Inside their flat, they winced at the incessant, distorted blaring of loudspeakers and Teutonic chanting in the streets.[3] People now openly shouted 'Jews – perish!', or even more bloodthirsty antisemitic jibes.

A few days after the *Anschluss*, when Jewish actresses had been made to clean the lavatories of the Josefstadt theatre, a nineteen-year-old girl was stopped by the Nazis on a street not far from her home. Barking out their

---

* Square of Heroes.

order, they forced her to get down and scrub the pavement. With gritted teeth and burning cheeks, she knelt and complied; disobedience was too dangerous. Her name was Ilse Epstein.

That day Ilse resolved to follow her school friend, a Jewish girl who had already left Vienna for Paris. Back home in Am Tabor, she started packing her bag. She would not stay to be humiliated again. In a few weeks she would be gone.

I learnt of this episode through one of my aunt's testimonies to a historian named Patricia Kalman.[4] As I read it, my own cheeks burned. This was not simply in anger at my mother's treatment. It felt so wrong to have stumbled upon such a significant personal event in the pages of an academic monograph. My ignorance of the life of the woman to whom I owed mine suddenly weighed heavily on me.

I shall always regret knowing so little about my birth mother. As I grew up, I gathered snippets of information about Ilse that gleamed like mother-of-pearl among pebbles. Black and white photographs showed her beauty: shining dark hair and a generous mouth. And she had green eyes, like mine. It was my grandmother, Edith, who told me this once when she looked at my eyes, so I can be confident of this fact at least.

I did speak to one other person who remembered my mother. It was 2011, and I was visiting the family friend who had wanted to adopt me on Ilse's death. Still as elegant as I remembered her from my childhood, she was now a widow in her nineties: her hair, in its French roll, was silver rather than blonde. She was the only person still alive, apart from my sister Claudia, who had known my birth mother. I wanted a last chance to glean some memories. As we chatted, she told me how much my mother had loved dancing. I had never known that; no one else had ever thought to tell me before. As I put my coat on to leave, I saw her eyes light up. The coat was velour, in a shade of grass-green. Smiling warmly, she said: 'Your mother had a green coat as well, you know.' My heart swelled.

The rest of my knowledge about Ilse is based on shakier ground. Tiny glimpses of her nature trickled through from my sister or stepmother, in rare unguarded moments of openness. Yet now I can barely recall these; they were so few, and spread over so many years. But of one thing I am sure:

Ilse was a tempestuous woman, whose moods changed by the minute. Late in her second pregnancy, Ilse had argued violently with someone; within hours of her tirade, I was born, three weeks earlier than expected. How must she have raged, then, at the Nazis' orders that day after the *Anschluss*.

How do you remove a citizen's right to exist? You make him or her 'other', less than human, a stain on your streets to be purged and forgotten like unwanted slogans.

In Germany, the Nazis had begun squeezing Jews out of society back in 1933. The first antisemitic legislation banned Jews from most professions. Two years later, Hitler's loathing for non-Aryans was embodied in the Nuremberg Laws. Aimed initially at Jews, but later Roma and Black people as well, these were designed to keep the German race 'pure'.[5] By 1938, over four hundred laws had been passed, limiting every aspect of Jews' lives. Within weeks of the *Anschluss*, these laws applied to the Epsteins as well, who were now Jews first, not Austrians. The family's identity, like that of their business, could not be disguised. In January, it became illegal for German Jews to alter their names. By April, the 'Decree against the Camouflage of Jewish Firms' banned the changing of business names also. Jews had to catalogue their possessions, and report any property above 5,000 Reichsmarks.*

Ilse was getting ready to join her Jewish school friends in Paris, the girls all hoping to find work there. She had made all the arrangements soon after her brush with the Nazis. The family knew of others taking steps to avoid the tightening noose of antisemitism. They had neighbours whose menfolk spent each night in a different household, constantly moving to avoid arrest. Many Jews guessed what lay ahead, and took control of their leaving. A Viennese journalist, Moriz Scheyer, later wrote of 'nine thousand suicides in the first five months' after the *Anschluss*. He described a placard pinned to the door of one 'well-respected Jewish family' who had chosen this desperate way out. 'Five Jews, who have killed themselves. Course of action highly recommended to others.'[6] The notice had been put up by the Nazis.

---

* Valued at around £30,000 today.

Scheyer also described a 'working-class woman, a nice, friendly-looking type, sitting opposite [him] in the tram … studying the … newspaper intently. Suddenly she turned to her companion and, with a sad shake of the head, said: "I really had no idea that the Jews were as bad as that."' [7]

Lisbeth's parents were angry at the readiness with which their country-men had embraced Nazism, and shocked at the acceptance of the racist lies appearing daily in newspapers. Above all, they feared for their future, and that of their troubled sixteen-year-old daughter. Less than a year had passed since her plunge down the lift shaft. Was an even worse danger approaching?

3

Vienna and Prague, May to August 1938: A Flippant Remark

Arnold could not hope to hold on to the family business. A month or so after the *Anschluss*, Lisbeth returned from school and was surprised to find her father at home. Stooped with defeat, he quietly told her how brown-shirted thugs had burst into his office on Volkertstrasse, demanding the papers to Arnold Epstein & Co. The firm had to be sold, for a pittance, to a more suitable, Nazi-approved proprietor: that is, an Aryan, not a Jew. On 24 May 1938, Germany's Nuremberg Laws took force in Austria, stripping the Epsteins of their citizenship and making the family stateless.[1]

Lisbeth saw her father's despair, and grew angry at how little Austria valued his loyalty. The man who had been ready to die fighting for his country in the First World War was now worth nothing. Meanwhile, at her Catholic school, Lisbeth was shocked by her classmates' behaviour. Some turned away when she or other Jewish pupils approached; others spat insults in their faces. She wondered if they had harboured these feelings for years, suppressing them until now when they were actively encouraged; or if they were just thoughtless kids, trying to fit in with the zeitgeist. Either way, she hid her feelings.

One morning in May, Lisbeth watched her father put on his hat and leave the flat. He was off to join the queue snaking down Seitenstettengasse, a narrow, cobbled street in the old Jewish quarter. Here, inside the Stadttempel, was the only source of help for Vienna's Jews. At number 4, above the heavy wooden door, a turquoise plaque with gold Hebrew lettering marked the offices of the Israelitische Kultusgemeinde Wien, the IKG. The organisation had been set up 90 years earlier by Franz Joseph, to provide his empire's Jews with cultural support. Hitler's government had commandeered the IKG, twisting its purposes to meet their ends.[2] It was the only Jewish organisation that they allowed to function, renaming it the Juedische Gemeinde, using the less euphemistic word for Jewish than '*Israelitische*'. Ostensibly there to help Jews leave the country, in truth the organisation became a conduit between the Nazis and those they vowed to be rid of: it provided an invaluable source of Jewish names and addresses. And later, when voluntary migration proved too slow, the Gemeinde was forced to arrange its members' deportation.

Arnold Epstein was going to the former IKG office to try to arrange his family's escape from Austria. He returned home with a questionnaire which was issued by Austria's Emigration Department. Lisbeth sat down beside him and watched as he began filling it out, in his immaculate, curlicue script.

The teenager must have looked on, heavy-hearted, as her father wrote under 'Occupations (specialised)' the words 'English and French correspondent' – an invented, or hoped for, career? On the next line he added 'sales agent for brushware, perfume and toiletries'. Under 'previous employment' he listed a string of positions: office manager at a machine factory, an official at Crédit Lyonnais bank as well as working at a bank in London, four years of war service, and a sales agent for the chandelier manufacturer, Alois Pragan. Lisbeth saw him put London and Paris under 'previous stays', both before she was born; she tried to imagine him there. She smiled at his adding Spanish to German, French, English and Bohemian as languages in which he was proficient. She was proud of her father's skills as a linguist – or, perhaps, of his ability to exaggerate them.

It must have been difficult for Lisbeth to watch this educated man write under the next heading, 'Present economic situation and monthly earnings', the words: 'Without job, without earnings'. Or to see his response to the question 'What plans do you have for your new residence?' which was simply: 'Any employment matching my knowledge'. All her father wanted was a country willing to restore to him the dignity of being able to work.

To increase his chances, he and Lisbeth walked each week along the Donaukanal to a building in the east of the city. By now, had they taken the tram, they would have been restricted to one of the seats at the back. Their destination was an ornate, white-domed observatory, whose art nouveau letters spelled out its name: 'URANIA'. Above, a huge plaque read: 'Built under the government of Franz Joseph I in the year 1910'.³ The Urania was now used for public education and lectures; hundreds of Vienna's jobless, now forced to retrain, attended classes there. Arnold had chosen bookbinding; Lisbeth took courses in leather craft and secretarial skills. These seemed transferable trades, wherever they ended up after Austria. And so, on the IKG form, under 'Has a new profession been chosen? If so, which one?', Lisbeth's father had written *Buchbinderie* – book-binding.

Above and overleaf: Photographs kept by Lisbeth of her leather craft class (and tailoring class?) at the Urania.

But where could the family go? Arnold had been to all the foreign embassies in the city to beg for a visa, to no avail. Now he entered his list of countries on the form: Australia, the USA, England (underlined twice), Brazil and Sweden. The only one with which the family had any link was America. Under 'any relatives abroad', Arnold wrote the name of an aunt in Brooklyn: Camilla Hartmann, at 1654 44th Avenue. How different their lives might have been if any of these countries had opened their doors, or Aunt Camilla had been willing to invite them to join her. But by 1938 the world was divided into two parts, as Chaim Weizmann* declared: 'those places where Jews could not live and those where they could not enter'.[4]

Hitler's poison was spreading. From 6–15 July 1938, an international conference met at Evian, in France, to tackle the problem of the many

---

* The Zionist and Israeli statesman, who would go on to be Israel's first president.

refugees trying to flee Nazi Europe. Roosevelt presided over delegates attending from 32 different nations. Golda Meir came from Palestine, but was not permitted to speak. Only two of the nations present agreed to increase immigration quotas to let in significant numbers of Jews: the Dominican Republic and Costa Rica. The US, mired in its own Great Depression, stuck firmly to its quotas.

The Evian Conference's response delighted Hitler, who saw his policies vindicated. He mocked the world's apathy: 'We say openly that we do not want the Jews. The democracies keep on claiming that they are willing to receive them – and then they leave them out in the cold; no one in the world wants them.'[5]

The last entry Arnold made was a list of family members hoping to emigrate: himself, Edith and Lisbeth. Ilse was about to go to Paris to join her school friends. Her passport was stamped with a pass out of Vienna on 11 July 1938. Four days later she reached Strasbourg railway station, where the border police added their stamp. Did Lisbeth hug her sister close as they said goodbye? I'd like to think that she did. Nor do I know if either girl imagined that this might be the last time they would see each other.

In August 1938, tired of waiting for a response from the Juedische Gemeinde and desperate for work, Arnold was driven to act. He set off for Prague, where his sister lived. Lisbeth waved her father off at the North Railway Station. In the stifling carriage, Arnold looked out at the passing meadows and mountains, dreaming of any opportunity that might await him beyond the Reich. With each hour of the five-hour journey, his expectations fell. By the time he disembarked at Prague's twin-towered station he was prepared to take anything. But his sister was blunt. There was nothing for him there. No possibilities, no openings at all. He stayed on in her apartment to consider his next move.

Back home in Vienna, Edith was not idle. She was blessed with a natural sociability, which Lisbeth wished she had inherited. Edith was charming and gregarious, and a great one for gossip. She had heard rumours, over kitchen tables and in the street. They had started that June, but she had chosen to ignore them. Now more of their Jewish friends and neighbours were taking heed. They were abandoning all they had in Vienna to seek a new and uncertain life on the other side of the globe.

None of the countries Arnold had written down on the form had offered him refuge. But had he filled in his list a few weeks later, he would have included another country, where one lone city held its doors open to all incomers, whether they had visas or not. Even Jews. Now Edith took notice of the rumours, and wrote to her husband in Prague. She would later insist that her suggestion 'wasn't that serious'. After all, she was well known for her flippancy.

Her letter simply said: 'How about Shanghai?'[6]

Vienna's Chinese consul general, Ho Feng-Shan, had been in post at the Chinese legation since spring 1937. As soon as he saw the effects of the *Anschluss* on the city's Jewish population, Ho started issuing entry visas to Shanghai like a host giving out party favours. Strictly speaking, these had been superfluous since 1937, when the Japanese invaded the port. Immigration control had lapsed; no one took responsibility for checking incomers' papers. But having visas proved helpful when getting passports reissued by the Nazis, or when trying to purchase tickets out of Austria.[7]

Whatever Edith's intention, Arnold took his wife's idea seriously. He went out and sold his diamond ring and gold watch. He then said goodbye to his sister and returned home to Vienna. They would never see each other again.

Growing up, I vaguely knew that my aunt had spent the war somewhere in China. But as with the rest of her past, she never discussed a word of this with me, and I barely knew which city she had lived in. A clue to this part of Lisbeth's story came from an unexpected quarter: a paperback book presented to me by my sister Claudia's husband. On its cover, a black and white photograph faded into cloud where the title appeared in large red letters: *Exodus to Shanghai: Stories of Escape from the Third Reich*. The photograph showed passengers disembarking from a liner, a naval officer on the gangway checking off a list. Other people, mostly men in hats and coats, waited on the quayside to greet them.

Seeing my expression, my brother-in-law said cryptically: 'Take a look at the index.' Suddenly a name jumped out at me. Three lines of entries referenced the married name of our Aunt Lisbeth.

I turned back to the beginning to see how Steve Hochstadt could have known Lisbeth. His acknowledgments revealed that he had interviewed a hundred former Shanghai Jews – refugees from Austria or Germany – about their wartime experiences. He thanked them for their generosity with both their time and their memories. *Exodus to Shanghai* was a distillation of the group's testimonies, compiled from the verbatim transcripts of thirteen interviewees. One of these was our aunt.

I was filled with excitement, but also with shame. Lisbeth had never breathed a word to either Claudia or me about her years in Shanghai. Yet she had clearly spent hours opening up to a stranger, a man who now knew more of her life history than we ever had. Had we not tried hard enough to find out?

Next to a short biography of our aunt was her photograph, taken by the author in the late 1980s. I read that the location was China, Hochstadt having accompanied a group of the contributors to his book on a trip there. Lisbeth's gaze was turned from the camera. A breeze was blowing her black hair up from her unsmiling face, which bore a look of determination.

Lisbeth on the Great Wall of China, 1989
(photograph courtesy of Steve Hochstadt).

Back home in Cambridge, I started reading my aunt's testimony. The words brought back her voice, its strange accent a blend of California drawl and guttural Viennese. I had always found her speech – like all her actions – frustratingly slow. A languid 'Hi!' or an elongated 'How *about* that!' if something faintly amused her, were the nearest she came to animation. Expressions of disapproval were more usual, accompanied by her smoker's catarrhal 'Ach' and a dismissive wave of her manicured hand. And now, in my hand, was her account of her last weeks in Vienna. I turned the pages, eager to discover what happened to her – and my – family.

The form that Arnold had filled in so neatly in May 1938 came to nothing. It was later processed by a nameless clerk, who scrawled across it in heavy handwriting and stamped it with two official marks. The first was the date, 30 January 1940, in the centre of the page. This cut across the second stamp: two large black 'S's, as sinister as a pair of venomous snakes.

Above and opposite: Pages from the IKG Emigration Department questionnaire, with Arnold's entries, May 1938 (Courtesy Archiv IKG Wien, Jerusalem holding, A/W 2590,45)

That August, the Nazis passed a new decree to help them identify Jews. Anyone whose names were insufficiently 'Hebrew' must have an extra name added to their papers. For women, this was 'Sara'; men had to add 'Israel'. Two months later, to remove any doubt about bloodline, another law rendered Jews' passports valid only if stamped with a large red letter 'J', for *Jude*. Surprisingly, this directive came not from the Nazis, but from the Swiss; their police were keen to stop Jews entering – and remaining in – Switzerland. The Germans had agreed to the idea with alacrity.

In October 1938, the Epsteins surrendered their passports for this enforced 're-validation'. They had to send other official papers for similar re-approval. A few weeks later, on 7 November, a German diplomat based in Paris, Ernst vom Rath, was shot by Herschel Grynszpan, a Polish Jewish teenager enraged by the Gestapo's brutal treatment of his parents and others like them. The Gestapo had seized thousands of Polish-born Jews, cramming them onto prison lorries as onlookers screamed *'Juden raus!'*

---

* 'Jews out!'

They were driven to the railway station and herded onto trains bound for Poland. When Grynszpan received news of his parents' plight in a card from his sister, he vowed revenge. Did the Epsteins know this, as they queued up outside the old IKG offices in the Stadttempel on 8 November to collect their newly validated birth and marriage certificates? The season's first flurry of snow was whitening the cobbles of Seitenstettengasse. Arnold, Edith and Lisbeth stood alongside hundreds of others, shivering in their desperation to leave.

No one queuing with the Epsteins could have known how much worse life was about to become. At 5.30pm the following day, vom Rath died of his wounds; the Nazis' revenge would be brutal and swift.

Above left and above right: Family papers revalidated by the IKG (Arnold and Edith's wedding certificate and Lisbeth's birth certificate), bearing the date 8 November 1938.

4

Berlin, June 1938:
An Unheeded Warning

In June 1938, in a different country, another man's life was coming under threat. No one could say that he hadn't been warned. But Berlin was his home, and he refused to leave his business in the city and his circle of faithful friends. Among them were many Gentiles, who still dared to associate with him. Why, then, should he believe the rumours and run from all that he loved, simply because he was a Jew?

Bruno Loewenberg was sitting at his favourite table in the bustling café on the Kurfürstendamm. His sketchbook and chalks lay on the table before him, lit up by the morning sunshine streaming through the café window. A curved-handled walking stick rested by his chair. As usual, his shirt was white and crisply pressed. At 47, Bruno was a man of particular habit and tastes. Every day, before opening his bookshop, he took the same banquette seat, with its view of the people walking along the sycamore-lined avenue. He ordered his usual small coffee – black and strong – and stirred in exactly two teaspoons of sugar, slowly and carefully. For him, this drink was no luxury, but a necessity of life. He had already had his first cup of the day in his flat. He often said that he only needed three things to be happy: a good coffee maker, a gramophone and a window looking out onto something green.

He had started going to this café because of its convenient location, a few streets from his flat. But now Bruno Loewenberg had no choice. Its large art nouveau windows were the only ones in this part of town free of signs with the words: 'No Jews permitted'. The Nazis' chokehold in Germany was tightening again. Two years earlier, Hitler had used Berlin's white-dominated Olympics to promote his party's ideals of Aryan superiority. When the Black athlete Jesse Owens won four gold medals, the furious chancellor declared that Owens's origins made him 'stronger than ... civilised whites', and proposed the exclusion of the runner's kind from all future games.[1] While Hitler's racism encompassed Black people and Roma, for Bruno the danger lay in the dictator's hatred of Jews.

The man drinking his coffee at his usual table never judged others by their outward appearance. He had no time for those who would judge him this way. His friends saw past his short stature and hunched back, the result of scoliosis since birth. Nor did they care about what the Nazis saw as Bruno's race. They carried on as usual, ignoring the growing signs of German hostility towards Jews. Their city buzzed with creative energy. Cabaret artists from Vienna still flocked to Berlin. New theatres were opening, Brecht was writing new plays and Reinhardt directing theatrical productions all across town.

Bruno in front of his bookshop in Berlin, on a postcard
sent in the 1920s

Bruno's crowd formed a Bohemian enclave, a rowdy group going from coffee houses to bars. Each sported his trademark style: one wore a distinctive hat, another a flamboyant scarf, a third was never seen without spats. They would philosophise and argue, trying to sell their paintings to each other. They would go to concerts and shows, loudly dissecting them afterwards over shots of spirits or glasses of beer. Bruno's choice of drink was neat vodka. He never took drugs, despite his friends' many offers: cocaine was to be found at every café table. He understood the nature of addiction, and it was not for him. He had seen how one of their group had succumbed to the drug. An impoverished artist in rags, the addict would go from table to table, begging for small change, a wild look on his face. When he had gathered a few marks, he would run to the pharmacy for his fix of cocaine. A few minutes later he would be back, carrying on the conversation exactly where he had left off, as he brazenly injected himself through his trouser leg. Everyone knew the artist carried his gear wherever he went; not an eyebrow was raised. The poor fellow lived in a bathtub in a friend's rented room.

The group was often seen at Clärchens Ballhaus on Auguststrasse, whose glitter ball sent light sparkling across the parquet dance floor. While many of them liked to foxtrot, Bruno chose to sit at a table upstairs. It was calmer in the grand mirror salon, with its chandeliers and oak panelling. Sometimes he ate schnitzel and boiled potatoes; other times he concentrated on the cabaret, and on one singer in particular. The woman with the finger-wave bob and wide kohl-lined eyes, captivating as an Egyptian cat. In 1922, she had become Bruno's wife. Seven years' later the marriage had ended. They had both been too young, he always said; it was not because she hadn't been Jewish. After all, most of his circle were Gentiles. The couple would stay friends for the rest of their lives.

Was it his unthreatening nature that drew women to him, or his humour and wit? Perhaps it was the warmth that shone from his brown eyes, or the mane of dark hair swept back from his forehead. Bruno Loewenberg was never short of female admirers. Just a few days before, one of them had made him a strange offer. She had wanted to introduce him, her 'beloved friend', to an important man whom she knew. She thought such a meeting would change that man's thinking – make him reconsider his opinion

Clara, Bruno's wife; Postcard he sent her before their marriage, showing his characteristic doodles.

of Jews. But Bruno had said no. He knew the identity of the man she wished him to meet, and saw no point. His name? None other than Joseph Goebbels.[2]

Bruno put his sketchbook aside and was draining the last bittersweet drop from his cup when he became aware of a movement beside him. A stranger at the next table was leaning towards him from his seat. He felt the man's breath on his ear as he whispered to Bruno:

'Listen, you shouldn't even go home to get your things, you should just leave as fast as possible.'

Bruno looked at the stranger as if he were crazy.

'Why?' he asked.

'Because we are planning to do terrible things.'

'How can you do these things?' Bruno asked.

The other simply said: 'We are developing ways.'

Bruno picked up his walking stick and left the café. He was still going to his workplace, his shop, just as he did each weekday morning. Why should he not?

By 7pm, he was back in his flat. He was listening to a Beethoven sonata while preparing his meal. A loud knocking at the door shattered the calm. Bruno opened the door, hands clammy, to see two men blocking the light from the hallway outside. They wore dark jackets and breeches that widened above high leather boots. Two lightning bolts on their collars and a death's head on their caps signalled the paramilitary *Schutzstaffel*, the Nazis' SS 'protection squad'.

'*Heil Hitler!*' one said. 'Come with us.' Nothing more.

Bruno stood quietly and thought for a moment.

'Should I take a toothbrush?' was all he asked.

The answer was the one he had feared.

'I think you should.'

He was not the only man arrested that night. On 14 June 1938, around 2,500 Jewish men were seized from their homes throughout the Reich.[3] They were a danger to the state, it was declared, and must be locked up. The grounds given were their previous convictions; for many, these were minor offences – little more than traffic violations – often from many years back. The timing of the disappearance of so many men was well planned.

That day, an addendum to the Nuremberg Laws forced all Jewish firms to be named and registered.[4] By getting rid of the owners before they could do this, and potentially disguising the Jewish roots of their businesses, it was child's play for the Nazis to steal the Jews' companies for themselves.

In the coming days and weeks, as thousands more were arrested, Bruno's friends would try desperately to find out where he had been taken. But none was able to discover the fate of the man with the twisted spine.

5

Vienna, November 1938 to May 1939: Fire and Compassion

On the bitter grey evening of 9 November, the Epsteins were at home in their flat, huddled together round their dining table. Finding fuel for the apartment's stoves was becoming harder. Despite the cold, they had little appetite for the clear soup with semolina dumplings that Edith had prepared. What they heard from their wireless was chilling. Joseph Goebbels, Germany's minister of Public Enlightenment and Propaganda, was making a speech on behalf of his Führer, now Austria's ruler too. A few hours earlier, Hitler had learnt of the death of Ernst vom Rath, the German diplomat, at the hands of his young Jewish assassin.

Goebbels's words were like a flame to blue touchpaper. While not explicitly condoning demonstrations of revenge, he declared 'insofar as they erupt spontaneously, they are not to be hampered'.[1] Citizens jumped at this invitation by the Nazi Party to express their strong pro-Aryan feelings. And so began the pogrom against the Jews of the Reich.

Vienna was brutally targeted. Crowds of Nazi supporters – Party members and ordinary citizens – rushed into the streets for an orgy of destruction. Hitler Youth and storm troopers could at last unleash their antisemitism; respectable, middle-class folk also joined in with enthusiasm. Officials of fire departments looked on, motionless, unless they saw non-Jewish properties under threat. The Epsteins, behind the bolted door of their flat, looked down from their windows. The night sky had turned orange, stained with dark plumes of smoke. Lisbeth trembled at the screaming; she could make out some of the obscenities being shouted as rioting Austrians wreaked havoc on Jewish businesses and temples. She heard glass shattering, and panes cascading from smashed shopfronts and sacred stained glass. Below, on the ground, thousands of shards glowed with the arsonists' flames, like light reflected from crystal chandeliers. This would give *Kristallnacht* – the Night of Broken Glass – its original euphemistic name, though the alternative name, the November Pogroms, is more honest. However it is known, the infamy of 9 November has never been wiped from the history books.

Neither Lisbeth nor her parents slept that night, the violence continuing until morning. By then, eighteen of Vienna's synagogues were in ruins. The contents of Jewish-owned shops were looted or thrown onto the pavements, drenched in water or ink, or burned to ashes. Jewish property lay destroyed throughout the city. The Stadttempel, where Lisbeth's parents had been married, was only spared because it stood in the heart of a mixed residential area, close to a significant church.

The Epsteins soon heard news that was even more disturbing. The crowds' violence had not only targeted property, but people as well. They had attacked Jewish men and women, dragging them from their beds to be humiliated and beaten in the streets. A hundred or more Jews died that night across the Reich, with a much higher death toll in its aftermath. Despite Goebbels's speech, everyone knew that the riots had been orchestrated by the Nazi Party: its members, in civilian dress, were seen spurring on the action. Little encouragement was needed. A newspaper report described how women stood by, clapping and screaming with laughter, holding their babies aloft to see Jews beaten senseless with lead piping. The reek of smoke and ash lingered for days.

Arnold's shop was already gone. But others whose businesses were looted or wrecked could claim no insurance money. Instead, the Jewish community itself was fined billions of Reichsmarks in reparation for the destruction caused by that night's violence. When Hermann Goering (the Reichstag president) heard that expensive imported glass would be needed to make good the damage, he fumed: 'They should have killed more Jews and broken less glass.'[2]

The horror of that night left Lisbeth's family in despair. They discovered that, in Vienna alone, 27 Jews had been murdered. Across the Reich, thousands of Jewish men were rounded up immediately after the pogrom. The Epsteins knew people who had been arrested, and were horrified when they learnt where the prisoners were being sent – the concentration camps that Hitler had set up since his first days in power. Thousands of dissenters, homosexuals and Jews were languishing in camps at Dachau, Buchenwald or Sachsenhausen, many dying at the hands of guards notorious for their brutality. Thirty thousand Jews joined their number in the days after the pogroms.[3]

A flood of new antisemitic laws was sped through to curtail Jews' freedoms even further. On 15 November, Lisbeth's education was suddenly over: like all Jewish students, she was expelled from her school. The family could no longer visit the cinema, theatre or concert halls, or – had they wished to – use any sports facilities. Arnold's driving licence was removed. German Jews had experienced this 'social death' far more gradually, over the previous five years, as Germany's antisemitic legislation had been insidiously growing since 1933. Its drawn-out nature disguised the threat, like the apocryphal frog unaware of its slow boiling to death as the temperature of the water around it is gradually raised. Many German Jews were in denial of any danger. But for Austria's Jews it felt as if the savage change in society's attitude had happened overnight. Another law gave Lisbeth a new cause for anger. She and Edith could now only shop for food at a specified hour, the one allotted to Jews in the late afternoon – by which time the shelves were almost empty. As they lined up for the scraps that remained, the pair were openly abused. Although it would be three years before the Reich's Jews were forced to wear the identifying yellow star, everyone knew the race of those queuing so late in the day. Lisbeth turned her head to avoid the spittle aimed at them; it was harder to avoid the venomous shouts of 'dirty Jews!'[4] Her heart raced and she clamped her lips tight: she knew that not holding her tongue would only make matters worse.

This may have marked the start of my aunt's facility to conceal her emotions. In those days when standing up to the hatred of antisemites could have had her arrested, or worse, it would have made sense for the teenager to suppress her fury. However angry and terrified she may have felt at the growing hostility around her, it was wise to stay silent. Only at home, behind closed doors, could she share her fears and confusion. But maybe she did not wish to add the burden of her thoughts to her parents' predicament? I wonder if the strength of this protective habit – this denial of emotion – that began in Lisbeth's youth led to it persisting for so much longer than it was needed.

Despite both women's fear, they knew that it was Arnold, not they, who faced real danger. As yet only men were being arrested. In Germany, Jewish women were staying behind as their men fled the country. Clinging on to their deeply held belief in German chivalry, these women refused to accept that their lives were at risk; surely no Nazi would physically harm them?[5] Now Lisbeth and Edith had to make the same heartbreaking decision. The pittance Arnold had received for his watch and his ring stretched to only one ticket: he must go on ahead to China alone.

Early each morning, Lisbeth watched her father leave the flat on his quest to get a visa. Her feelings were mixed. While part of her hoped that this time he would succeed, she dreaded the thought of his abandoning them. His destination was the office of the one man in Vienna actively helping the Jews: the Chinese consul general, Ho Feng-Shan.

For the last twelve months Consul Ho, in blatant defiance of orders from the Chinese ambassador in Berlin, had been offering a means of escape to Vienna's persecuted Jews. He had granted thousands of them visas to Shanghai. His compassion for others surpassed concern for his own safety, earning him the title, decades later, of the 'Chinese Schindler'.[6] For people still awaiting their re-validated papers, Ho ignored all the rules. He handed out promissory notes for a visa even to those with no passport in which to stamp it. The Epsteins were lucky in this regard: they had collected their reissued passports on 25 November 1938. Yet more queuing in the snow, but this time outside the consulate of the Czechoslovakian Republic, as this was the country of Arnold's birth. There an unsmiling official had stamped and handed over their new documents. Lisbeth's heart sank when she saw, on the first page, the black swastika-bearing eagle dwarfed by a large red letter 'J'.

My grandfather returned many times to queue outside Ho's consulate, waiting to secure the means to leave Vienna. The lines were so long that scuffles sometimes broke out between those vying to get inside Ho's office. But Arnold's patience eventually paid off. In May 1939, exactly a year after he had filled in the IKG emigration questionnaire, he had both his visa and a ticket for Shanghai.

At around this time, Ilse had decided to leave Paris. She had discovered she was not legally allowed to work there, and so set sail for England. She left Dieppe on 21 May, landing in Newhaven later that day.

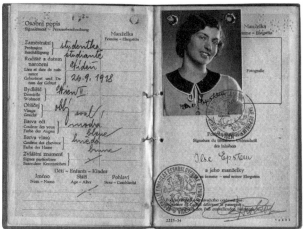

Ilse's passport showing her entry visa to the UK, May 1939.

It turned out that my mother's move from Paris saved her life. Not one of Ilse's Jewish friends in the French capital survived the war. I shivered when I learnt how narrowly my mother had escaped death in a concentration camp, simply by choosing London over Paris. It reminded me of Kate Atkinson's novel of slipped time, *Life After Life*, where a trivial decision proves a pivotal turning point in a character's life, over and over again: a seemingly random choice may alter everything that is to follow. Had Ilse stayed in France, I might not be here to write this book.

The Epsteins' apartment was awash with advice and hastily wiped eyes as the family prepared for Arnold's departure. Edith fussed around her husband as he packed the single suitcase permitted by law. He carefully selected those items he considered essential for his new life in China. In his wallet was the government-allowed sum of ten Reichsmarks*; he left the rest of his cash for his wife and daughter. Lisbeth bit her lip and clenched her hands as she looked on, trying to hide her anxiety. The spring sunshine could not warm her that day.

Arnold's journey began with the train from the Hauptbahnhof to Trieste, the Italian port from where most emigrant ships sailed. Edith and Lisbeth bid their farewells at home. They did not want to waste money on the cab back, nor did they relish saying goodbye in front of the Nazi guards patrolling the station.

As Arnold stepped out of the taxi, he saw every platform filled with uniformed men. Although his papers were in order, he knew Jewish men were prime targets for officials' aggression. As he looked for his train his heart was pounding, and it barely slowed as he climbed the steps to his carriage. Inside, he kept his eyes lowered until he found the seat bearing his number. When he put his suitcase up on the rack, his head suddenly swam with the enormity of what has happening. He might never see his homeland again; even worse, when would he next hold his wife and daughter? He sat down on the hard, upholstered seat and put his head in his hands.

---

* Around £62 today.

6

Buchenwald, June 1938 to July 1939: 'Only the Birds are Singing'

In neighbouring Germany, another Jew was also desperate to leave Europe. A man with even less reason for hope than Arnold Epstein.

His luxuriant head of hair was gone, replaced by a sheen of coarse stubble, making his long ears more apparent. He was not alone in having felt the scrape of the razor at his skull: the thousands imprisoned with him had also been shaved to the skin. For some, at the start, this aspect of their situation distressed them the most. But that would soon change. The man took it silently; his focus was on staying alive. Although hunchbacked and short, he had powerful shoulders and arms, and inner strength as well. He would need both in the labour camp.

Bruno Loewenberg had been born almost half a century earlier, in the seaport of Stettin, on the River Oder.* His father, a ship's chandler, loved painting the vessels he supplied with equipment. Franz Loewenberg captured the insignia of each one he saw – a white funnel with a blue field, a golden star and the company badge – in precise watercolours. The lad looked on in awe, and his passion for colour and creativity was born.

---

* Stettin is modern-day Szczecin, now part of Poland. Bruno Loewenberg was born there on 16 December 1890, when the city was part of the German empire; it had previously been Danish, and Swedish. Whatever its identity, it had never welcomed Jews.

The boy's ancestors had lived in the region since medieval times. In those days, Jews were forbidden to live in the city, forced to live in the countryside under a Gentile dignitary's protection. A noble landowner – Graf von Loewenberg – had deigned to take on Bruno's Jewish forebears, imposing on them his surname.[1] The boy grew up with his dearly loved sister, as well as a clan of aunts, uncles and many cousins. His father was neither rich nor poor, but able to afford his son's visits to the orthopaedic institute. Bruno went there daily for his dose of remedial exercises. Unstrapping the uncomfortably tight leather corset that he was forced to wear for years, he crouched and stretched, moved and twisted, all to the therapist's instructions. But the therapy failed. Bruno's spine – severely bent to the left ever since his birth – refused to straighten by one single inch. He would live with this scoliosis for ever, growing up with a pronounced hump on his twisted left shoulder.

The daily exercises made him strong. Despite his curved back and lack of height, Bruno could run and fight as well as Stettin's other harbour boys. At first his peer group was merciless, throwing rocks at the boy in his strange leather garment. One evening, back home, he flung the detested thing off, vowing to never wear it again. After that the boys accepted him; his courage, kindness and loyalty earned their respect and affection. This never changed, as his wide circle of friends would attest. Bruno never grew taller than five feet four inches, as his back remained bent, but his shoulders were strong and broad. His natural warmth continued to attract others. They recognised the wisdom and wit in his eyes, revealed when he swept the thick brown hair back from his forehead. Only the insensitive (or those issuing passports) ever used the word 'hunchback'.

On the June day that the Nazis forced him out of his home, Bruno had been transported to Buchenwald. At its entrance, the wrought-iron gate displayed in huge Bauhaus lettering the motto *'Jedem das Seine'*.* Like Dachau, it was not yet a death camp. Prisoners could be released if they had proof of a means to leave Germany, or if the Aryan 'buyer' of their business needed their knowledge to run it.[2] But every day, casual murders

---

* 'To each what he deserves'.

took place; it was part of the system's routine. The sadistic nature of SS guards – often only seventeen to twenty years old – in Dachau and Buchenwald was already being reported in the British press in October 1939. Some prisoners went mad, while others feigned attempts at escape, to be shot and so released from the agony of living.[3] Inmates like Bruno learnt to numb themselves to it.

In the barracks, where Bruno slept under straw, he met a company of actors and cabaret performers from Vienna. The camp had plenty of philosophers and writers, politicians and poets as well. The bookseller had always enjoyed debating and philosophising. But now the topics preoccupying the prisoners were basic ones. 'Where do I sleep?' 'What do I have to cover me?' 'What soup will I eat?' And the darkest, 'Will I die here?' Such questions took over their thoughts, displacing their old lives' more metaphysical musings. Only occasionally did they recall these. One of Bruno's friends from Berlin, a politician named Heinemann who had been in the senate, was in the camp when Bruno arrived. The two managed to come together for each day's labour, holding the same handle on the same crate of sand that they hauled up and down the stony ground. And in whispers they revisited those abstract dilemmas that had once seemed so important. Heinemann knew he would never leave the camp alive: his captors had already sworn he would die there.

And death was at hand, every minute. Men were beaten senseless for the slightest misdemeanour, or for not working hard enough. Each man became hyper-aware of those around him, constantly assessing what they were planning to do, and to whom. This way some could survive. Their day started at four in the morning, shivering as they washed over wooden basins, before being counted. Their one meal, on long tables, was bread and a bowl of meatless soup. It was eagerly devoured. If someone died at the table – of hunger, or sickness – all around grabbed for his bowl. The weakest of them, which included many of the artists and actors, were sent to work in a barn, to darn socks, or given meaningless tasks to fill their time. Work was everything.

Somehow, Bruno managed to get chocolate in the camp, and he hid a piece under his top bunk mattress to eat alone every night. Had he been caught, his life would have been over; instead the chocolate helped him survive. Another twist of good luck came in a strange guise: one day his hand became infected after he cut it open on a rock. He was taken to the camp's makeshift hospital, where a camp doctor operated to take out the pus. But no anaesthetic was used; the pain made him faint. Afterwards, the guards threw him out of a back door into a field, where he awoke to find twenty or thirty others with bandaged limbs. He soon realised that his injured hand was a blessing. This, together with awful sciatic pain, meant he could do no heavy labour until it healed. The men sat on the ground together, doing the work the guards had given them, despite being barely conscious. After the operation, Bruno was given a basket of twigs and some sharp glass splinters. He was ordered to shave the bark off each twig. Holding the splinters between his knees and working with his uninjured hand, he eventually filled a second basket with shavings of wood.

Rest was unknown in the camp. Not a moment was free from toil. But instead of labouring in the icy wind outdoors, Bruno was now sent to join the others – the weak or the privileged – darning socks in the barn. No relationship could develop between the prisoners, no connection was allowed: they were forbidden to talk. Bruno felt as if a thick blanket had enveloped each person in darkness. The once ebullient performers and composers from Vienna – the librettist Fritz Löhner-Beda, the cabaret actor Fritz Grünbraum and the composer Hermann Leopoldi among them – were darning beside him. They sat together, downcast and silent, all expression of art now extinguished. The barn was home to some mice almost as hungry as the men. Bruno had a crust of bread in his pocket. He gave the creatures a few crumbs; each day they came back for more. His friendship with the mice was the closest he came to humanity in that soulless place. Beside the barn door, the authorities had put up a sign: '*Nur die Vögel singen*' – 'Only the birds are singing'. A warning that no human voice should ever raise itself in song.

Towards the end of that year, the camp changed its philosophy on singing. It already had a talented band, created from the professional musicians among the thousands of prisoners. The commander now decided he needed a Buchenwald anthem. Since he knew he had composers as well as players in his camp, he set up a competition to write one. A prize was promised for the best song.

Two of Bruno's new Viennese friends, Löhner-Beda and Leopoldi, wrote the winning march. With its uplifting words of freedom, destiny, and saying 'yes' to life, *Das Buchenwaldlied* greatly pleased the commander. He had the orchestra play it morning, noon and night. Every afternoon, the prisoners would hear the band playing as they returned to their barracks through the big gate. Its rousing words filled their ears as they gathered on the parade ground for 5pm roll call, each man lined up to be counted. Those marked out for punishment, for whatever offence the guards had noted, were strapped to whipping posts across from the band. Then an SS man counted 25 beats, in time to the music, as his hefty partner delivered that number of lashes to each man's back and behind. This was the music allowed in the camp.

The anthem's creators never got the prize they had been promised. Leopoldi miraculously survived not just Buchenwald, but Dachau as well. Immediately after the war he went to New York, where he resumed his successful career. In 1947 he returned to his native Vienna, where he stayed until his death from a heart attack. That was 1959, when the composer – an eternal optimist – had reached his allotted three score years and ten. The librettist, Löhner-Beda, was not as lucky. After Buchenwald, he was transferred to a work camp near Auschwitz, where, in 1942, he was beaten to death.

In July 1939, after thirteen months in the camp, an incredulous Bruno was summoned and told he could leave. His sister had managed to buy him a ticket out of Germany; he never discovered how she had acquired it. Jews were allowed to leave Nazi-occupied Europe until their escape was prohibited on 23 October 1941; that month saw the start of their deportation to camps in the east.[4]

Bruno's joy was matched by his exhaustion. Along with others due for release that day, he lined up at the gate of the compound. All were made to swear to say nothing of their experiences. If Bruno spoke to one soul, the guards threatened, they would send a submarine to catch him, wherever he might be. His last memory of the camp, as he stood beneath the letters

Jedem das Seine, was the furious guard bellowing. For as Bruno had signed his name on the exit papers, he had committed a terrible crime. He wrote 'Bruno Loewenberg', leaving out the middle name 'Israel', required by law to show to all that he was a Jew.

The small group of freed men hiked for hours through the woods surrounding the camp. They were heading for the railway station at the city of Weimar, eight kilometres away. They were free, yet still shivered inside. Then each went his own way.

Bruno Loewenberg headed first for Berlin. There he went straight to the home of the woman who had saved him. The moment she opened the door, his sister flung her arms around him. She tried to hide her shock at his shaven head, and disgust at the smell: her brother's filthy clothes reeked from the de-lousing chemicals the camp guards had sprayed on them. Soon Bruno was sinking into his first bath for over a year – now elevated to the highest of luxuries. After he finally dragged himself out of the water, he dried himself with a soft towel and slid a clean white shirt onto his back. He found a dark tie and suit, and in this outfit posed with his nephew for a photograph, his arm lovingly placed on the grinning nine-year-old's shoulder. The resemblance between them was striking. Bruno would treasure the photo for the rest of his life.

Above left and above right: Bruno's sister, and Bruno with his nephew, on their reuniting after Bruno came out of Buchenwald. To my regret, I do not know – nor shall ever discover – either of their names.

Bruno stayed with his sister as long as he dared, while he sorted the paperwork for emigration. His first step was to visit the city's branch of the French shipping line, *Messageries Maritimes*. There, on 26 July 1939, a French official stamped his passport with an emigrant visa to sail. His destination was handwritten in vibrant green capitals. Another stamp forbade the bearer from lingering in France for more than *'quinze jours'*. Three days later, armed with this means of escape, Bruno walked to Berlin's grand lime tree avenue, Unter den Linden. At number 61, in the Deutsche Bank building, another official stamped his passport, this time in heavy purple ink. The heading was *Reisefreigrenze* – 'travel allowance limit' – which showed the amount of cash Bruno could take out of Germany. The figure beneath was ten Reichsmarks.[5] With his papers complete, Bruno went to the nearby office of the Chemins de Fer Français to buy a train ticket from Berlin to Marseilles, via Kehl. He spent a last night at his sister's, his heart heavy at the inevitable separation.

The rail journey seemed endless, only sweetened by his recent memories of his nephew and sister. He even dozed off at times, when his exhaustion

Above and overleaf: Bruno's passport with stamps including his visa to sail to Shanghai, July 1939.

got the better of his fear. Finally on 30 July 1939, Bruno Loewenberg stepped off the train at the French port of Marseilles. There he stood and stared at the huge ships moored in the harbour. As he breathed the salty air deep into his lungs, his father's colourful paintings of ships' livery floated before him. He could barely believe he was free. Or that, a few days later, one of the liners before him was to take him to safety. To a new life, far distant from Europe. On his passport's new visa, the bright green letters spelled out the name SHANGHAI.

7

Vienna, July 1939 to January 1940: A Miraculous Phone Call

The flat on Am Tabor was quieter than ever. Lisbeth and Edith sat at the dining table, sipping their tea, thinking of new ways to save money. They had sold nearly everything, except the most basic essentials for living.

They had both been heartened by the latest news from Ilse, who was now settled in England. After applying for jobs as a governess or a domestic servant – the only type of work for which refugees like her were eligible – she had found a position as a maid in London. If only her mother and sister had any chance of earning anything themselves. With no means of earning an income, they had only one option left. They must give up their flat.

In July 1939, just as Bruno Loewenberg was leaving Germany, Lisbeth and Edith packed up their few possessions and moved from Am Tabor to a smaller apartment. Their new home was flat 13 at 4 Schwertgasse, in Vienna's first district, south of the Donaukanal. It lay steps from Judenplatz, the square at the heart of the city's medieval Jewish quarter. The apartment building's ornate iron gateway and wide stuccoed hallway gave a false air of grandeur; the rooms inside were tiny.

Lisbeth and her mother now had two simple goals: to survive, and to effect their escape. Jewish women as well as men were now being dragged from their homes without warning or reason. Some were seized for deportation on trains bound for Nazi-Occupied Poland. The Juedische Gemeinde were suggesting that Vienna's Jews should volunteer for transports to Poland, to form communities there.[1] No one knew what befell these volunteers on arrival, but dark suspicions were growing. The Epstein women wisely ignored the advice.

Lisbeth continued her evening classes at the Urania, although her new skills in leather craft and shorthand typing led to no work. At the same time, Edith kept up her pressure on the Juedische Gemeinde for financial assistance to make the journey to Shanghai. They were both greatly relieved when a letter from Arnold confirmed his safe arrival. He told them briefly that he had found accommodation in the cheapest part of the city, a Japanese-run district called Hongkew. It was dirty and overcrowded, but its low rents attracted many penniless European refugees like himself. The women wrote back with any news they could muster to try to keep his spirits up. But as each letter took several weeks to arrive, these exchanges were frustratingly sparse.[2]

By now – the middle of 1939 – Shanghai was being flooded by refugees fleeing Hitler: two thousand were arriving there each month. If that rate continued, the city was in danger of being overwhelmed. In August 1939, the Japanese authorities – urged on by Shanghai's Jewish leaders – introduced new entry restrictions, effectively ending the port's open-door policy.[3] Strangely, it was Edith, not Arnold, who first learnt on the grapevine that one of these restrictions was a ban on more immigrants entering Hongkew. Sharp as ever, she wrote and told her husband that he was more likely to get their entry papers if he moved to a different part of town. Lisbeth later recalled: 'When my father first came, he did live in Hongkou*, like everybody else. And it was difficult for him to get that paper, to ask us to come. We heard that if you do not live in Hongkou … it might be easier to get that guarantee, so we did write him again.'[4] As usual, Arnold took his wife's advice.

Summer progressed, but despite the sunshine, Europe was sensing the dark shadow of impending war. As the Germans and Soviets signed a non-aggression pact, Britain and other Western powers began mobilising their troops in anticipation of German advances into Poland. On 1 September,

---

* After the Second World War, Hongkew's spelling was changed to Hongkou.

Lisbeth and her mother's worst fears were confirmed. Huddled by their radio, they heard the news that Hitler's forces had indeed invaded Poland. Two days later, Britain and France declared war against Germany. Which meant on Austria too. The Epsteins were suddenly on the wrong 'side' of the conflict. Instead of offering protection against the Nazis, the Allies would be sending bombs. Could they not see how much the Epsteins also hated Hitler? Never had Lisbeth and her mother felt so scared, and so alone.

Across the Channel, Britain's declaration of war on the Axis powers affected Lisbeth's sister too. The 21-year-old Ilse had met another Viennese refugee, an architecture student three years younger than herself. His name was Josef Meller. Family lore relates their first meeting in London as taking place at a gathering of left-wing sympathisers (knowing my father, I imagine it was a talk put on by the Workers' Educational Association rather than a collection of conspiratorial Trotskyists).

The couple may have spoken German together, but in public they now had to learn the language of their new country. Refugees like them were given a booklet on arrival which offered guidance on how to behave. Point 1 advised the immediate learning of English 'and its correct pronunciation'. Point 2 warned: 'Refrain from speaking German in the streets and in public conveyances and in public places such as restaurants ... and *do not talk in a loud voice*' (italicised in the original).[5] Some quarters of British society still viewed these foreigners with hostility. In those grey days of rationing and food shortages, and the recent Depression, many feared the refugees were after their jobs. The Jews fleeing Europe were not welcome. Nothing had changed since the Evian Conference: prohibitive quota systems for entry kept most countries' doors closed to many of the victims of Nazism.

What's more, as soon as war broke out, German-speakers like Josef were considered 'enemy aliens'. They were classified into one of three groups: my father fell into the least dangerous (and most common) Category C – considered a genuine refugee from Nazi oppression.[6] At this point, only a few hundred (all Category A individuals) were detained. Instead, in October 1939, Josef was sent to a transit camp near Richborough, Sandwich. He was one of 4,000 young refugees offered temporary housing there, in Kitchener Camp. The men were allowed to come and go, and treated warmly by the locals. But Ilse was separated from her boyfriend.

When I went through the documents in the box with the sunflower clasp, I regretted the fact that I know so little German. I remember, when I was very little, Ruth pointing out the parts of my face – *Nase* and *Auge* and *Augenbraue* – with Claudia standing beside me. But my sister was very resistant to Ruth's efforts to teach us. She said she did not want to be different from the other children at school – an understandable attitude, and common among the children of immigrants. The German lessons stopped. I later chose Latin at school on the advice of teachers who knew I was interested in studying medicine. But I grew up hearing German spoken around me, especially when my parents were arguing, and picked up some words and their pronunciation. On the other hand, I think I missed learning some English colloquialisms known to all my friends. I also grew up thinking that the name of the plant in our garden with its showers of lovely purple flowers was 'visteria'.

Looking back, I now think my parents may have been somewhat relieved that our German tuition turned out to be short-lived. They – like many refugees – wished to distance themselves from the land of their birth. It was ironic that, years later in 1971, the London German School opened on a site very near our Petersham home. I remember that my parents found this rather unsettling, with mixed feelings about being surrounded by speakers of their native tongue.

In Vienna, the Epstein women were growing more and more desperate. Their circle of friends was shrinking as so many Jews had already left. When would their turn arrive? They checked the letterbox in Schwertgasse over and over for news from Shanghai. Then in October 1939, the letter came. With trembling hands, Edith opened it, to find the immigration papers and guarantees that Arnold had finally obtained for them both. His move from Hongkou had paid off. They stared at the papers, eyes as wide as their smiles.

The weather changed sharply. Autumn was replaced by one of Europe's coldest winters on record; temperatures were the lowest for a century in many parts of the continent. Snow came early to Vienna that year, and people hurried through the streets with heads down and coats wrapped tightly around them. Consul Ho was still issuing visas, but now only one ship a month was leaving Italy for the East.

All Lisbeth and her mother needed now were their tickets to sail. But competition had never been fiercer. Those Jews who could afford it were resorting to bribery, offering any valuables they still owned – Impressionist paintings, Persian rugs or fine jewellery – to steamship agents. Such goods would be of no use to them anyway: the Nazis stopped people taking them out of the country. The Epstein women had nothing left to sell but, by tightening their belts even further, scraped enough money together for their fares. Mother and daughter became familiar with every steamship company in Vienna, as well as the travel bureaux on the Ringstrasse; every day, they lined up to try to get tickets. But each time they reached the front of the queue, their hearts sank as they were told the last ones had just gone. Lisbeth later recalled: 'I can still see us waiting in line for tickets, tickets, and people bought tickets just before us, last ticket sold, everyone went back home without tickets.'[7] Even Edith's charm failed to move the officials behind the counter. Each day they returned home empty-handed, and with heavy hearts.

On 7 November 1939, Lisbeth's mother had reached the limit of her patience. Arnold had found work in Shanghai; nothing else was stopping them now. Edith wrote to the Juedische Gemeinde, pleading for their help:

I would like to ask the Community to help me to obtain two tickets for Shanghai. My husband has found a job as a teacher at an English College for Refugees. He writes: 'A bright future would be secure here if you finally would be here.'

He has already sent us the immigration papers. I could come up with about 500–600 RM, which the Community could use to buy the tickets.* I implore you to give me and my daughter the opportunity to live a humane life at my husband's side.

My husband travelled without any support of the Community to Shanghai, paid his taxes for 30 years to the Israelite Community and joined the World War from 1914–18 as Rittmeister.

I do ask for any support,

Yours sincerely, Edith Epstein, 1, Schwertgasse 4/13

---

* 500–600 RM is equivalent to around £3,000–£3,600 today.

While Lisbeth and her mother awaited a reply, yet more paperwork had to be sorted. There were all kinds of inspections, involving more queuing each day. One day they were sent to line up at a beautiful building on an estate formerly owned by the Jewish family, the Rothschilds, now commandeered by the Nazis. Lisbeth and Edith climbed an elegant staircase 'right out of an opera by Mozart' that led to a room filled with Nazi officials. She would never forget the mismatch between the expressionless men and their ornate surroundings, as they either stamped people's passports or sent them away with neither a stamp nor any hope, but just a cold, cruel look.[8]

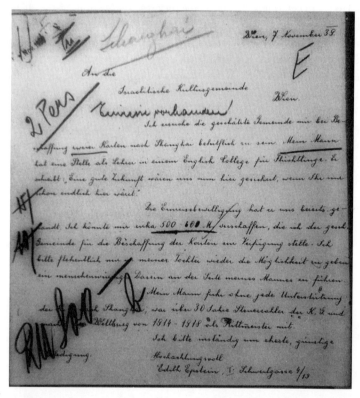

Above and opposite: Edith's letter to the IKG requesting help, and IKG notes showing Arnold's date of travel to Prague (Courtesy Archiv IKG Wien, Jerusalem holding, A/W 2590,45).

On 24 November the two women crossed the bridge over the canal back north up to Leopoldstadt, to 3 Schiffamtsgasse. At the district's finance offices, under the hard stare of a tax office official, they signed a document headed *Steuerliche Unbedenklichkeits-bescheinigung*. A long word for a huge act of relinquishment. The paper was the women's tax clearance certificate, without which they could not leave Austria.

Hitler not only wanted to rid the Reich of its Jews, but also to extract all their money. His government repurposed a levy intended to stop wealthy citizens from evading tax by living abroad. Now the Nazis used the *Reichsfluchtsteuer* – Reich Flight Tax – to penalise emigrants fleeing persecution. Edith's signature on the document proved she had paid the Flight Tax, and any others still owed to the state. With this declaration, she signed

Edith and Lisbeth's Flight Tax papers, November 1939.

away the family's rights to their lifetime's acquisitions in Austria, as well as all future claims of any inheritance by future descendants. Once assured that the women had handed all their goods to the state, a notary counter-signed the document, affirming that he had no objections to them leaving.

Another month passed with no news, and New Year's Eve was approaching. There were few celebrations; Lisbeth and Edith had neither the will nor the money to mark the close of that dismal year.

But then January came, and with it the telephone call that changed everything. When Edith picked up the receiver, someone from the Juedische Gemeinde said simply: 'If you give us all your cash, we can get two tickets for you.' Without hesitation, Edith gave them all she had: having saved a further 200 RM, this now amounted to 800 Reichsmarks*.

Within days, Lisbeth and her mother held in their hands two tickets to sail to Shanghai. They were to leave the port of Trieste on 7 February 1940, on the *Conte Rosso*. Lisbeth's emotions were in turmoil again: intense joy at the prospect of seeing her father, but deep anxiety at this uprooting from her homeland. Just turned eighteen, the little security she had known was about to vanish. Ahead lay a journey across 11,000 miles of ocean, into an alien world. But there was no time for introspection.

In one way packing for their new lives was easy. The law only allowed each refugee to take one suitcase with them, as well as a prescribed amount of jewellery: a watch and wedding ring, one neck chain and just one pair of earrings. And money required no thought. The pair had no cash, apart from the ten Reichsmarks each could take out of Austria. But how could Lisbeth decide which items to take? She must have agonised over the best use of the limited space, packing and repacking as she reassessed her selection. Perhaps her mother advised her to forgo her prettier clothes in favour of more practical ones: Arnold had told them of Shanghai's icy winters. Did she listen to Edith, or smuggle in a favourite yet frivolous item? Which books or childhood mementos should she take, which prized photographs or letters? And could she squeeze in those sandals and those boots? What could Lisbeth bear to leave behind, with no guarantee of ever seeing it

* Around £5,000 today.

again? She must have kept photographs of herself and her sister as children, and portraits of her parents, as these remained in the box I inherited.

When they were ready to leave, Edith let in two Nazi officers; everything they were taking had to be meticulously itemised, and the inventory handed over for inspection. Lisbeth's hands shook as she opened her case, the stony-faced men looming over her. Only after the officers had checked off the list and approved it for emigration could the women's luggage be sealed.

The pair valued their lives over their possessions. They were not risk takers. But they knew of other refugees who were more daring. Some hid diamonds or other treasures, sewn deep into the hems of their clothing. They heard of one little boy, made an unwitting smuggler: he carried a long chain of pure gold in the bunting around the pillow he clutched to his chest. His mother's gold rings were hidden in his teddy bear's nose. Others converted their cash into gold, then persuaded trusted jewellers or goldsmiths to turn the metal into everyday items. Solid gold buttons or belt buckles were disguised with cloth coverings; handbag decorations gleamed, undetected, with real gold.

On the morning of 6 February, the Epstein women climbed into the cab for the railway station. They were breaking no rules; their cases held the permitted allowance, and no more. Any value in the contents was purely sentimental.

Few people were about, it was so early. Lisbeth looked out of the cab to take in her last memory at their apartment building. She took a deep breath, trying to crystallise an image of Vienna's beauty to engrave in her memory. The streets were silent under a blanket of snow that shone in the pale winter sun. She did not see a single person along the way.[9]

When the pair reached the station, pandemonium took the place of tranquillity. Passengers crowded the platforms; Nazi guards in leather coats stood everywhere, legs astride, ready to pounce on anyone whose papers or luggage showed the slightest infringement of the rules. But Edith's wallet held the final document they needed to leave Austria. A small sheet was headed *Abmeldebestätigung* or 'deregistration' document, and dated the day of their departure on their tickets: 6 February 1940. The exit paper was marked valid until 10 March 1940. As if my aunt and grandmother would linger in Vienna a day longer than necessary.

That sheet wiped the women out of existence, as far as Austria was concerned.

Close inspection of the tiny document shows both women's official *'Reichskleiderkarte Nr.'* – clothes certificate numbers, used on ration cards for the purchase of garments like socks, sweaters and dresses. Had they stayed any longer, even this meagre benefit would have been snatched away as, the very day that they left, a new law deprived Jews of these cards. The paper bore another chilling detail. In front of the handwritten name 'Edith' someone had added 'Sara'. My grandmother's Old English name, unlike her daughter's Hebrew-derived 'Lisbeth', was not deemed Jewish enough by the Nazis.

When I noticed this tiny detail, I felt sick. I must have looked at the flimsy half-page in Lisbeth's box a dozen times before the significance of that 'Sara' really hit me. This evidence of a Nazi law I knew of in theory had so much more impact when I saw it applied in black and white to someone in my own family. How much more viscerally I understood the Nazis' intent from this small slip of paper than from all the history books I had read.

At last Lisbeth and her mother, scarcely able to believe it, stepped onto the train for Trieste. Like Arnold before them, they kept their eyes lowered to avoid attracting attention and being turned back. As they sat down in their places, both were shivering with fear. As long as they were in Nazi territory, every guard walking through the carriages could prove lethal. They had heard of other refugees undergoing brutal searches, and being arrested if illicit items were found. At the Brenner Pass with Italy, Jews were forced off the train for inspection. Every piece of luggage was opened and searched. If no contraband was found, men and women were separated and strip-searched. Jews about to board German ships had artificial legs removed and smashed open, and the wigs of Orthodox women were ripped off and searched for hidden valuables – deliberate humiliations.

The women sat rigid and motionless as their train neared the border with Italy. They hardly dared breathe. Suddenly the door to their carriage was flung open. They both looked up, paling, as the uniformed guard leant in. To Lisbeth's astonishment, the German control not only ignored both their luggage, but said to them warmly: 'Have a good trip.' She was stunned, never expecting 'humanity' from a uniformed guard. She and Edith 'could have taken the whole world' along with them!

Mother and daughter settled back in their seats, relaxing at last. Lisbeth let her turbulent thoughts wash through her as her pulse slowed back to normal. She barely dared imagine the home that lay ahead. What would they find, a month from now, when their Shanghai fantasy would turn into reality?

Edith and Lisbeth's deregistration document, showing 'Sara' added to Edith's name, February 1940.

8

Bruno the 'bookman'

He had never given up hope. He had refused to be destroyed by the starvation, humiliation and beatings he endured for thirteen months in the camp. Or by awakening four hundred times to the same dread crushing his chest. And his hope had paid off: his life was once more his own. True, it had been transplanted to Shanghai's alien landscape, but it now had purpose again. His recovery had begun.

By late September 1939, Bruno Loewenberg was getting used to the humid warmth of Shanghai. The stubble on his head was softening, as new greyer hair grew in. His eyes were less often clouded by tears, and – during moments when he could shut out the past – began to shine with their former warmth. No longer a number, he was a man; and more than that, a *bookman*, the word he would use to describe himself for the rest of his life.

The voyage on board the *Messageries Maritimes* vessel had been no luxury cruise. His sister's life-saving gift, which had rescued him from the hell of Buchenwald, had only stretched to a third-class ticket in steerage. He had no cabin, but slept alongside a hundred other people within a large room. On the last leg of the journey, between Hong Kong and Shanghai, their ship had been turned back to Europe. The date was 1 September; the French had just declared war on Hitler, and needed the vessel for military purposes. Bruno and the others were disembarked at Hong Kong, where British officials promptly interned all the Germans as enemy aliens.

Compared to his previous internment, Bruno's time imprisoned in Hong Kong was a breeze; he declared later, one 'should always be interned by the

British!'¹ For ten days he and the other 'prisoners' were kept in a school, where they ate meals delivered daily from a nearby hotel. All they had to do was to say 'here!' during the countings that took place every morning. Once the British realised that these Germans posed no threat at all, they found them a ship to continue their voyage to Shanghai. Which is where Bruno's new life began.

Above left and above right: Bruno on release from Buchenwald, compared to how he had looked during First World War service, twenty years earlier.

Bruno in Shanghai in 1940, with his hair regrown.

Bruno never imagined he would ever start a business in Shanghai. But here he was, in his newest venture in the heart of the city's International Settlement – the prime territory, with its elegant Bund river frontage, that British and American merchants had seized almost a hundred years before.* In the mid-nineteenth century, the British and US naval victories in the Opium Wars led to the two 'unequal' treaties of Nanjing and Tientsin, which forced the Chinese to open Shanghai and four other ports to international trade.[2] Since then Westerners had settled within their own protected enclaves in the city, from where they continued, as best they could, to replicate the lifestyles they had left back home. The English-speaking among them called themselves Shanghailanders, to contrast themselves with the city's native residents, the Shanghainese.[3]

Bruno's business was called the Lion Bookshop, a name that came from the family surname bestowed by Count von Loewenberg.† The second-hand bookshop occupied a room in a multi-tenancy house at 328 Moulmein Road, on the corner of Bubbling Well Road. Bruno, a shrewd businessman who made the most of his limited resources, soon added a lending library as well. Not far away was one of Bruno's favourite places, the Café Louis, whose German-style cakes made it popular with many other sweet-toothed customers. Louis Eisfelder and his family were also refugees from Berlin, and had arrived in November 1938, opening the café a few months later. Café Louis' tagline, beside a hand-drawn logo of a shield bearing a coffee cup and pretzel, was 'specialists in fancy cakes, chocolates and marzipan'; they claimed to be the best continental confectionery in Shanghai. Not surprising, since some of their pastry chefs had been trained by a French *pâtissier*. Perhaps more surprising was how skilfully the Chinese chefs learnt to cook German-style meals, despite being taught by the owner's sister, Bertha, who 'never learnt a word of English or Chinese'.[4]

---

* The word Bund means 'any artificial embankment'; in Anglo-Chinese ports, it was the embanked quay along the shore. In *Tales of Old Shanghai*, Graham Earnshaw writes that it has been called 'the most mispronounced word of all. It is not pronounced in a Germanic way: it has Sanskrit origins, and the Shanghailanders pronounced it to rhyme with "shunned".'

† *Loewe* or *Löwe* means 'lion', while *berg* is 'mountain'.

Like many of the city's immigrants, the Eisfelders rented their premises from Silas Hardoon, the Sephardi* landlord once described as 'the richest man East of Suez'.[5] His mansion, a few doors further down Bubbling Well Road, was surrounded by hectares of secluded gardens, screened from prying eyes by a long brick wall over three metres high.[6] Other moneyed residents chose to live in villas in Frenchtown, the Concession settled by the first French merchants in 1849. A smaller district than the English-speakers' International Settlement, Frenchtown was seen by some as a more elegant address.

While many went to Café Louis to drink hot chocolate or tea, Bruno preferred its excellent coffee. He also enjoyed the cakes and hand-made chocolates, sometimes even ordering the whipped cream and strawberries offered as accompaniment to their pastries.[7] The owner's teenage son, Horst, later wrote that *anything* could be bought in Shanghai if one had the money, a fact all refugees soon discovered for themselves.

Bruno regularly combed the city to find the stock for his bookshop. His last days in Berlin had left no time for him to salvage any possessions from either his shop or his apartment. Had he tried, the door of each building would in any case have been slammed in his face by its new Aryan owner. Here in Shanghai, Bruno's favourite place to source books was Seymour Road, which was a short walk westwards along Bubbling Well Road: the length of its six blocks was lined with second-hand stores. Such thrift shops were springing up fast, as the city's German and Austrian immigrants sold off the valuables they had been able to bring in before the luggage limits were imposed. A Jewish charity, the International Committee (IC), set up the first emigrants' thrift shop to help the refugees make a little cash.[†] Fur coats – which were prone to mould in Shanghai's damp climate – porcelain,

---

* Sephardi Jews originate from Spain, Portugal, North Africa and the Middle East, in contrast to Ashkenazi Jews, descendants of those from France, Germany and Eastern Europe.

† The International Committee for Granting Relief to European Refugees was usually referred to simply as the IC, or the Komor Committee after Paul Komor, its co-founder. The IC was funded mainly by Sir Victor Sassoon, a businessman and member of the Baghdadi Jewish Sassoon family, who had come to Shanghai in the 1920s.

silverware, candelabras, cameras and jewellery could be bought for a song. All nationalities came to these shops, including the Japanese, who were especially keen to get their hands on the rarer items.

People soon recognised the distinctive broad-shouldered man with the stick, scouring the goods being sold along Seymour Road. But he was disciplined, keeping his focus on books – in particular, those written in German, of which there were many. Some refugees had crated up entire libraries to send on before leaving. Others arrived weighed down by suitcases crammed with their favourite reading matter.

Bruno always had a good eye for what might sell. His shop in Berlin, and before that, Paris, had been famous for rare, antiquarian works, including many art books and prints. He had held small exhibitions of contemporary painters, often the Expressionists so hated by Hitler's party, who saw such work as an offence to the German race, a corruption of Teutonic culture. They called it 'degenerate art', a view that made no sense to Bruno. Now he set about rebuilding his stock. The German-speaking immigrants' books were expensive, as they were high quality, so he bought cheaper pirated editions for more 'everyday' purchases. Shanghai was China's leading centre of printing and newspaper publishing, with a thriving press.* The city was also famous for cheap copies of foreign books. Since the Chinese recognised neither foreign patents nor copyrights, no one considered such pirating either wrong or illegal. The city's presses rolled out vast numbers of low-priced, flimsy volumes, near-replicas of popular books written in English, shortly after their publication in Britain or America.

Bruno quickly discovered how the 'pirates' could print copies of books so hot off the press.[8] As soon as a new bestseller reached Kelly & Walsh, the large American bookstore in Shanghai, an 'informer' from a rival Chinese-run shop would tell its managers. They would then send someone out to buy it. Representatives of all the other Chinese bookstores would meet to agree how many copies they should get 'reprinted'. Within days, as if by magic, copies of the English-language book would fill their

---

* The refugees also created new German-language newspapers themselves, helping to keep people informed of the progress of the war back in Europe.

own shelves – identical to the original apart from the missing copyright page. Bruno readily bought these near photocopies, alongside more costly imported ones. True, the pirated books soon fell apart, and the thin paper between their hard covers was blotted with cheap newsprint. The quality of the illustrations was abysmal: whether half-tone or full colour, they usually came out as a solid blob of ink on the page.[9]

But Bruno knew his customers did not care. They were happy to get their hands on these pirated editions, being both short on funds and keen to learn English – Shanghai's lingua franca for schools and business since the days of the first British and American settlers. The city's philanthropic Jewish support committees organised English classes for the newly arrived German-speakers. They took place at the hastily set up camps – known as *Heime* – for those immigrants without homes, as well as at the SJYA School.* The English-language editions that Bruno sold were cheap, helped the refugees learn the language more quickly, and lasted just long enough to be read, keeping everyone – apart from the original publishers, if they knew what was going on – happy.[10]

The German's book business was proving a success. By 1941, the Lion Bookshop and Circulating Library was reported in SMC police files to be 'a fairly sound business'.[†][11] And, just as in Berlin, Bruno soon collected a wide circle of friends.

One of whom would change the course of his life.

* Shanghai Jewish Youth Association.

† The SMC was the Shanghai Municipal Council, the city's Western-run authority, with representatives from all the powers who had settled in Shanghai after the Opium Wars. These foreign powers were Great Britain, the United States, France, Italy and Portugal.

9

February 1940: Exotic Harbours and Flying Fish

The twin yellow funnels of the *Conte Rosso* gleamed in the winter sunshine as Lisbeth and Edith each carried their single suitcase up the gangway. A short while later, the Italian liner's massive engines throbbed into life, and there was no going back. Lisbeth leant against the white railings, watching the distance between herself and the dockside increase, and the buildings shrink away. Slowly but inevitably, her past was dissolving from view.

It was 7 February 1940. The two women had spent the previous night in Trieste, in simple accommodation arranged by the local Juedische Gemeinde. Lisbeth thought the Italian port was 'the most beautiful place in the whole world'; its grand seafront piazza faced the sparkling Mediterranean waters where ships lined up under vast cloudless skies. The air was lighter and the sky bluer than in Vienna; no wonder painters flocked to Italy, she thought. But she also knew that her reaction came more from the freedom the port represented than its physical qualities. She could breathe freely at last: Lisbeth was no longer afraid for her life.[1]

Once the *Conte Rosso* – named after the fourteenth-century Count of Savoy who wore nothing but scarlet – was in open water, the women found the staircase leading down to their accommodation. Edith had booked one of the 250 second-class cabins that slept three people. The liner offered suites or cabins for nearly 2,500 passengers, plus space for the crew of four hundred. Originally launched as a transatlantic steamer in 1922, taking tourists on luxury cruises between Italy and New York City, she had been sailing the Trieste–Bombay–Shanghai route since 1932. Now she and her sister ship, the *Conte Verde*, had a new role, offering escape to thousands of Jews seeking the haven of Shanghai. Lisbeth and her mother were lucky that their tickets had come through while Italian ships were still allowed through the Suez Canal, the shortcut that sped passage from Europe to the East. A few months later, in June 1940, Italy would enter the war as an ally of Hitler, and the British would close the canal to Italian ships, leaving only the Trans-Siberian Railway as a route of escape.[2]

Not surprisingly, every cabin was taken. Among the *Conte Rosso*'s passengers were 150 of the last Jewish emigrants still able to leave a Reich now at war.[3] Many of them had been forced to buy first-class tickets – the only ones left – even though once on board they had neither the funds nor the dress to fit in with their fellow travellers. Many of the wealthier passengers had little sympathy for these misfits, and made no effort to hide their disdain. Even some of the higher officers snubbed them.[4] Moreover, the refugees had been made to pay return fares, since no one could guarantee that they could land in Shanghai.[5] Yet everyone knew that this journey was only one-way.

The two women followed the stream of other passengers and soon found their cabin. It was quite cramped but, to Lisbeth's relief, it was clean and neat. Although she and her mother were only travelling tourist class, they soon realised that, compared to what they had left behind, four weeks of luxury lay ahead. Unlike the poorest on board, they were not confined to the cramped space of steerage below deck. Lisbeth was free to explore almost the whole ship, apart from the few areas reserved for those with first-class tickets. For her, the coming voyage shimmered with the safety of a comforting dream, however transient.

The eighteen-year-old must have delighted in exploring the liner's many decks and public spaces, soon discovering the different areas set aside for eating and drinking, lectures and sports. She would have admired the lavish Italianate décor, whose elaborate sculptures, carvings and columns were intended to recreate the feel of an old Venetian palace. The main dining salon and lounge were finished in fifteenth-century-style solid oak and embossed leather panelling, while the smoking room was decorated in chinoiserie. Because the *Conte Rosso*'s route crossed many sun-warmed oceans, the designers had unusually included a system for dining outdoors: the forward part of the main promenade could convert to a vast open-air restaurant. An Olympic-sized swimming pool attracted many, although Lisbeth was still reluctant to expose her badly scarred leg.

The ship's food and hospitality was a highlight of the voyage. Lisbeth could hardly believe what they were offered: the dining room allocated to their cabin class served three full meals daily on cloth-covered tables. Compared to the meagre pickings back in Austria, 'where Jews got nothing', Lisbeth felt like a guest at the Ritz. Whenever she sat down on a deckchair, a passing steward would offer hors d'oeuvres or a cool drink. While other Jews may have struggled to overcome their distaste for *trefe*[*] food, this was not an issue for the secular Epsteins. *Porc avec pommes, bouillabaisse* … the two women had no qualms about putting pragmatism before piety.

At night-time, mother and daughter stood together on deck. They marvelled at the intensity of the stars brightening the inky-blue sky, and at the glittering of the flying fish leaping up from the waters. The month at sea felt like a holiday to Lisbeth; for the teenager, whose life had so recently been blighted by fear, the journey was 'absolutely gorgeous … an outstanding experience'. In Bombay, bananas were brought onto the ship, picked straight from the tree. Lisbeth could not believe the fresh taste and perfume of the fruit; she had never tasted one like it before. But the dark shadow of war was inescapable, even here. Along with the other refugees suspended between Austria's horrors and the unknown ahead in Shanghai, Lisbeth could not pretend this was just a pleasure cruise. Harsh reminders of reality pierced the temporary feeling of ease, like spiky horsehairs poking through an old sofa. And while Edith found it easy to relax and socialise with fellow passengers, at times her daughter found their presence, and behaviour, disturbing.

One pair of refugees made a lasting impression on Lisbeth. She and Edith were sipping tea in one of the ballrooms when she noticed two young men, who were smoking and laughing by the baby grand on a dais at the

[*] Non-kosher.

edge of the room. The one seated at the piano was playing 'Die Moritat von Mackie Messer',* while his companion, glass in hand, sang along with great gusto. His guttural German suited the ballad's harsh lyrics:

> Und der Haifisch, der hat Zähne;
> Und die trägt er im Gesicht;
> Und MacHeath, der hat ein Messer;
> Doch das Messer sieht man nicht.†

Lisbeth knew where the young men had been only days before boarding the ship. Their gaunt faces were still etched with hunger, sharp cheekbones jutting through pale skin, their shaven heads darkening with stubble. Bony wrists projected from the piano player's sleeves as he moved his hands over the keyboard.

Lisbeth turned to her mother and asked: 'How are they able to enjoy themselves, and sing, and be so happy? It seems like a contradiction to me.'

Her mother replied: 'Well, it's *because* they came out of the concentration camp that they are happy.'

At that time, it was still possible for prisoners to be released from places such as Buchenwald and Dachau, though only if they had proof of their means to leave the Reich. Any murders that took place within the camps, though deliberate, were random and on a small scale. But the camps' role would change: the full horrific mechanisation of the death camps would come into force the following year. Without their tickets to China, the two young men might well have been destined for the gas chambers.

Was Edith surprised at Lisbeth's question? With her own carefree nature, she may have underestimated the effects of the last few years on her daughter. Since the age of sixteen, Lisbeth had experienced so few moments of levity; when faced with it now, was she no longer able to recognise it?

---

* 'Mack the Knife'.

† 'And the shark, he has teeth / And he wears them in his face / And MacHeath, he has a knife / But the knife you don't see.'

The *Conte Rosso*'s journey crossed the Mediterranean, the Red Sea, through the Gulf of Aden and into the Arabian Sea and the Indian Ocean before reaching the South China Sea. She stopped at many anchorages en route, notably the ports of Aden, Bombay, Singapore, Manila and Hong Kong. But the two Epstein women, like others whose passports were stamped with a large letter 'J', were not allowed to disembark. There was always the risk that some would try to jump ship, even though few countries were prepared to accept any Jews. Although she never once set foot off the ship, Lisbeth felt as excited as if she had travelled to each destination, and craned her neck across the viewing deck's railings at each harbour.

At some of the *Conte Rosso*'s first stops, like Alexandria or Port Said, people would come on board to sell or give items to those confined to the decks. Lisbeth watched as Arab vendors shook their heads in disappointment that the refugees could not afford even the cheapest wares. Representatives of Egyptian Jewish communities also came on board, but they offered the émigrés gifts – of light clothing, money and cigarettes, even underwear.[6]

On other ships, Jewish emigrants had been luckier, being able to go ashore to explore the ports of call. However, a family member was often asked to stay on board to prevent anyone from absconding. At ports where Jews were allowed to disembark, the penniless refugees were often surprised by the kindness of strangers. A young German refugee, Ernst Heppner, left his ship with others at Port Said, and met some local Jews waiting to take the group to an old house near the harbour. They followed the Egyptian Jews up a rickety staircase into a room where they saw tables covered with second-hand clothing. The teenager was bewildered. Never before in his middle-class life had he been deemed poor enough to need charity. Overcoming the shock of his new status, he took the clothing. On the way back to the ship, Arabs tried to sell him fresh dates. When they realised he was penniless, they gave him some of the fruit in exchange for a few cigarettes he found deep in his pockets.[7]

People respond to stress in different ways, and Lisbeth found some of the refugees' behaviour on board quite disturbing. A few were plainly in shock. They had become unable to speak or interact with others, and appeared to be in an almost catatonic state.[8] Others found sleep impossible, pacing the ship's deck all night. One refugee on board described these insomniacs as 'people that were wasted, wasted ... People that were psychically so terribly hurt that they walked like animals ... like the freedom-loving animals ... in the zoo. They were walking slowly, like ghosts.'[9] Many could not shake off their grief at having to abandon older relatives, or their fear that Gestapo agents lurked in the ship's shadowy passageways – and, in fact, German officers, including Gestapo members, were on board some of the émigré ships.[10] These damaged souls slunk around the ship, ground down to the point where Lisbeth wondered if they had begun to believe themselves no more than the subhumans – the *Untermensch* – of Nazi rhetoric.

Lisbeth tried not to be disturbed by such depressive behaviour, and must have had sympathy for them, even those whose relief at escape spilt into disorder and rowdiness. She heard the rumours flying around the ship of married women sneaking off to the cabins of officers, or that of the ship's doctor, emboldened by their liberation. People seemed to change as soon as the ship had passed the Suez Canal. She saw other refugees become aggressive, actively picking quarrels and starting fights that forced the Captain's intervention.[11] Such wildness was not surprising. After months or even years of fearful living, people were bursting with long-suppressed feelings. Like molten lava building up within a long-silent volcano, at some point their emotions were bound to explode.

Lisbeth Epstein, however, stayed calm. Perhaps this trip marked the start of her coolness, her detachment. Perhaps it had started much earlier. But she was wary of others, and slow to trust them. No records show if she made any friends during the voyage. However, she kept two tiny black and white photographs, with crimped edges, taken on board. She and Edith are on deckchairs, a smiling, clean-shaven man beside Lisbeth – he could be Indian or Sri Lankan. Edith is elegant as usual, wearing a sundress and her painted Cupid's bow smile. Lisbeth's black hair is cut in a childish bob that barely covers her ears. She is dressed in a dark, puff-sleeved top, and fashionably wide-legged trousers that hide the shape of her legs. In one picture, Lisbeth's eyes are narrowed against the sunshine gleaming off the waves; in the other, they are downcast. In both, she is leaning sharply away from the man sitting by her.

Lisbeth and Edith on the deck of the *Conte Rosso*.

Lisbeth may have simply been shy, rather than unwilling to get close to others. Not everyone is born outgoing and sociable. Yet the society she grew up in was known for its haughtiness. The Viennese were even more confident than other Austrian citizens, often stereotyped as being reserved, unfriendly and cold. Growing up in the capital, Lisbeth had been surrounded by these feelings of entitlement, as much part of her city as the whipped cream on her hot chocolate. Well aware of the background and class of her fellow passengers, she would not have been alone in any snobbishness. Many of the émigrés on board retained their prejudices from home despite being, quite literally, in the same boat. They did not fail to spot the slang some passengers used, which gave away their roots. Other divisions remained: the Germans viewed their Austrian brothers with disdain. Berliners mistrusted the Viennese, full of airs and graces, their honeyed words fake and phoney ('*Sie sind falsch*'), 'too polite … too gracious'.[12]

The refugees were united, instead, by a shared curiosity – if not anxiety – about their destination. Some had literally no idea what Shanghai was. As one later declared, they 'could have been going to Mars or Jupiter …'[13] Lisbeth, along with many others, went along to the ship's lecture room to hear talks on Shanghai. She already knew the city was no East Asian backwater. She had seen photographs of the thriving metropolis, and the sweeping Bund where trams and cars drove past skyscrapers to rival any in New York, Paris or London. But she needed to know more. She loved facts and statistics, and these lectures provided plenty of material to fill her thoughts.

Lisbeth heard that the port stood at the mouth of the 3,000-mile River Yangtze, making it a fought-over trading hub. That it owed its international nature to the nineteenth-century settlers – from Britain, France and America – whose greed for trade forced its gates open after the two Opium Wars of the mid-nineteenth centuries. She learnt of the unequal treaties these foreign 'barbarians' signed, giving them unprecedented rights to live and carry out business in China. These included extraterritoriality, an arrangement protecting the foreigners from Chinese jurisdiction, allowing them to answer only to their own countries' laws. It was Shanghai's 'tangled web of extraterritorial rights and Chinese jurisdiction' that made protection against fraud near impossible – contributing to the city's later notoriety as a centre of lawlessness and crime.[14]

She gawped at the size of Shanghai's population, which numbered over 4 million, including at least a million Chinese refugees from the 1937 war with Japan. And at the diversity of the city's population, which the lecturer explained was based on a 1935 census carried out by *Fortune* magazine. The article analysed the city's Shanghailander population (the 'white men and their predecessors' to whom the city's 'power and the glory' belonged), beginning by firmly 'Excluding [the] 25,000 Russian exiles (*whom as a group Shanghai does not classify as white men*)*', which included many White Russians who came after the October Revolution of 1917. *Fortune* also excluded the 30,000 Japanese residents, whose army had 'laid waste half the city in 1932'. This left around 19,000 Westerners, including British, American, French, Danish, Italian, Spanish and Dutch, and 1,600 ethnic Germans – a different group from those German-speakers who were now fleeing Hitler.

As well as these, a further 6,000 residents were listed in a footnote as 'Polyglot odds and ends', bringing the total to almost 50 different nationalities. These included some Lisbeth had never even heard of: who on earth were the Tonkinese? She smiled at how the 343 Poles included among the 'odds and ends' were described, as 'largely Russians in disguise'.[15]

---

* Author's italics.

One fact she took comfort in was that there were already many Jews in Shanghai. But, the lecturer pointed out, the community was divided in two, according to their origin. The longer-established group of Jews were Sephardim, with roots in the Middle East; these numbered around 700. They included wealthy Baghdadi dynasties, like the Hardoons, Kadoories and Sassoons, whose fortunes had first been made in Iraq and India, trading cotton and opium. Once the port of Shanghai was opened to foreign traders in the mid-nineteenth century, these men saw the opportunities offered and quickly ascended the city's social and economic ladder. The second Jewish community was larger, but poorer. The 6,000 Ashkenazi Jews came, like Lisbeth's family, from Eastern Europe; they included many Russians. Their businesses were far more modest, coming from humbler roots than their Sephardi brothers. Although they had begun arriving in China at around the same time, their reason was to escape the poverty and pogroms of their homelands. The arrival of the Central European Jews fleeing Hitler was about to treble the size of Shanghai's Ashkenazi population.

It was clear that Lisbeth and the other émigrés on board were following a well-trodden path: Shanghai had long welcomed other countries' rejects and misfits. Some of these incomers were of dubious morals, out to make a quick fortune and then leave; others were desperate to escape pogroms, destitution or the arm of the law. The city's open-door policy had its downside. By accepting so many adventurers and fugitives, fortune hunters and smugglers in the 1920s and 1930s, Shanghai had earned a shady reputation. 'Sin city' became notorious for lawlessness, prostitution and gambling. A place of decadence and drugs, gang warfare and violence, and one where kidnapping happened daily. In the Badlands – a no man's land in the city's Western districts beyond the settlements, notorious for its opium dens, brothels and gangsters – 'a foreign woman was robbed of her fur coat … at 3:00 in the afternoon', and mobsters snatched children for ransom from schoolyards.[16] Its very name was synonymous with the act of kidnapping.* And this was to be Lisbeth's new home?

---

* The verb 'to shanghai' was coined in the nineteenth century by the Americans, from the days when men were dragged, drugged or tricked onto ships desperate for extra deckhands. It referred to the nautical practice of getting crew for a vessel by rendering men insensible to get them on board. To 'shanghai' has since been widened to mean to abduct, constrain or compel, or coerce or trick (someone) into a place or position, or into doing something.

Those attending the ship's lectures became ever more anxious. Next they learnt of a different kind of threat: the city's inhospitable climate. Of its enervating humidity and frequent typhoons, its regular flooding with filthy river water that spread germs as fast as gossip. Despite Shanghai's modernity and world-leading progress in printing, higher education and cinema – the city was home to a thriving movie industry – its sanitation was sickeningly primitive. Infections were rife. The audience paled as they listened, Lisbeth among them. But when the lecture was over, and people rose to leave, most agreed with resignation: their only hope was Shanghai. To paraphrase the words of a refugee interviewed decades later: they may have known little about what they were getting into, but they well knew what they were getting out of. [17]

And so many plans were made on board the *Conte Rosso*. Wherever refugees gathered, there were animated discussions of hopes for the future. Many refused to be cowed, staying positive and dreaming up schemes for the life that was drawing nearer each day. Some had brought practical items with them, which they planned to sell soon after landing: tinned sardines, anti-malaria pills, cameras or work tools. Many formed strategic alliances, hatching ideas for joint enterprises. As 'nobody liked to eat Chinese', new acquaintances combined their skills in cooking and business, aiming to open German-style restaurants in Shanghai. [18] Rather than chop suey or noodles, they would offer *schnitzel*, sauerkraut and sausage. For the versatile and robust, and those prepared to take risks with new partners, the voyage buzzed with ideas, fuelled by solidarity and kinship. Some, more gregarious than Lisbeth, even met their future husband or wife during the month suspended between homes.

'What will we find? How and where will we live?' [19] Such questions were still uppermost in many refugees' minds, Lisbeth among them. Despite knowing Arnold was waiting to greet them, her concerns became less easy to ignore as China drew inexorably closer. The luxurious dream was being eaten away, like a sandcastle dissolved by the tide. In its place she sensed a dark unknown presence looming ahead. By 8 March 1940, the four-week voyage was over. The Epstein women's cocoon of comfort, perched precariously between West and East, was about to unravel.

10

8 March 1940: A Shocking Reunion

As Lisbeth and the other passengers leant against the railings of the *Conte Rosso*, their animated chatter faded slowly into silence. I imagine a chill sweeping over them. It would not have come from the light spring breeze rising off the dank waters lapping the sides of the ship, but from the desolate landscape lying before them. Gaping holes showed grey sky through skeletons of concrete apartment blocks. Streets were littered with smoke-blackened ruins.

Not long before, Lisbeth and the others on deck had been watching a string of verdant green islands glitter past along the coasts of the East China Sea. After these had faded away, the Yangtze's flat hinterland had replaced them, with its sprinkling of small rural farmhouses. Now, the tide having turned, the *Conte Rosso* was edging out of the Yangtze's sprawling estuary and into its urban tributary, the Whangpoo river. The filthy waterway was bringing them into the heart of Shanghai. They watched the dockside drawing closer. Along the shore, a line of ugly buildings squared up to them: oil storage tanks, a power plant, wharves and *godowns*, or warehouses. But it was what lay beyond these that must have sent goosebumps down Lisbeth's arms. Destruction and debris, as far as the eye could see: mounds of charred wreckage scattered across the mud. Corrugated iron lay in jumbled heaps beside piles of splintered wood. Shop signs dangled from doorways opposite telegraph poles that looked like they had been driven into at speed. Blackened shells of houses stood beside empty spaces like rotting teeth in a cavity-filled mouth.

What lay before the young woman was the aftermath of the battle of Shanghai, a conflict of almost three years earlier. The fighting between disciplined Japanese and poorly trained Chinese soldiers had flattened many parts of the city; fierce hand-to-hand and house-to-house combat was later described as 'the most intense conflict since Verdun in World War I', and 'Stalingrad on the Yangtze'. After three months' fighting, the Japanese overcame their opposition, leaving 300,000 Chinese and 40,000 Japanese dead.[1] Worst hit were the densely populated districts north of Soochow Creek, the industrial areas of Hongkew and Chapei, sending thousands of terrified Chinese civilians fleeing for protection within the foreign settlements. Instead they were greeted with blows from police batons wielded by the British, American and French. The scorched-earth policy of the retreating Chinese had finished off the devastation. Both districts housed the poorest Chinese, the power behind the city's cottage industries and sweatshops; Chapei also had the northern station of the Shanghai–Nanking railway. Little wonder they had borne the brunt of enemy fire. As well as dropping bombs from the air, the Japanese had shelled the city from warships on the Whangpoo and the Yangtze. Although Lisbeth had read of the conflict, only now did she witness its reality.

I cannot say if she was watching all this with her mother beside her, but I imagine them staring across the water in silence. Rubble littered the streets, which criss-crossed away from destroyed wharves and buildings. A few shadowy figures were drifting through the remains, like ghosts in a desolate landscape.

Although she did not know it, Lisbeth was looking at the southern edge of the district her father had left only a few weeks earlier. This undesirable strip of land had first been claimed by the Americans back in 1848 as their foreign settlement.[2] Its swampy land and industrial river frontage, nothing like the stately Bund, made the American sector the poor relation of the International Settlement proper. This was Hongkew, the most crowded and impoverished part of the city. It was also where the Japanese had set up base after their 1937 victory, and it was now Emperor Hirohito's men who dominated the district, which they spelled Hongkou. From a huge barracks there, the Japanese Naval Landing Party, a 3,500-strong force of marines, controlled almost all of Shanghai. Only the two protected foreign-run concessions, of the English-speakers and the French, stayed untouched; even the Japanese dared not provoke the Westerners.

But the invaders had authority over the rest of the city. Their bayonet-wielding soldiers stood rigid at checkpoints throughout Greater Shanghai. Japanese officials now also controlled who entered the city. In August 1939, responding to the anxiety of Shanghai's leaders – both from the Municipal Council and Jewish groups, including prominent men like Sir Victor Sassoon – over the flood of refugees entering from Europe, they clamped down on immigration. Only those with funds – US$400* – jobs or relatives awaiting them could come in. By October, anyone meeting these conditions who wished to live in the Westerners' International Settlement could only move to one district: Hongkew. This was also the sole place most refugees could afford, and now it was completely full to newcomers.[3] Lisbeth's father had been living in the Ward Road *Heim* there, but to get entry papers for his wife and daughter, he moved out of Hongkew. Only later would Lisbeth learn how close she had come to living among those shattered streets.

The *Conte Rosso* turned slowly now, to navigate the Whangpoo's sharp southward bend. Lisbeth likely reached for her handkerchief as the stench wafting up from the brackish waters hit her nostrils. A potent mix of decaying fish, factory smoke, rancid rubbish and raw sewage created a welcome that none with her on deck would ever forget. Early in the mornings, the night-soil boats would have added to the smell, their stinking loads of human excrement from the city's primitive lavatories to be used as manure on the mudflat fields miles upstream.

The river around Lisbeth was alive with vessels. Hundreds of dark-sailed cargo junks, fishing trawlers and barge-like single-oared sampans steered up and down; some were now circling their ship. A flat-bottomed boat rocked beside the *Conte Rosso*, its impoverished Chinese occupants straining their home-made net to catch the spray of swill, rinds, crusts and bones being spewed from a porthole. Further along the Whangpoo, grey warships loomed beside the embankment, the red and white Rising Sun flying from each. A discreet distance away, British, French and American gunboats displayed their

---

* Today equivalent to around $7,800 or £6,460.

own flags. Further off, a row of ocean liners bore the standards of half a dozen different nations. They brought memories of a long-vanished world, where people travelled freely, on luxury trips to exotic locations.

Had Lisbeth turned her head towards the opposite bank, on the port side of the ship, she would have had a quite different view. Here lay Poodong, Shanghai's industrial dockside, with its factories and *godowns*. Low, windowless mills belched aubergine-coloured smoke. Out of sight, Chinese workers toiled to increase the profits of Western companies like Jardine Matheson, British-American Tobacco and Standard Oil trading here in the East. Blue-clad sweating labourers, crammed together cheek by jowl, made all manner of goods: textiles and clothing, fireworks and beer, and endless curios for export. Lisbeth again narrowed her eyes to see what lay past the factories. The eastern hinterland offered glimpses of rice fields fading into the distance.

The *Conte Rosso* continued on, and Lisbeth would have heard the passengers' chatter start to rise in response to the changing scenery to starboard. The desolation and rubble were behind them, replaced now by leafy parks and public gardens. And suddenly, another sight was emerging, one she recognised from the guidebooks. Even more breathtaking in real life, the mile-long waterfront of the Bund curved out before her. Here was a city unashamed of success! And yet, she would have remembered from the lectures, just a century earlier it had been a muddy riverside path used only by boat pullers. Then British settlers appeared, and piled it high with stones and solid earth to stop the Whangpoo waters encroaching. Thanks to their engineering, the sludgy path had been transformed into this metropolitan roadway.*

Before Lisbeth and the others lay decades of imperial opulence embodied in granite and marble. The sweep of grand buildings proclaimed Shanghai's unequivocal status as East Asia's commercial hub. There were banks and trading houses, and impressive hotels; from their Victorian style, many dated back to the days of the port's first Western traders. Art deco towers

---

* This was the process of 'bunding'. Rena Krasno described how the 'muddy, flat bank upon which the yellow Whangpoo river always tried to encroach' was reinforced in this way.

from the 1920s shaped the skyline. Lisbeth's heart must have leapt as she recognised the pyramid roof of Sir Victor Sassoon's Cathay Hotel from the black-and-white photo in her guide book, and realised that it actually shone with green patina. Would she ever see inside the famed 'Claridges of the Far East'?

But any reveries were shattered by the ship's tannoy blasting out an announcement. A crackling voice was explaining the procedure for passing through customs and picking up their bags. Lisbeth felt the ship slowing down, and within minutes heard the graunching of the massive anchor dropping into the mud. The engines finally fell silent. I imagine my aunt and her mother looking across the jetty at the building they were being told to enter. The imposing white granite Custom House had a distinctive clock tower. Its classical British-built clock face was the largest in Asia. Nicknamed 'Big Ching', when the clock's two hands became one, its machinery chimed noon with the same melody as Big Ben.

The two women watched the ship's crewmen unload endless piles of luggage for transfer to the Custom House. Lining up patiently with others in their cabin class, they awaited the tender that would take them to the landing stage, from where they would walk across to the white building. All they had to their names were two suitcases, the clothes they were wearing, their small allowance of jewellery and ten Reichsmarks each.

Lisbeth helped her mother out of the small boat and onto the jetty. They were about to step onto dry land for the first time in a month. The ground swayed alarmingly beneath her legs as she followed the other passengers onto the Bund, and the building's entrance. Doric columns guarded an ornate iron gate, bearing 'Custom House' in heavy gold letters. Lisbeth's chest must have tightened as she caught sight of the uniformed men beyond the gate. Once inside, she may have studied the marble floor tiling, to keep her eyes from any official. But none of them gave her or Edith a second glance; no one cared if these latest immigrants had identification papers or passports. Breathing sighs of relief, mother and daughter slipped into their new city unchallenged.

The lack of checks was strongly criticised the next day in a police report entitled 'Central European Jews – Arrival of s.s. "Conte Rosso" on March 8, 1940'. Detective Sergeant Frederick Arthur Pitts complained of 'the complete lack of cooperation and organisation displayed by the Lloyd Triestino offices and the officers of the s.s. "Conte Rosso" ... in matters relating to the disembarkation of Jewish refugees from Europe arriving on this steamer. ... No separate and detailed lists of Jewish arrivals were available for the use of the Committee representatives [waiting to 'instruct refugees on board as to how they should proceed'] while the passports of the refugees had not been collected by the ship's officers and were thus still in possession of the Jews themselves.' He went on: 'It is difficult to describe on paper the confusion that reigned... Suffice it to say that certain of the refugees left the steamer without handing over their passports'.[4]

Within moments of stepping back onto the pavement, Lisbeth's relief was replaced by a nerve-jangling dizziness. She would never forget that first assault on her senses – a jarring mixture of smells, sights and sounds. On top of the river's decaying stink came the oily stench of street food being fried in stalls all around her. She thought she would never be able to breathe again. Looking this way and that, she reached for her handkerchief again, nauseous from the heavy odours of sweat, incense and cooking oil. She would soon learn the names of the food she saw being hawked: the long *you-zha-qui* – strips of twisted dough deep-fried in peanut oil – and the round *tsi-ven*, sweet sticky rice balls stuffed with a *you-zha-qui* in its centre. She watched a vendor shape a rice ball with a steaming cloth, then use the cloth to wipe the sweat that was dripping off his brow.[5] Her stomach heaved as much as her head ached. From that moment on, she vowed never to touch street food.

'Has there been an accident?' Lisbeth whispered to her mother. She could not believe the number of people thronging the waterfront – more than she had ever seen in one place before. She felt breathless again. 'Something must be going on; there cannot be that many people, like ants, constantly moving.' Dozens of Chinese labourers were hauling luggage between ship and shore.[6] The wiry men's backs were bent double under the weight of huge steel and leather steamer trunks, a feat demanding as much skill as strength. The trunks were lever-balanced by a broad strap across each man's forehead; one wrong movement could jerk his head back, instantly breaking his neck.

Lisbeth would also soon learn that crowds and hubbub were normal. That day on the Bund she saw wharf workers in rags, and longshoremen, long-robed merchants and sailors; there were well-dressed compradors and *taipans*.* Keeping order over this miscellany of humanity were tall Sikh policemen in red turbans, employed by the British authorities. Countless rickshaw men battled through the crowds, their cries for customers clashing with the screech of unoiled barrows; the Chinese believed that the wheels' piercing squeak would frighten off any bad spirits. Some wheelbarrow pullers carted piles of freight, others balanced a clutch of factory girls on their way to or from work. On either side of the Bund's central reservation – where the rich parked their cars – pedestrians and rickshaws jostled for space among the swirl of vehicles.

Lisbeth and Edith pressed together as close as they could, scanning the crowd for the one familiar face they both longed to see. Then Lisbeth saw a man approach. Something about him reminded her of Arnold, but her brain refused to recognise the shrunken figure. 'Isn't that Papa?' she whispered, again. For a moment, neither woman was sure, it was so difficult to believe the man before them was Arnold, 'because he had lost so much weight', and looked so 'impossibly' thin. But it was indeed him. He embraced his wife tightly, unable to let her go; it was the first time they had touched in nearly a year. Lisbeth stood by, almost in shock, unable to weep.

The gaunt figure, whose grey hair had aged him beyond his 50 years and whose face had a strange pallor, now spoke. His voice was weaker than Lisbeth remembered. He told them he had rented a place off Weihaiwei Road, on a street named Yang Terrace in the International Settlement. At this Lisbeth's heart rose, only to fall again seconds later at what her father said next. They were to travel there in separate rickshaws, which meant trusting a stranger to take them to the correct address. The eighteen-year-old, just a month out of Vienna, grew even paler than usual. She could not believe what her father was asking. She later recalled the horror of that

---

* Compradors were Chinese buyers who handled the Chinese end of foreigners' business affairs; *taipans* were foreigners who were the heads of businesses in China. 'Comprador' comes from the Portuguese for 'buyer', and its use dates from the opening of the five Chinese treaty ports established after the first Opium War.

moment: 'How can you do that? Here in a place where we have no idea where we are, we are landing in a new continent, and how do we know this man is going to bring us there?' She was loath to trust 'this strange Chinese character running in front of a strange vehicle'. But there was nothing to be done. Arnold had already summoned the rickshaws, and was paying the pullers the agreed fare.

Lisbeth Epstein reluctantly climbed into the rickshaw, which set off with a jolt through the streets of their new home. She could barely believe what was happening, her head spinning as the unfamiliar landscape swirled round her.

11

The mid-1930s:
Shanghai Millionaire

'Me no worry – me no care!
Me go marry millionaire!
If he die – me no cry!
Me go marry other guy!!'
— Refrain from a popular Shanghai
song of the late 1940s

The city that Lisbeth found herself in had been immortalised in a board
game that the Chinese had shamelessly copied a few years earlier from the
American original. *Shanghai Millionaire* was identical to *Monopoly*, but its
locations were in Shanghai, laid out according to the best and the worst
addresses. The most expensive thoroughfare was, of course, the Bund
rather than Boardwalk (or Mayfair in the UK version); next came Nanking
Road – the Oxford Street of the East. Another prized location was Bubbling
Well Road, where Bruno would open his bookshop. Although the Jewish
refugees could not afford to buy the board game, some of their children
made copies, and played it for hours in their new home.'

History books in Lisbeth's ship's library offered fascinating gossip
concerning Shanghai's many real millionaires – of which it had more than
its fair share. Originally recorded as a mere 'fishing stake estuary', by the

The Shanghai Millionaire board game set up for play. (Source: *The Bell Family Collection*, Special Collections and Archives, University Library, California State University, Northridge)

sixteenth century Shanghai had grown to be 'a small county seat, a walled fishing town'.[2] After 1843, when the port's gates were officially opened to Western merchants, the city became a magnet for fortune hunters: 17 November that year saw Shanghai become one of the five treaty ports set up along the Chinese coast by the Opium War victors. First British, Americans and French, and later Russians too, wasted little time finding opportunities to make money. For the next 90 years, the city at the mouth of the Yangtze offered rich pickings for those with the wit and the ruthlessness to succeed. Its amoral atmosphere drew in the world's speculators and outcasts. Its many legal systems – which were different for each foreign jurisdiction, including the Japanese – made protection against fraud near impossible, attracting many with less than scrupulous intentions. Adventurers hoped to make a quick buck, then leave as quickly as possible. Few planned on making damp, disease-infested Shanghai their permanent home.

But the city drew more respectable businessmen too. Intriguing characters, Lisbeth thought, like the Hardoons, Kadoories and Sassoons, Sephardi Jews whom she heard mentioned in the ship's lectures. Using their wealth to speculate in the Shanghai 'boom', they bought up land and transformed the city's skyline. One developer had begun building on the port's watery soil back in the 1920s, investing millions in the place. His name was Ellice Victor Sassoon, known to all as Sir Victor. An English-educated socialite, he came to embody the image of Shanghai as a thriving metropolis of glamour and cocktails. The ship's books showed photographs of him, dinner-jacketed, leaning on the stick he had used ever since being injured in a First World War plane crash; his other props were glamorous young women.

Of Sassoon's many buildings featured in a Shanghai guidebook, the one Lisbeth liked most was the pyramid-roofed Cathay Hotel on the Bund. From its high penthouse suite, Sir Victor would look down on the waterside embankment. Anyone who was anyone either stayed at, or was seen in, the Cathay. Since the mid-1920s, long-distance luxury cruises had set their passengers down on the jetty. By 1929, Sassoon had built an establishment worthy of greeting the richest among them. His ten-storey art deco hotel, with its copper-green roof, stood on prime waterfront land – as *Shanghai Millionaire* attested, the triangular block between Nanking and Jinkee Roads off the Bund was the city's most valuable. The 'last word in luxury', the hotel had air conditioning, water piped into the hotel from the Bubbling Well springs just outside the city, and a shopping arcade offering the fanciest foreign goods for sale in Shanghai. Every celebrity visiting the city passed through its revolving doors into the gilt-and-Lalique lobby. Even those sleeping in cheaper places, like the non-air-conditioned – but still grand – Astor House hotel over Garden Bridge in Hongkew, would drop in for a visit. One of the Cathay's first guests was a flu-stricken Noël Coward, who had stayed in one of its suites in 1930, where he was said to have written *Private Lives* in four fever-fuelled days.

The ship's library books painted a picture of a city that the refugees realised was no more. Two decades earlier, before the stranglehold of war gripped her throat, Shanghai offered a whirlwind of hedonism to those who were carefree with their cash. It became 'the most decadent city in the world', a place of 'riotous abundance'; 'the pleasure capital of the Orient'.[3] But it was also beset by extremes: of poverty and wealth, capitalism and Communism. And it was ridden with snobbery. The latter arrived with the British, alongside their favourite foods, drinks and architectural styles. Their elitism was intimately bound up with antisemitism, which led to their balking at dealing with some of Shanghai's most influential men, the Baghdadi Jews. This even included its highest-profile, 'striking' and 'pukka-pukka' millionaire, Sir Victor Sassoon. To the British, his religion represented a real social disadvantage.[4] As one Shanghailander confessed: 'He was Jewish but one couldn't very well snub a man who played golf with the Prince of Wales. It was a perplexing topic at the Club, I can tell you'. They deigned to call the wealthy Sephardi philanthropist and businessman, Lawrence Kadoorie, elder brother of the equally philanthropic Horace, 'almost one of us'.[5]

Yet, for Shanghai's British residents, no Jew was really close enough to their kind to be accepted. Jews were banned from that bastion of International Settlement society, the Country Club at 651 Bubbling Well Road. The club barred Chinese as well, no matter how plentiful their silver dollars. It was easier to gain entrance to the elite club if you were a visitor to Shanghai than if you were Jewish or Chinese. Visitors could be 'proposed and seconded by two or more members' for admission for 'a period not exceeding ten days'.[6] Not even Sir Victor's years at Harrow and Cambridge and long-standing allegiance to Britain could counter the ban. It applied, too, to a distinguished city family, the McBains: the first Mr McBain had made the cardinal error of wedding a Chinese woman.

Sir Victor was not one to be cowed. After all, it was he – a famed horse lover – who declared: 'There's only one race greater than the Jews, and that's the Derby.'[7] After the Country Club's rejection, and another refusal of a table in one of Shanghai's swankiest nightspots, he took his revenge. At 444 Bubbling Well Road, near both unwelcoming venues, he built the city's first air-conditioned nightclub. Ciro's was deliberately less exclusive than the starchier British-run venues, and became popular with Western businessmen and Chinese mobsters alike. The Kadoories responded to such rebuffs with similarly positive steps: they converted one of their elegant properties – a balconied, Renaissance-style villa covering 1,800 square metres – into the Jewish Country Club. This stretched from 702 to 722 Bubbling Well Road, the span of twenty standard properties.

The ship's books told of the lives of two other 'Shanghai millionaires' with Jewish roots. Emily 'Mickey' Hahn and Morris 'Two-Gun' Cohen crossed paths in Shanghai in the 1930s; they would both also return to their homelands on the same ship in September 1943. Hahn was an American socialite and writer, while the Polish-born 'Two-Gun' spent his youth as a London delinquent.

'Mickey' Hahn was a great favourite of Sir Victor, who saw her as a kindred spirit. No one could fail to recognise her at any social gathering: her constant companion was her pet Singapore gibbon, Mr Mills. Named after the Malayan who had sold Emily the ape, he always perched on his mistress's shoulder, from where he would watch over the evening's proceedings. Lisbeth would have smiled at pictures of the unlikely companions, and at the fact that Mr Mills's costumes, including a 'Sunday coat lined with otter fur', were made to measure by a Russian Jewish immigrant who owned a children's toy shop and dress salon in the French Concession's Avenue Joffre.[8]

Morris Abraham 'Two-Gun' Cohen's story was stranger than fiction. A long-time resident of Astor House, the city's first British-built hotel, he came to China by a circuitous route. The grifter, adventurer and gun-runner ended up as the bodyguard of the Chinese Nationalist leader, Sun Yat-sen. His criminal tendencies began as a youth, leading to 'Fat Moishe', as he was then known, being sent for a spell in a reform school in west London: the Hayes Certified Industrial School for Jewish Boys. On the eighteen-year-old's release in 1905, his despairing parents dispatched him to a Saskatchewan ranch. Instead of benefiting from the healthy outdoors, Cohen honed his troublemaking skills, learning how to use a gun, gamble and hustle. Some years later, he moved to Alberta where he added a military training to his amateur boxing skills.

A chance encounter in Saskatchewan drew 'Two-Gun' into a circle of Chinese revolutionaries, part of Sun Yat-sen's anti-Manchu resistance movement and a forerunner of his Nationalist Kuomintang Party. Later Cohen met the Chinese Nationalist himself when Dr Sun came to Canada to buy arms, and the Jewish grifter soon became Sun's personal bodyguard, although he preferred the title 'aide-de-camp'. He earned the role because he was 'an excellent marksman, sincerely supported the Chinese revolutionary movement … and was utterly indifferent to his own personal safety'.[9] In 1922 Cohen left Canada for Shanghai, to escape his huge debts. This is where he earned his most famous nickname. After a bullet nicked his right arm in a gunfight, he taught himself to shoot with either hand; from then on, he openly carried a pair of Smith & Wesson pistols and became 'Two-Gun'

Cohen. He declared that the Jews and Chinese have much in common, including the fact that both 'make good friends but damned bad enemies'.

Readers of the ship's history books learnt that Shanghai's millionaires included Chinese businessmen as well as Westerners. One of the less salubrious was Du Yue-sheng – also known as 'Big Ears' Du, since his ears stuck out 'like panhandles' from his large shaven head.[10] His villa in Frenchtown, as city people commonly dubbed the French Concession, housed 'three wives, nine cars, eighteen chauffeurs, three bodyguards and dozens of servants'.[11] Du ruled the city's spectacularly profitable underworld, and his 'gigantic and efficient' gangland organisation made people fear him greatly. His specialties were 'opium-smuggling, gun-running, silver-smuggling, operations in the gold-bar market, white slave traffic, kidnapping, shooting anyone for a price (ten dollars to one hundred dollars, Chinese dollars, depending on the importance of the troublesome one).'[12]

'Two-Gun' Cohen and 'Big Ears' Du were born in the same year, 1887. They had little else in common and could not have looked more different. Cohen was stocky and broad, in his double-breasted suit and fedora. Du was a skinny drug addict, with a shuffling gait, two-inch-long opium-stained nails and empty, dead eyes that made strangers stiffen. W.H. Auden and Christopher Isherwood – who visited the city in 1938 – described Du's feet, in particular, 'in their silk socks and smart pointed European boots' as 'inexplicably terrifying'.[13] The gangster bribed his way into appearing an upright, even philanthropic, member of Shanghai society. His entry in the city's 1933 edition of *Who's Who* described him as 'a well-known public welfare worker'.[14]

I wonder how much Lisbeth read of Shanghai's history before setting foot in that land so far from her home. Did she know of 'Big Ears' Du and his addictions to drugs and crime; or that this Shanghai Millionaire's impoverished background meant he never learnt to read? How different from herself, and her fellow immigrant shipmates on the *Conte Rosso*, for whom reading would prove a lifeline out of the bleak reality into which they had sailed. By the time the refugees set foot on the Bund, they had little left but their literacy – and whatever books they had brought with them. They would treasure these cultural links to their lost homeland more than diamonds or pearls.

12

8 March 1940: The Journey to Weihaiwei Road

After a handful of years hauling passengers through the streets of Shanghai, most rickshaw pullers were totally spent. Skeletally thin, apart from bulging calf muscles whose snaky veins looked ready to burst, their hearts and lungs could take the strain for only so long. The bodies of most gave out long before middle age. But without this work, starvation was likely to have killed the men sooner.

As she shifted from side to side in the hard-seated contraption, Lisbeth knew nothing of this. She had never seen a rickshaw before; now she had to trust that this one was taking her to Weihaiwei Road. Soon she, like other Shanghailanders, would come to rely on the efforts of a wiry Chinese man to take her around the city. Many Westerners viewed the puller as more animal than human. But this first ride shook Lisbeth more than just physically. Head aching with anxiety, she had already lost sight of her parents – the crowd was too dense. All she saw – and could smell – a few feet from her face, was a 'strange Chinese character', dragging her through an alien landscape. The swirl of people around her made her dizzy again. To distract herself, she focused on the buildings they were passing. Her mother had taught her to navigate by landmarks; this ride was a good place to start.

As he set off from the Custom House, Lisbeth's rickshaw puller turned northwards up the Bund, and on her left was a grand cream and red building. This was the six-storey Palace Hotel, an establishment whose beds she would never sample: its single rooms cost $12, while doubles were $24, and 'suites by arrangement'. Even less likely to go inside were the figures she glimpsed crouching outside its doors, her first sight of Shanghai's poorest. War and famine had created a penniless underclass, living in tragic conditions. Every night, families weakened by hunger huddled in doorways along the Bund, while each day saw thousands quietly scavenging, living and dying by the polluted waters of the Whangpoo river.

Two famous beggars had made this a viable career, becoming so familiar to locals that they had their own nicknames. Seated on the pavement in front of the Palace Hotel, one had driven a nail holding a lighted candle into his shaven skull; his nickname was 'Light in the Head'. Nearby sat the woman who cried without pause and so copiously that small pools formed around her hunched body; she was known as 'the Weeping Wonder'. Others increased their wretchedness by faking wounds with pig's blood, or genuinely maiming themselves – or their children. Some slung corpses, which were plentiful on Shanghai's dangerous streets, over their chests to increase people's compassion. Thieves careless enough to have been caught by the Japanese police waved their handless stumps at passers-by, in the hope of a few extra coins.

Lisbeth must have felt horror mixed with pity at seeing Shanghai's maimed and destitute souls. But such feelings would soon fade with the passing of time, as they did for everyone else. While she was painfully aware of these unfortunates' plight, her compassion had limits; she must look out for herself.

Just past the Palace Hotel, the north–south Bund joined a major route westward through the International Settlement. Formerly called Dah Ma Lo, the British renamed it Nanking Road in the mid-nineteenth century.[*] They adopted a more pragmatic system of road names over the picturesque Chinese ones. All main Settlement roads at right angles to the Bund were called after Chinese cities: as well as Nanking, they chose others like Foochow, Canton and Peking. North–south roads, parallel to the Bund,

---

[*] *Dah Ma Lo* means 'Great Horse Road'.

were named after provinces, such as Hunan, Szechuan and Shantung. The French names were different again, honouring illustrious dignitaries or citizens, *à la* Rues Impériale, Cardinal Mercier, Lafayette, or Avenues Roi Albert and Foch.[1]

Now Lisbeth's rickshaw swung left into Nanking Road. She immediately saw why the guidebook had called it the Oxford Street of the East. It was crowded with shoppers, and the soundtrack had switched from that of a buzzing waterside to a city's traffic-filled hubbub. Tram bells clanged, merchants cried out and songbirds chirruped from their cages. Food sellers carried huge wooden tubs on bamboo poles balanced across their bent shoulders. Lisbeth could make out the savoury smell of steaming chicken broth and noodles cutting through the heady perfume of incense. On each side of the street, pagoda-roofed shops displayed red and gold sign boards; fluttering banners bore indecipherable Chinese characters. Had she been there at night, she would have seen the road ablaze with neon lights, 'increasing in brilliance and intricacy of design'.[2] Here, in broad daylight, the rickshaw passed silver- and goldsmiths, dealers of porcelain and silk, and countless curio shops. Homeless orphans ran the length of the road, pulling at the skirts or sleeves of Westerners, or tapping at car windows. All Shanghai knew their mantra: 'No mama, no papa, no whisky soda!'

As the puller continued westwards down Nanking Road, Lisbeth saw larger shopfronts that looked just like European department stores: Hall and Holtz, Weeks and Co. and Lane Crawford. A little further along, new signs indicated the city's large Chinese-run stores, the 'Big Four': Sincere's, Wing On, Sun Sun, and The Sun. These ornate, neoclassical buildings near Nanking Road's junction with Chekiang Road embodied Shanghai's Jazz Age boom of the 1920s. Some of the large department stores on Nanking Road had a sadder history. Sincere's had opened in 1917; twenty years later, on Saturday 14 August 1937, its Corinthian columns had been demolished and 170 shoppers killed by one of four stray Chinese bombs. Aimed at the Japanese armoured cruiser *Idzumo*, the bombs had fallen short, landing instead on the 'safe' foreign settlement. Sun Sun, like the others, was more than just an emporium; it had its own radio station and ballroom, even hotel accommodation. Lisbeth blinked as she passed rows of enticing window displays.

Her rickshaw puller pressed on, weaving her past Sincere's and Wing On, through the chaotic jumble of people, bicycles, trams and motor cars. Now they were passing a string of British-looking buildings of Victorian red brick. On her right Lisbeth saw an imposing town hall, followed by another colonial building. The sign at its entrance read 'Louza Police Station'. Although she did not know it, Lisbeth was looking at the birthplace of China's anti-imperialist May Thirtieth Movement.

Since late May 1925, the British-run Louza Police Station had become notorious in Shanghai. A Chinese labour activist had been killed by the foreman of a Japanese-run cotton-mill. Student sympathisers on their way to attend the martyr's funeral were arrested, and their trial set for 30 May. On that day, more far-left students gathered to protest about the case, armed with nothing more than anti-Japanese pro-labour signs. When their ringleaders were arrested and jailed in the Louza station, two thousand protestors turned up outside its doors. The chief of the Municipal Police was enjoying a day at the Shanghai races, leaving an anxious deputy to face the mob. At around 3.30pm, the deputy made a fatal decision. With hundreds mobbing the station, no one heard the warning that he would shoot if they didn't disband. He snatched a rifle and fired at the crowd outside the door. His Sikh and Chinese policemen followed suit, opening fire on the unarmed protestors, killing twelve people and wounding many more. The British act of aggression lit the touchpaper that sparked a wave of Chinese anti-imperialist and anti-Japanese unrest. Communist-backed labour strikes and anti-foreign riots quickly spread throughout China, under the banner of the May Thirtieth Movement. [3]

Lisbeth would have baulked at the complexity of Shanghai's politics; so many factions were vying for control. As well as Communists and Nationalists opposing one another from within, Western powers and the Japanese held sway over different parts of the city. When the Epstein women arrived in 1940, Shanghai was a shadow of its mid-1930s exuberant self. Japan's victory in the 1937 conflict over Chiang Kai-shek's Nationalist army had destroyed its heart. In addition to killing hundreds of thousands of Chinese, Japanese forces requisitioned the delta's fertile paddy fields, raising rice prices to riot-inducing heights. Japanese troops took over all of Shanghai, apart from the two protected foreign settlements which now formed a 'solitary island in the sea of Japanese occupation'.[4] Everywhere else in the municipality – that is, the 320 square miles of the old walled Chinese city and the districts stretching beyond the Westerners' land out to the gangster-filled Badlands – was in the control of their new Japanese rulers.[5]

But the city was also pulled apart by home-grown discord. In the early 1920s, Shanghai had become the centre of China's Communist movement. With headquarters in the city's International Settlement, the Communists fought hard for workers' rights until, in April 1927, they were brutally suppressed by Chiang's right-wing army, with the assistance of Du Yue-sheng and his mobsters. By 1940, the Japanese had the upper hand. They set up a so-called Chinese government in Nanking, led by an ex-Nationalist named Wang Ching-wei.[*] Another fierce anti-Communist, Wang believed that with Japanese backing he could defeat both Western oppression and the Communists. In fact Wang was a collaborator, and the regime in Nanking was a puppet government of Japan. Meanwhile, Chinese Nationalism still flared up in protest against the Japanese invaders.

Shortly after passing Louza Police Station, Lisbeth's rickshaw was at Nanking Road's junction with Thibet Road. To her left lay the largest expanse of green she had seen since arriving. From its curved white fencing, she realised it must be the city's racecourse. Paid for by the Settlement's wealthy residents, the twelve-acre grounds enabled the British and Americans to carry on playing their favourite sports. There was a swimming club, cricket grounds, golf course, bowls club and tennis courts, plus a baseball field for its American patrons. As important as their need for cricket and golf had been the need to maintain their social life, which is why racing figured prominently here in Shanghai. Each May and November, spectators packed into the grandstand, eager to gamble their American or Chinese dollars on the tiny Mongolian ponies that raced in the course's three-day meets. The Chinese themselves were often baffled by the energy and time many Westerners devoted to their various sports, often played under Shanghai's hot sun.

---

[*] Known as Jingwei in the modern Chinese spelling.

Nanking Road ended as the rickshaw reached the racecourse, transforming into a new road, which followed the curve of the course, and was described by a contemporary guidebook as 'one of the "seven most interesting streets in the world"'.[6] It stretched almost two miles westwards, to the suburbs, and the Badlands. More romantically, at its end also lay the ancient Jing'an temple and, beside it, the mystical bubbling well.* For centuries, sightseers had journeyed to look over the well's four low stone walls, whose corners were decorated with unidentifiable creatures. But the visitors had eyes only for the frothing waters below. Fed by gaseous springs, these had the power – legend said – of miraculous healing.

Lisbeth would never see the road's legendary well. By 1940, it had dried up, and was nothing more than a small walled enclosure in the middle of the road, filled with rubbish and reeking black mud. But now as she travelled west for the first time, along 'uptown's' main thoroughfare, Lisbeth watched the landmarks pass by. First came the soaring monolith overlooking the racecourse, the art deco Park Hotel. In 1935, its 24 storeys had piqued Sassoon's competitive spirit, since it dwarfed his Cathay Hotel by some 72 feet. Next came the Carlton Café, run by Al Israel, a saloon bar owner from San Francisco. The boxing matches Al once hosted on his café's roof garden had been so bloody that they had incurred the wrath of Shanghai's Municipal Council. Lisbeth knew nothing of this; her mind was focused on the question of how far they were from Yang Terrace, her new address.

Suddenly she was flung to one side as the puller veered again to the left; they were turning south alongside a graveyard. As she looked into its grounds, Lisbeth was surprised to see headstones lettered in Hebrew. This was the city's first Jewish cemetery, named the Israel Cemetery when built the century before. It was now better known as 'Mohawk Cemetery', for the rickshaw was bumping down Mohawk Road. This unlikely name came from Henry 'Mohawk' Morriss, a British-born tycoon who bought Shanghai's influential *North China Daily News* in 1901. His home – Mohawk Lodge – stood a little further down from the cemetery. Morriss was a

---

* Or *Chin-Ngan*, meaning 'tranquil repose'.

great lover of racing and gave his horses Native American names, such as Minnehaha and Shawendassie, which led to his nickname. The mogul's tastes rivalled those of fellow millionaire Sir Victor Sassoon; like Sassoon, his fortune was due at least in part to the opium trade.

Just as Lisbeth started to despair of ever reaching her destination, the sweating puller slowed down and eased his rickshaw to the right, which took them at last into Weihaiwei Road. The puller slowed to a halt, then bent over, panting. The journey had taken less than twenty minutes, but to Lisbeth it had seemed an eternity. She carefully stepped out of the rickshaw, her legs suddenly shaking. She looked round for her father. All she saw, as she stood in front of a high stone gateway, was a crowd of ragged beggars sprawled on the pavement. They were outside number 497 Weihaiwei Road, one of two entrances leading into Yang Terrace.[7]

Lisbeth would never forget the sight of the filthy beggars, with open sores and weeping wounds; she would soon learn that they lived at this gateway. At noon every day they would be offered a bowl of thin rice soup by the Salvation Army, who ran a soup kitchen there. This was the only help Lisbeth ever saw offered to the city's destitute, and it warmed her heart to that charity ever after.

Suddenly the other two rickshaws appeared at her side, and the teenager's anxiety calmed into relief. She watched her parents get out, and felt her pulse quicken as they linked arms to walk towards their home. She followed Arnold and Edith through the stone entrance, hardly daring to imagine what lay on the other side. What she saw made her smile. They had joined a short curving lane, which led to a well-tended garden, with lawn, trees and shrubs. She could see white camellias and smell fragrant roses. Opposite the garden stood a terrace of attractive red-brick houses, each three storeys high. Lisbeth counted four pairs of semi-detached homes in the terrace. Arnold stopped at the first. At number 1 she saw a sign in capital letters that read: 'Shanghai Health Studio: Medical Cosmetics and Herbal Treatment. By Appointment Only'. The other half of the pair was number 2. Arnold's gesture indicated that they had reached their destination.

Lisbeth followed her parents up the stone steps that led to the front door of the house, aware of her heart thudding. At the top step she hesitated. She hardly dared to find out what her new home was like.

13

Shanghai 1940: The Bookshop on Bubbling Well Road

The Lion Bookshop was bound to succeed. Bruno Loewenberg knew that refugees like himself, far from home, yearned to blot out the world in which they now found themselves. Books provided longed-for oblivion, however temporary – a respite from the alien life these new immigrants faced.[1] Their pages offered a tie to the past; not just through their words, but their characteristic smell also evoked memories, as do the garments of loved ones held to the face of the bereaved. And to feel the texture of the cream paper, to see the familiar colours and images on old dust jackets, to flip through well-thumbed pages – all these small acts carried the refugees back to their homelands in Europe.

Bruno was the first European refugee in Shanghai to set up a second-hand bookstore that incorporated a lending library as well.[2] He had financial help from a German Jewish woman, Dora Schein, who had come to Shanghai before 1937 and who co-owned the library together with her husband. Members paid a small subscription to join; for each book borrowed they paid an additional fee of a few cents, depending on the length of the loan. These modest charges were within reach of almost everyone. With this small but regular income, Bruno grew his business and continued to feed his customers' appetite for distraction from the chaos around them.

The Lion Bookshop soon drew in non-refugee readers too: Japanese, established German residents and other nationals became regular customers. As its small ad showed, the shop stood at '328 Moulmein Road, Corner Bubbling Well Road', which made it easy to find: everyone knew Bubbling Well Road. Moulmein Road, though much smaller, was also a shrewd business choice. It was home to many Jewish organisations, including the Shanghai Jewish Club at number 35, a major venue for Russian-Jewish recreational activities.[3] Close by stood the city's branch of the Jewish nationalist youth movement Betar, which promoted sports and Zionism with equal vigour. Next door was the American YWCA club, which had once been home to a wealthy British doctor. The twin of Bruno's building, it was a substantial, red-roofed mansion, with five pairs of decorative windows looking out onto large lawns.

How Bubbling Well Road had changed over the last 90 years! Mid-nineteenth century settlers had known it as a quiet country avenue lined with willows and plane trees, bordered by creeks. The Western *taipans* and wealthy Chinese who lived in its European-style villas used it for weekend family outings: they would ride to its western end in their landaus and broughams to visit the celebrated well beside the Jing'an temple.[4] Now its bucolic peace was replaced by a commercial street's clamour. If Bruno walked a few steps from his shop, he would see the crowds visiting the road's cafés, restaurants and hotels. The Majestic Hotel was famed for tea dances – but sold more whisky than tea. Of the road's many social clubs, Bruno's favourite was the one at number 444: this was Sir Victor Sassoon's inclusive club, Ciro's, which welcomed Jews like himself. If he were out for a stroll, Bruno would pass grocers, barbers, Chinese furniture shops and pet stores, as well as beauty salons and butchers, dressmakers and dairies, curio shops and furriers. He sometimes stopped at the Siberian Fur Store, to practise his few words of Russian with its owner, a Jew named Gregory Klebanov, who shared his passion for vodka. For the more health-conscious, Bubbling Well Road had sporting goods suppliers, physicians and pharmacists. At number 770, Health-Rays Limited offered treatment for 'neuritis, rheumatism, bronchitis, etc. or skin diseases'.

The Lion Bookshop thrived, despite growing competition. Although other libraries might try to match its stock, it was Bruno's charisma that made the business succeed. He had a warmth that never failed to draw people to him. Buchenwald had taught him what mattered in life; he now appreciated the simplest of pleasures. He knew the value of friendship, and this knowledge gave a light to his eyes that the people who encountered him recognised as special. Men and women alike were charmed by it, and by the humour in his rich, deep voice. As he gestured with his long fingers to underline his philosophies on life, music and art, his listeners were held rapt.

Conversation and debate were among Bruno's favourite things, so he made them a central part of his bookshop. As the library became well known, it drew in many youngsters. Bruno welcomed them warmly, and – recognising that, for many, their education had been abruptly cut short – had an idea that would keep them returning. He was soon making enough money to sponsor a series of debates and lectures from guest speakers that were designed to interest young people.[5] These attracted dozens of young German-speakers, mostly in their late teens, but also a few in their twenties, and soon the group of young adults was meeting up regularly for the talks. The Lion Bookshop soon became 'a mecca for refugee teenagers wanting more than the basic curriculum offered at school'.[6] A regular library user who went to the talks was Horst Eisfelder, the Berlin teenager whose parents owned the Café Louis.

Bruno would suggest suitable books for anyone in the group who wanted to speak on some specific topic. As well as employing a female assistant to check people's books in and out, he hired a highly intelligent Czechoslovakian former journalist, famed for his skill at debating, to help run the discussion groups. The man used to explain that 'a good journalist must be able to demonstrate clearly and logically the very opposite point of view and argument which he propounded the day before.'[7]

There was no difficulty finding people willing to contribute to the discussion groups; Shanghai was overflowing with refugees eager to talk about their former areas of expertise. The newly arrived Germanic community was top-heavy with well-informed, middle-class professionals, including experts on art, literature and architecture. Many were delighted to find a young audience desperate for culture and knowledge. Some of the youths later said that the library provided the only education they received during their time in Shanghai.

Among the speakers were former editors of Prague's liberal-democrat German-language daily, the *Prager Tagblatt*, whose existence was ended with

Hitler's invasion of Czechoslovakia. The journalist who organised the talks had also worked at the influential newspaper; he gave lectures on history and politics. Painters discussed aspects of art, recalling the days before Hitler when they could create as they pleased. The noted architect, Richard Paulick, gave talks on his work at the Bauhaus, where he and his colleagues had designed houses on modern lines, notable for their distinctive flat roofs. Although he was not Jewish, he had been forced to flee Berlin after being labelled a cultural Bolshevik. His father was a prominent labour leader, which inflamed the Nazis further. In April 1933, members of Hitler's brown-shirted SA made an attempt on both their lives.* Paulick fled to Shanghai the following month, arriving as 'the first German refugee in June 1933'.[8]

Since Paulick lived at 871 Bubbling Well Road, quite close to the library, he regularly offered his apartment as a venue for talks.[9] On other evenings, the discussion groups met in the Café Louis after business hours, or in the homes of other refugees.

Even after Buchenwald, Bruno Loewenberg always claimed he was not politically minded. Perhaps this was how he had turned a blind eye to the growing danger in pre-war Berlin. The talks he enjoyed most were on art, refusing to accept that any of it was 'degenerate'. Although he still kept his sketchbook to hand, he saw his creations as mere scribbles, and preferred to enjoy the talent of others. He watched his customers browse the shelves of the Lion Bookshop, chatting to new friends they were making in this Germanic haven so far from home. The man at its heart was content with his new life in Shanghai. What choice did he have, and what good was despondency?

Each night he returned home to sleep in the small space that he rented in a house not far from the library, past the stone gateway that marked the entrance to Yang Terrace. As he lay down on his mattress within the balcony, he closed his eyes and dreamt of coffee on the Kurfürstendamm. He tried to recall the smile of his sister and the wide grin of her son during their last fleeting reunion in Berlin. Those faces now seemed so distant, as if from a different life altogether.

---

* SA stands for *Sturmabteilung*, 'Storm attachment', the Nazis' paramilitary wing.

14

March 1940: A Couch for a Bed

I imagine Lisbeth entering the house on Yang Terrace: as her eyes adjusted to the dimly lit hall, the first thing that hit her was the smell, a mixture of fusty damp, and unwashed clothes, mingling with the odour of cooking oil seeping from one of the rooms.[1] The wallpaper – brownish with a faded geometric design – was curling off the walls. Large areas of its pattern were obscured by spreading tentacles of mould, the result of Shanghai's humid climate. A sepia print of the Prater's giant Ferris wheel, icon of the amusement park, hung on a nail, put there partly to stop the paper from completing its fall. Lisbeth could make out low voices, speaking German as well as Yiddish. A caged bird chirruped insistently from behind one of the closed doors across the hall.

A few steps ahead of her, her father and mother were already ascending the staircase. Lisbeth glanced at the rooms each side of the hallway. She wondered who lived on this ground floor, and on which floor her bedroom would be. The terraced house looked so promising, opposite its civilised gardens; its red-brick and slate felt reassuringly European. Now, pulling her hand back from the sticky balustrade, her hopes were beginning to fade. Her left leg felt heavy, and slowed her down as she climbed the stairs.

Arnold stopped on the first floor and beckoned his wife and daughter into a room on one side of the staircase. Lisbeth noticed again how grey his hair had become, and the sickly hue of the skin across his sharp cheekbones.

'This one is ours,' he said as he unlocked the door.

Lisbeth followed her parents and looked round the room. It was barely half the size of their drawing room back home; its walls were the colour of nicotine. She had caught the bitter smell of tobacco on her father's clothes when they first embraced; the same aroma now enveloped her even more strongly. But the room was bright: the early afternoon sun penetrated the grime on the large sash window, and gleaming particles of dust danced in its beams. She looked out of the window, beyond the wide-alcoved balcony with its stone overhang, onto the rose garden below. People in Western dress were walking past, and for an instant she forgot where she was. Then reality hit her, and she turned back to the room.

A small table and three unmatched chairs took centre stage, the table set for the family's first meal together. So much had happened since they had been apart; where would their conversation start? Across from the window, a small charcoal stove revealed the room's source of heating, plus a hot plate for cooking. Lisbeth saw a tall thin wardrobe, which she guessed would be large enough for her parents' few garments. She wondered why it was in here, rather than their bedroom. Then she noticed a small double bed squeezed into the alcove formed by the balcony. A wave of unease ran through her until she spotted, above a sofa, a shelf with a few photographs and other familiar mementos from home. She moved closer.

There was a photograph of Edith, wearing a white dress, her black hair up and her smile painted immaculately. One stiff studio photograph showed herself and Ilse, aged four and eight years, at the Weitzmann studio at 9 Praterstrasse, Vienna. The photographer had posed them carefully, draped in satin and each given a necklace to wear. Lisbeth's was a string of plain wooden beads, while Ilse had a pendant on a shining gold chain. Frozen in time was Lisbeth's attempt to pull her sister's pendant towards her own chest, her eyes gazing wistfully at the camera from beneath a harshly cut fringe.

Lisbeth wondered what her sister was doing at this very moment. She knew that Ilse had left Paris and was now living in some foggy London suburb. Was England proving more welcoming than France? Were people more understanding of the Jews fleeing Hitler, and offering them work? Had her sister yet found a position as a governess or domestic servant? Middle-class women like her could not expect any employment more prestigious than that; they had to be grateful for any means of earning a living.

Lisbeth and Ilse as little girls with necklaces, 1926.

A soft voice drew her back to Shanghai, and the present. Her father was speaking, though his words made no sense.

'The screen is to give you some privacy,' he was telling her.

She looked from him to the sofa, beside which stood a decorated Chinese screen. The couch's sagging centre suddenly matched how she felt, as she understood what her father meant. This room was all Arnold had been able to afford. Lisbeth was to sleep on the sofa, while her parents had the bed in the alcove. The room, just this one room, was the family's new home. Their home in Vienna suddenly felt very far away.

Over the following weeks, Lisbeth grew accustomed to life in what she now knew was 'a very good neighbourhood'.[2] They shared the boarding house with six other sets of tenants: a sign at the front door explained that visitors should ring the doorbell between one and seven times to attract a specific household's attention.

She placed her few possessions on the shelf over the sofa, treasured ties to her past. Among them were a few books: slim volumes of romantic poetry by Heine, and works by von Hofmannsthal, whose writing she loved. She had also brought more photographs, and treasured postcards, that she would keep safely for the rest of her life.

As time passed, Lisbeth's horror at their one room eased. She came to realise that others put up with far worse. She and Edith were fortunate that Arnold had been in Shanghai since the previous year, and that he had found decent work. Not as a bookbinder, as he had put down on his immigration form, but better: he was a history teacher at a school for refugee children. There he could make good use of his English, as lessons were taught in Westernised Shanghai's favoured language. Nor could his wife and daughter have imagined stepping onto the Bund without him to greet them and take them to their new home. Many immigrants were not as lucky; they arrived in their heavy woollen suits with no one to meet them. They spent their first night in China on hard camp beds, sleeping besides scores of others in a makeshift reception centre set up by Sir Victor Sassoon. In 1938 Sir Victor turned over several floors of his Embankment Building, a grey curving block of offices and homes for the wealthy, into a place for 'processing' penniless Europeans. The vast building stood on the eastern side of Garden Bridge, occupying a quarter of a mile of Soochow Creek, called by some the busiest river in the world. The landmark of Broadway Mansions, twenty storeys of art deco sandstone also built by Sassoon, loomed up on the other side of the bridge.

Sir Victor's generosity provided the refugees' children with daily milk, and the Embankment Building even offered the homeless immigrants an indoor swimming pool.[3] But after *Kristallnacht*, the number of Jews proved too much even for Sassoon's spacious halfway house. From early 1939, a new solution was found, which Arnold had turned to when he had landed that June; he had been taken, along with hundreds of other immigrants, to a drab housing block in bombed-out Hongkew, the district north of Soochow Creek. Arnold spent three months in the building at 138 Ward Road, moving only when Edith alerted him to the new laws forbidding further immigration into that part of the city. The block was the first of five refugee camps – or *Heime** – run by Jewish charities in the city. Their funding came from two sources: Shanghai's wealthy Sephardi community and New York's American Jewish Joint Distribution Committee (the AJJDC, often referred to as the JDC or simply 'the Joint').[4]

The camp had been set up in the January before Arnold's arrival, converted from an old Russian barracks. The other four *Heime* quickly followed – improvised conversions of schools and barracks so damaged by the 1937 conflict that no one else would live there, housing 2,500 destitute European refugees and feeding another 8,000. The Sephardi families gave generously to their Ashkenazi friends; some had never met a poor Jew before now.[5] They were a last resort for the most desperate, or those who believed that their stay in Shanghai would only be temporary.

Entry in *Emigranten Adressbuch* p. 44 showing
Arnold's Ward Road address.

---

* From the German for 'homes', despite their lack of any feeling of homelessness.

Decades later, in March 2004, my sister Claudia and I travelled to China together. This was an ambitious undertaking for us both. Although used to occasional short trips to Europe together, this was our first venture to such a distant and different land. A friend had left us the use of her flat in the former French Concession, and asked her driver to take us wherever we wished. What an amazing opportunity to explore the Shanghai streets and locations that Lisbeth and our grandparents had known in the 1940s!

The flat was spacious and light, filled with Chinese furniture and pictures. In the evening, we could cool off in the shared swimming pool. The building stood in a peaceful boulevard in old Frenchtown. The ex-Concession's ancient walls still had gaps through which we could peer to glimpse ornate villas in shaded gardens. I could picture colonial types or wealthy Chinese gaily sipping cocktails as they waved cigarette holders around. Yet just a short walk from the building, the whole atmosphere changed. The calm was replaced by people yelling and motors roaring, and the smell and steam of street cooking; the air was thick with car fumes and cigarette smoke. The streets were crammed with cyclists and pedestrians, often loudly expelling mucus onto the pavements from their throats or finger-pinched noses. The rickshaws were gone, their place taken by a dizzying number of bicycles, whose riders balanced crates of fruit or electrical goods across overladen handlebars, ringing their bells as they wove between the traffic. Horn-blaring taxis zigzagged through people rushing who-knew-where.

One of our first destinations was the *Heim* on Ward Road, where our grandfather had spent his first few months in the city. Although many of Shanghai's roads had been razed to make way for the city's relentless facelift, Hongkou's streets were less altered than most. The local government was even starting to preserve some historic buildings and shop signs to publicise the story of the Jews who had found refuge there. As my sister and I walked along a pavement shaded by plane trees, we spotted, above an old wooden doorway, some faded lettering. As I made out the words, the hairs on my arms rose again: they advertised 'Horn's Imbiss Stube'*, and Café Atlantic.

---

* Snack bar.

The old German signs remaining in Hongkou.

Not far away was Hongkou's main road, which Lisbeth knew as Ward Road, but was now Changyang Lu. We stopped at number 138, where we found the entrance to our grandfather's first 'home'. Here stood Shanghai's original *Heim*, the temporary camp that had housed the penniless refugees fleeing Hitler. As we gazed through the gate at the large building with its stained concrete walls, now criss-crossed with telegraph cables, tears came to my eyes. Suddenly our ancestor's shadowy life stared back at us, in solid bricks and mortar. I imagined Arnold among the hundreds of destitute men, women and children, in his thick European clothing, and pictured him as one who ate and slept in this drab, soulless place. My throat tightened as I turned away, thankful that he had stayed there for only a few months.

Lisbeth heard her father's descriptions of Ward Road with horror. Arnold told her of the camp's crowded dormitories, where married couples slept in different areas from single folk. With no storage space or even nails in the wall to hang clothing, refugees shoved their suitcases under steel bunk beds, or used them as tables. The proud teenager also hated the idea of taking charity from others. The thought appalled her, as did that of lining up with other people for a bowl of thin vegetable stew, or meat soup so lacking in fat that it left no stain if spilt on one's blouse. Her room suddenly seemed luxurious compared to one full of strangers, sleeping so close you could smell their bodies and hear their noises at night. Even worse was the camp's makeshift sanitation. For the girl used to the lavender soaps her father brought home, the thought of communal washing made her shudder. One *Heim* she heard of had only two ancient lavatories for more than four hundred people.[6]

Spared any first-hand experience of the *Heim*, Lisbeth soon valued her home's own facilities. People told her: 'You don't know how lucky you are! You have running water. You have good toilets!'[7] They were right. Unlike many Chinese-built houses, the British-style one in Yang Terrace had its own modern plumbing, and the Epsteins shared indoor showers and toilets with only tens, rather than hundreds, of residents.[8] Others faced the ignominy of having to use that most primitive of toilets, the 'honey bucket'. This – common throughout the poorer parts of the city – was a wooden bucket kept in a fetid outhouse. Each day it would fill up with urine and excrement, and then be put out at night for collection by the 'honey-pot man'. The sounds of his rattling 'honey cart', pushed before him at arm's length in the small hours, and the cry of 'Myah kai, myah kai', signalled his nightly arrival.⁹ After his wife had scraped and swabbed the bucket with a coarse brush dipped in the previous day's dishwater, he would return it to the outdoor throne room. The pungent contents of these honey buckets would be sold to outlying farms, for whom this night soil served as prized fertiliser. Small wonder that fruit and vegetables had to be individually washed with a special soap, or soaked in chemicals, before they could be eaten.

As the days passed, Lisbeth became more accustomed to her surroundings. The household had its own staff – an *amah* to help with the infants, and a servant for the most menial tasks. At first Lisbeth felt uncomfortable with the name used to describe him, which was 'boy', despite his being an adult Chinese. The name was a legacy of the Western settlers of almost a century before, whose colonial attitudes to local people normalised such disrespect.

Despite her initial unease, Lisbeth decided that the 'boy' could teach her some of the ways of Shanghai. She followed him in the mornings when he was sent out to buy boiling water to add to their teapots. She was surprised to discover that hot-water shops stood on nearly every street corner. Each was tended by a man who boiled water in huge iron cauldrons encased in cement.¹⁰ It was cheaper to go to these vendors than to use electricity at home. The 'boy' showed Lisbeth the different bamboo tokens exchanged for the water, costing one, two or three cents. Each cent token bought a single ladleful. He was repeatedly warned to check that the water was really boiling before bringing it home. Everyone knew the danger of unboiled water. Every drop had to be boiled before use to remove the assortment of organisms that thrived in the Whangpoo. Typhoid and cholera were rife. One refugee couple Lisbeth heard of learnt the hard way that a water filter was little defence against cholera: choosing that over boiling their drinking water had killed them both.

The 'boy' showed Lisbeth the best district to shop for their food, which was over the bridge in Hongkew, where everything was much cheaper than in the International Settlement. It was also a manageable twenty minutes' walk, although if Lisbeth's leg was too painful, she could take a rickshaw or even the electric tram. The service connecting Hongkew with the rest of Shanghai had been cut during the Japanese conflict of 1937, when the locals had fled the area. Now the trams were running again, and the Chinese were returning.

Lisbeth and her mother shopped at both of Hongkew's big markets. At the junction of Boone and Woosung Road was the purpose-built Hongkew Market, Shanghai's largest, attracting shoppers from miles around. Before the fighting began in 1937, farmers had brought their fresh produce and poultry there daily; food was scarcer now, but could still be found. The municipal market was in the heart of the refugee enclave on Chusan Road, German-speakers lived side by side with Chinese families, the street full of children playing, vendors haggling, barbers shaving customers and people cooking. Lisbeth liked the municipal market, known to most locals as Die Markthalle. Japanese bombs had destroyed its three-storey concrete structure in the summer of 1937, but through the back-breaking effort of the European immigrants, the burnt-out skeleton had been restored to a thriving market. Hooks dangled stringy cuts of pork and beef, scrawny chickens and pigs' bladders, alongside ducks with dangling necks and offal still dripping with blood. Lisbeth tried not to inspect these too closely. Wicker baskets overflowed with piles of melons and cabbages, yams and other produce she did not recognise. Yet when shoppers kvetched about the prices in her native German, or Yiddish, Lisbeth felt almost as if she were back home.

As in Vienna, Edith prepared all the family's meals; Lisbeth's lack of interest in cooking had not changed here in Shanghai. To both women's relief, Arnold was slowly putting on weight, and seemed to be getting a little stronger. Lisbeth kept encouraging her father to eat, while nagging her mother to follow all the culinary rules to stay safe. She eyed every item of food or drink they brought home with suspicion, knowing how each posed a threat to their health. It was not just the water that held invisible dangers: she learnt to slice bread thinly in order to expose the parasitic worms that were lurking within, and poured rice vigorously onto a plate before passing it to her mother for cooking, so that the insects inside would wriggle up to the surface.

A different sort of hazard was associated with rice, but this came from a scam enacted by food sellers who knocked door-to-door at refugee houses in Hongkew. It involved a whole cast of characters: a young Chinese man, a group of local accomplices and a screaming child. The young man would deliver a bag of rice to the home of a Jewish refugee, who would swear she had not ordered it. The man would assure her that it was already paid for, and so she would accept it in front of a crowd of Chinese. Shortly after, the man would return, agreeing it was indeed delivered in error; the woman would hand back the rice. Half an hour later, a crowd would appear outside the refugee's home, a wailing Chinese boy at its centre; a policeman would soon arrive to investigate the commotion. The bewildered refugee would be taken to the police station, where the boy's incomprehensible complaints were translated. He would accuse her of taking his bag of rice without payment. Since all the 'witnesses' would swear they saw her do this, she had no choice but to find the money for the goods she never kept.[11]

If they could ever afford meat, Lisbeth made sure it was fresh. The 'boy' had taught her how the 'chop' – the official stamp – on its surface showed the grade of the beef, mutton or pork. Purple meant top-quality produce, while blue indicated second-grade meat.[12] She also learnt to recognise the ingenuity of the Chinese boys offering noodles at prices that were truly 'dirt cheap'. The lads chased after grocery trucks, then slashed holes in the sacks of noodles on the back. When they swept up their loot from the street, they made no effort to separate the noodles from glass, stones and dirt picked up at the same time. Lisbeth or Edith could do this later at home, slowly and with care. Money was tight, but time was plentiful.

Those first days turned to weeks, and then months. Lisbeth had no choice but to accept this life, which was so alien to the one she had left behind in Vienna; she had to make the best of it. She wondered if she would meet any people her age, with similar interests and dreams, or would her fellow refugees all be too absorbed in their own problems to befriend her? As she settled down at night on the couch, she thought of Vienna's wide streets and the department stores with their fancy Christmas window displays. How she would love just one more glimpse of Café Demel and its white-aproned staff ... But at least she and her parents were alive. Who knew what had befallen their Jewish friends and relations who had not left? Her family had escaped the threat of men in jackboots, but this new city came with its own set of dangers. She wondered if she could ever feel at home here.

15

Spring 1940: Lingerie Shops and Corpses

In her first few months in Shanghai, Lisbeth 'did not do very much', as she later recalled. She had time to explore the streets near her home, to get the lie of the land. Yang Terrace lay inside the city's Western-run International Settlement proper, the scant two square miles that the Japanese dared not touch. Its pavements were lined with plane trees and sycamores, so she could window-shop in the comfort of shade. As well as its Weihaiwei Road entrance, Yang Terrace had another gateway from Yates Road, running south at right angles. It was nicknamed Petticoat Lane by the British, or Pants Alley by the Americans, thanks to its many lingerie shops. Lisbeth stopped at the windows displaying garments in 'silks and satins and silver', embellished with embroidered crêpe de Chine and lace. Although the city's guidebook for tourists considered their prices very reasonable, the comparison was with goods sold in Europe and America.[1] For refugees like the Epsteins, such items were priced far out of reach.

At the top of Yates Road was Love Lane. Lisbeth avoided walking there after dark. As its name suggested, it was the Settlement's most well-known brothel district. At number 80 was the St Anna Ballroom ('Dancing Nightly, 8pm to 2am'), famous for its swing bands and home to XQHA, one of the city's five foreign-language radio stations. Another no-go area for the eighteen-year-old was Rue Chu Pao San in Frenchtown, a short street off Avenue Édouard VII near the French Bund. Its countless bars and clubs attracted crowds of sailors, soldiers and prostitutes; alcohol-fuelled fights were so common that the street was known as 'Blood Alley'. A British soldier described it as 'a thoroughfare entirely dedicated to wine, women, song and all-night lechery', those drawn there 'easy pickings' for thieves.[2] The contrast with her home in Vienna was remarkable, but Lisbeth grew accustomed to her 'wild' new city surprisingly fast. She knew it was rife with gambling and prostitution, but later said that she never saw any opium.

Very quickly she learnt where *not* to go. It was impossible to miss all the warnings to new refugees issued by Jewish relief organisations. One such group was the Speelman Committee, which had been set up in 1938 as refugee numbers swelled, and whose lectures were full of practical suggestions.[3] Lisbeth paid attention to the warnings: not to venture into the old Chinese city, or the Japanese part of Hongkew, 'Little Tokyo';[4] to steer clear of the unsmiling Japanese guards at the city's checkpoints. Other practical advice – 'don't carry any valuables and don't trust policemen' – was unnecessary: she had no valuables, and avoiding men in uniform still came naturally.

Lisbeth Epstein's new city had one thing in common with Nazi-run Vienna: the value of life was dependent on one's race. Here it was destitute Chinese people, not Jews, whose lives counted for nothing. In 1933, the bodies of more than 5,700 Chinese 'beggars, indigents, still-born female infants etc.' were left on vacant lots for collection and burial by benevolent societies. What killed them was never stated; only this total, recorded under the heading 'Exposed Corpses'. Thousands more deaths went unnoticed; in Shanghai there was no compulsory registration of deaths.[5] To her horror, Lisbeth soon saw this for herself. She learnt to walk carefully to avoid the small bundles wrapped in newspapers and placed on the pavement – the tiny stiff bodies of Chinese infants whose parents had no money to bury them.

Seeing these paper-wrapped bundles must have hit my grandmother especially hard. For Kerstin Timmerman's research into Vienna's archives uncovered more information that I had never known about my family. Kerstin's email starkly listed a number of facts about the Epsteins. Point 5 read: 'Daughter Gertrud born on 11 Nov 1915 in Vienna'. I was amazed; this was the first I had heard of another sister. On reading the full document attached to the email, I discovered why. Page 4 showed that Gertrud had died on 29 December 1915; the 'cause of death was a seizure'.

I returned to Kerstin's email. When I reached the last point I had to reread it to take in its words, which I stared at in disbelief: 'Twin (Son) was stillborn

4 Jan 1922 in Vienna'. That was my aunt's birthday too; so Lisbeth had been a twin. On that day, Edith had been delivered of a son as well as her daughter. There was no record of the dead baby's name. I thought of the two healthy sons I had given birth to, and my heart ached for my grandmother. Had Lisbeth known this? Like so much else in her life, she never spoke to me of it; had her mother ever told her? I have heard that a twin senses its sibling's presence in the womb, as the pair float together in the darkness. And that if one of them dies, even around the time of the birth, the survivor may for ever mourn the bereavement. Could the death of her brother, even if never discussed, have begun the crushing of Lisbeth's spirit so early on?

Had Lisbeth known of the stillbirth of her twin, or Gertrud's death, those tiny corpses on the streets of Shanghai must have been even more painful to see. Edith would certainly never forget the death of her only son; or her first child, born and then gone just a few weeks later. She would surely always mourn her lost babies, and these frequent reminders of infant mortality must have reopened those wounds.

The initial horror of such casual brushes with death wore off shockingly fast. Like other Europeans who spent time in Shanghai, Lisbeth would learn to step over the tragic little parcels. Larger bodies were more difficult to ignore. Corpses were left to lie on the streets, waiting for collection in the early morning by the Blue Cross Benevolent Society truck. The truck collected around 80 bodies each day.[6] After outbreaks of cholera, these trucks would be heaped with dried-up bodies, their eyes rolled back and black mouths gaping. One corner in the city was known for its piles of corpses; it was here that starving beggars and those infected with cholera crawled off to die. Early the next morning, the Municipal Council's rubbish carts would collect their spent bodies for disposal in Hongkew's crematorium.

Lisbeth must have hated walking past this grim corner and looked away. Just as horrible was the sight of bodies hanging from ropes in doorways or, worst of all, the grimacing heads neatly positioned on doorsteps, the grisly remains of dissidents executed by the Japanese.[7] Since the 1937 invasion, the plight of Shanghai's Chinese had worsened, with many more in poverty. Thousands crammed into Red Cross camps, offered only rice gruel for sustenance; thousands died there – especially children – of dysentery or cholera.[8] Unaware of the cruelty that the Nazis were inflicting on non-Aryans back in

Europe, Lisbeth could hardly believe the callousness with which death was treated here. Yet she gradually 'learnt that life is very cheap when you live in the Orient'. Even her neighbours, fellow Jews, behaved differently here: 'If a beggar died in the street in front of a house, people would push him to the next house. This was because if somebody died on your premises you were supposed to pay for the funeral.'

Chinese lives may have been valued the cheapest, but Lisbeth knew that death came as surely to Jews as it did to the Shanghainese. She and her neighbours made every effort to heed the countless health warnings. For some Jews, hypochondria is a natural part of life; here in this hazard-filled environment, her family and their neighbours' leanings towards anxiety and fastidiousness were, at last, warranted. The habits of hand washing and cleanliness, which had been drummed into them since childhood, may have even saved their lives. The refugees boiled water, avoided milk and unwashed fruit, and scrubbed and disinfected whatever they could. They grew paranoid about the danger lurking in every insect and pest-ridden creature. They knew a mosquito bite could deliver malaria. Even worse was the bite of a flea from a rat's carcass. If this led to swollen lymph nodes, which burst and oozed foul-smelling pus, it meant the victim had caught the deadly black plague.

Some neighbours of Lisbeth appeared to become masters of microbiology. They soon bored those within earshot with their knowledge of infectious diseases, such as the difference between typhus and typhoid – both rife in Shanghai, and debilitating, potentially even deadly. But, as the new experts told Lisbeth, since their causative agents entered the body quite differently, different strategies must be adopted to avoid them. She listened patiently when people began to explain, for deep down she knew their words were important.

Typhus's nickname was 'jail fever', which gave a clue to its origin. Its bacterium, *Rickettsia typhi*, was spread by the rats and mice that thrived in unsanitary places like prisons. Hordes of these rodents scuttled through the city's rubbish-strewn streets, their fur carrying hundreds of fleas and lice along with them. The insects swelled as they feasted on their hosts' bacteria-rich blood, then passed the germs on to the next human they bit. Within days, the victim's chest would flush with typhus's telltale rash. As the pink spots spread across the body, a raging fever set in. If untreated, typhus so inflamed the blood vessels that the damage led to delirium and death. No wonder people blanched at the threat of being sent to Shanghai's prisons. They knew that confinement in the lock-up at Hongkew's Wayside Police Station, a rat-infested bunker, was a potential death sentence.

The pink rash of typhus was easily confused with that of the similarly named typhoid. Jewish refugees were more likely to contract this than typhus; its agent was everywhere. *Salmonella typhi* contaminated all types of food, as well as drinking water and milk. Shanghai water was deadly; bacteria flourished within the city's primitive sewage system and the filthy Whangpoo.

For some, typhoid infection caused only mild malaise. They showed no symptoms, and so went on to pass the infection to others. Only those obsessed with personal cleanliness were protected – which included most of the Jews. For them, hands could not be washed too meticulously after using the toilet, nor water boiled too long, nor food cooked too thoroughly. Nothing was eaten unpeeled or un-disinfected. No one dared risk a serious attack of typhoid; its fever and blinding headache, pain and debilitating diarrhoea could prove fatal. For the vulnerable – the very old or young, or the already infirm – it could lead to a lassitude that could drift into death.

While Lisbeth was aware of these dangers, she tried not to brood on them. There were other things in life, after all! She had found a good source of distraction, which Arnold had introduced to her and Edith soon after their arrival. Just around the corner from their home was the lending library on the corner of Moulmein and Bubbling Well Road. The whole family became keen subscribers, and Lisbeth started to go there often, for there was little other entertainment. They knew the owner by sight: the Berliner with the hunched back was also a neighbour, living a few doors further down Yang Terrace.

Like many other refugees, Lisbeth and her parents leapt at the chance to buy or borrow volumes, both in their mother tongue and in the English they were striving to learn. Reading reminded them that their homeland had once offered more than antisemitism: a rich literature and elegant poetry. Bruno Loewenberg's business helped many Europeans keep their sanity in Shanghai. Lisbeth and her parents visited the red-roofed villa on Moulmein Road each week. They would wait at the front desk as the young woman who helped Bruno entered the details of their loans in a large ledger. The teenager would watch closely as the girl recorded each withdrawal made and the fee received.

Lisbeth had another means of escape once any chores had been done. She liked to walk eastwards from Yang Terrace, then take a rickshaw to the northern end of the Bund. There, where Soochow Creek flowed into the Whangpoo beside Garden Bridge, lay Shanghai's Public Gardens. Soon after their reunion, she and her parents had posed for photographs there, against a backdrop of branches spreading from a golden rain tree.

Lisbeth, Edith and Arnold in the Public Gardens, Shanghai 1940

Years later, on our visit to Shanghai, my sister Claudia and I stood in these same gardens as we prepared to cross Garden Bridge. I had seen the city landmark (now named Waibaidu Bridge) in many photographs, but had not expected the thrill of the sight in real life. Its distinctive girders were unchanged: criss-crossing steel in two humps like no other bridge I had seen before.* By half closing my eyes, I could easily imagine the Japanese guards, decades earlier, who had threatened the disrespectful with their razor-sharp bayonets. The hairs rose on my arms as I recognised Broadway Mansions' bulk ahead of me on the other side of the bridge. Staring at Sassoon's art deco apartment building, I found it miraculous to think that my aunt would have looked at exactly the same rust-coloured building when she stood at this spot. Yet how different Lisbeth's Shanghai experience must have been from our leisurely stay.

---

* I later learnt it was a rare 'camel-back truss' bridge.

In the late 1930s, the bridge across Soochow Creek linked two different worlds. On the Bund side lay the Western quarter; across the creek was the Japanese enclave, 'Little Tokyo', home to 30,000 Japanese – civilians as well as militia – and their marines' permanent barracks. Their guards now manned part of the bridge, perpetuating the atmosphere of fear that began after their forces took control of much of the city in 1937.

Although it was not the only bridge that linked the International Settlement to Hongkou, after the 1937 conflict, Garden Bridge was the only one open to vehicles as well as foot passengers, and was certainly the busiest.[9] At first, the Japanese banned the British and other foreigners from Western settlements from crossing over at all. Wearing dark uniforms with white leggings, and helmets like metal bowls, expressionless soldiers would emerge from their wooden hut halfway across. They scrutinised anyone wishing to enter Hongkew, demanding papers, passes and deference. But soon after their victory, the Japanese relaxed their policy and began encouraging British and American businesses and ex-residents back over the bridge, to live, shop and pay taxes there. In February 1938, they published a list of inducements to encourage people back, including discounts on food, and free sake to those prepared to drink to the health of the Japanese emperor, Hirohito.

The list also included the regulations to be followed, notably when crossing Garden Bridge into Japanese territory. The proclamation 'requested' that everyone crossing from west to east 'respect the Japanese sentry on point duty at the Garden Bridge and at street corners by giving him a gentle bow, and wishing him "GOOD MORNING"'.[10] Hats had to be removed, and a bow from the waist made to the guards, before one could continue across on the appropriate side. Any infringement would invite varying degrees of punishment, according to its gravity or the mood of the guard. Bowing too slowly, or not deeply enough, could lead to humiliation with slaps, blows or even bayonet thrusts. The Chinese were those most at risk of repercussions from the guards' sadism. They had to bow especially deeply; failure to do so incurred a scream of 'zulu'.* One Chinese cobbler who forgot to bow was shrieked at by the Japanese soldier, then slapped in the face until blood

* Pig.

gushed from his nose. Even a Japanese businessman, who forgot to remove the cigarette from his mouth when he bowed, was 'pummelled and slapped' mercilessly by guards on the bridge until he collapsed. Others suffered worse fates, being bayoneted and then hurled from the bridge, their bodies swept away by the currents below. If Westerners like Lisbeth witnessed – or suffered – any such brutality, they knew not to react.

Although their guards could be brutal, the Japanese bore no special grudge against the city's Jews; no one ever felt they were antisemitic. On the contrary, many Japanese had respected the community ever since 1904, when a Jewish banker named Schiff had loaned the empire of Japan $200 million, which helped bankroll the country's war with Russia.[11] They viewed the Jewish people as clever and powerful, and actively encouraged the newly arrived immigrants to join the expansion of their part of the city. They even made sure that all the European refugees were regularly vaccinated against the city's many infectious diseases.[12] This attitude from the authorities was a welcome – if strange – experience for those fleeing Hitler, who were more used to being reviled by those in uniform.

Lisbeth loved returning to the Public Gardens beside the bridge and, on humid June days, she joined others strolling among the lawns to enjoy the cool breeze. She would daydream, eyes half closed, their lids' lining glowing orange in the sun. She imagined herself back near her home in Am Tabor, among the chestnut avenues of the Augarten. There, in centuries past, the young Amadeus had conducted matinée concerts to the delight of Viennese residents, who also enjoyed many of Beethoven's works. No such music here, she thought, as she reopened her eyes. The gardens and waterway were lively with movement. Semi-mesmerised, she stood and watched the river traffic glide back and forth. She knew her 'not doing very much' must come to an end. She could no longer ignore what was glaringly obvious. Arnold's salary had been enough to cover the cost of his meagre diet and his cheap cigarettes. But now he had two more people to feed, one of them a teenager. The financial pressures on the family meant only one thing: Lisbeth's weeks of idleness must come to an end. But as she tossed and turned in the humidity of the oppressive Shanghai night, she asked herself again and again: what kind of work could she do?

16

Little Vienna's Ingenuity: Soap, Bratwurst and Strudel

'Welcome to Shanghai. Now you are no longer Germans, Austrians, Czechs or Roumanians. Now you are only Jews. The Jews of the whole world have prepared a home for you.'[1]

As Lisbeth stood by the Public Gardens at the north end of the Bund, she looked across the iron-girder bridge towards the place where she hoped to find work. The place where most immigrants – to whom the words of welcome were directed – had settled. The 'Now you are only Jews' speech was spoken by a member of the IC, one of Shanghai's Jewish relief organisations, the month after she arrived. By spring 1940, the refugees' new Chinese 'home' had expanded greatly since the arrival of the first two or three hundred people a few years earlier. The two surges of immigration from Europe, after the *Anschluss* in March 1938 and after *Kristallnacht* a few months later, had brought over 15,000 destitute Jews to Shanghai, at least half of them crowding into Hongkew. They were all now competing for jobs. Lisbeth knew she had to join in the struggle.

Whenever she crossed Garden Bridge to go north of Soochow Creek, Lisbeth silently thanked her father for finding Yang Terrace. The first time Arnold had taken her to Hongkew, the assault on her senses echoed the shock she had felt when stepping off the *Conte Rosso*. Here in this war-ravaged district, the stench of rotting rubbish, cooking oil and, from some alley houses, the wooden 'honey bucket', overwhelmed her. The noise was relentless. Voices shouting in Chinese – the local Wu dialect, Shanghainese, a fast-growing and distinct language from Mandarin Chinese – battled with tinny radios emitting ear-splitting music from every doorway. Lisbeth soon became familiar with the constant shuffling of clinking mah-jong tiles on wooden tables, against the background chat of the players. As well as their conversation, of which she understood not a word, she caught snatches of Yiddish, German and sometimes Polish from Hongkew's newest residents. Had she stayed until nightfall, her skin would have crawled at the tissue-paper rustle of cockroaches and rats scuttling across floorboards.

In the bleak district of Hongkew – the 'wrong' side of Garden Bridge – food was cheaper and rents were often 75 per cent lower than anywhere else in the city.[2] Unlike Yang Terrace, with its spacious-feeling gardens, parts of Hongkew felt claustrophobic to Lisbeth. Its drabness was threaded with narrow alleyways like capillaries snaking through the body. This network of lanes crammed the maximum number of people into the available space, housing 100,000 Chinese side by side in dreary intimacy. Each lane was a gloomy passageway, accessed from a gate off a much wider main road, lined with multi-occupancy houses on each side. The gates were closed at night, often guarded by tall Sikh policemen, giving the lanes a strangely medieval quality.

Lisbeth felt sorry for the families she saw in their dark, airless rooms. Their only view, save the washing lines flapping grey garments across the ten-foot-wide alley, was into the rooms of the families opposite. And while the presence of so many Japanese in the district deterred many, the city's poorest inhabitants couldn't be choosers.

But the area also had its good side, one that drew in the Epsteins and many others. A large part of Hongkew buzzed with a vibrant new atmosphere. Alongside 'Little Tokyo' lay another foreign enclave, centred around the streets radiating from the *Heim* on Ward Road. In the two and a half years since the first German refugees had arrived, their community – now numbering 8,000 and well-supplied with architects, draftsmen, engineers and builders – had painstakingly rebuilt many of its bombed-out streets. Brick by brick, powered by sweat and determination, the refugees had transformed the charred ruins into a thriving facsimile of their home. Hongkew now had its own 'Little Vienna'.

Lisbeth enjoyed wandering the rebuilt streets, breathing in the familiarity of these German-style shops here in the midst of the poorest Chinese. She and her mother soon discovered the delights of Little Vienna, an unlikely home from home, which they saw as 'a resurrected flourishing little village'. It drew bargain hunters from around the city, offering every business and all type of goods imaginable: grocers, bakeries, pharmacies, plumbers, locksmiths, barbers, tailors, milliners and cobblers. Artisan butchers sold bratwurst and other sausages, whose smoky, garlicky flavour, rich with herbs and pepper, was almost as good as those they were used to. Who cared if the veal or beef had been replaced by pork? This was no place to try to keep kosher. The smell of frying *wurst* transported passersby back to Vienna or Berlin. Craftsmen bakers sold *tortes* topped with fruit and cream; cafés, bars and restaurants served crispy schnitzel and vinegary fermented cabbage, to be washed down with sharp German lagers or sweeter, more malty, bocks. The best chocolates could be bought at the Café Louis, while the Vienna Bakery had tangy *apfel strudel*, bursting with its apple and raisin filling. Edith looked approvingly at the thin crispy pastry; she always said it must be rolled thin enough to be able to read a newspaper through it.

For those with the money, in Little Vienna almost any type of food could be bought. The cheapest food was Chinese, but the Epsteins preferred European fare, like the 'Viennese' sausage and sauerkraut at Delikat at number 23 (offering *'Beste Wiener Kueche'*),* or the soft liver dumplings in broth served at Café International at 81. Cream cakes were to be found at Hesky and Gerstl's Tearooms at 252 Chusan Road; there were even milkshakes or ice creams sold at the milk bars, which were new to the Chinese, who never ate dairy. For the hardest up, there was always coffee made from a second or even third brewing of grounds sold on by the Café Louis, or a hot dog from the *Würstelstand* parked by the kerbside.[3]

---

* Best Viennese cuisine.

Some of Hongkew's revived restaurants and nightclubs also offered live music. Two favourites were the Roy Roof Garden above the Broadway Theatre, and the White Horse Inn – whose name came from an Austrian opera – on Ward Road. The Epsteins enjoyed reminiscing about home with the latter's Viennese Jewish owners. Rudolf Mosberg and his wife had been determined to bring a taste of their homeland to Shanghai.[4] For Lisbeth and her family, it was not just the enjoyment of finding familiar foods; it also felt good to speak their mother tongue with others who had shared their recent experiences.

Hongkew's European-style establishments not only fed refugees, but also Shanghailanders and Japanese intrigued by the new cuisine, as well as providing work for the immigrants. It was not surprising that Lisbeth began her search for work in Little Vienna. As she walked through its streets, she would have noticed that most of the German-speakers in the area were far older than she was.[5] With middle-class backgrounds much like that of her own family, they were largely professional people, white collar workers and even artists of various sorts. The community had a glut of journalists, lawyers and medical practitioners; the refugees were spoilt by the number of doctors, dentists and ophthalmologists competing for patients. They often worked in shifts, sharing tiny 'offices' with others of the same profession. Their numbers also made their prices affordable.

Displaced Europeans seemed to settle into life here surprisingly easily. While a few still reeled from culture shock, or appeared listless, most remained motivated, even optimistic. Many did so by convincing themselves that China was a temporary solution, a mere stepping stone on the way to the golden lands of America or Australia. I don't imagine Lisbeth being among them. She was focused on the present. But finding work was not easy. Clerks and executives, accountants and bookkeepers were two-a-penny. Even had she aspired to such jobs – a stretch beyond her secretarial course at the Urania – these were often done by Western-trained Chinese willing to work for impossibly low wages. And Shanghai was no longer thriving. In Japanese hands, it was facing economic crisis as overseas investors pulled out their money and international trade was in decline.

Lisbeth was clear about what work she did *not* want. Never interested in domestic chores, or waiting on others, she was reluctant to ask in Little

Vienna's cafés or restaurants. Instead, she kept her eyes open for work that might keep her hands clean, or better still, use her mind. There had to be something among the variety of immigrant ventures; after all, these included many novel money-spinning ideas. Some refugees with an interest in rare used stamps had brought their collections from home, introducing this new trade to the city.[6] A man from Germany had brought a set of paint-filled rubber rollers carved with flower patterns that provided an instant wall covering, solving Shanghai's problem of permanently peeling wallpaper at a stroke. Others earned cash with manual skills that Lisbeth did not possess. They mended bicycles or typewriters, or set up small manufacturing and assembly plants in Hongkew; one plating shop used electricity generated by four bicycle riders.[7]

Lisbeth had heard stories of other enterprising Jews. Two friends, working out of one of Hongkew's many ruins, had started making soap using equipment bought from a junk dealer. Sir Victor Sassoon was so impressed by their efforts that he bought up their entire output and set them on the road to success. But the teenager had been more intrigued by another tale. She had been told about a man who noticed that Chinese pharmacies sold many snake serum products. These were anti-wrinkle treatments (early forerunners of Botox) that exploited the muscle-paralysing toxins contained in the venom. The refugee set up his own snake farm, harvesting the valuable serum that he then sold on to the city's drugstores.

Lisbeth would not have minded working in a chemist's. But none responded to her enquiries. She turned back to her search. So many refugees were still without work, even after a year of desperately trying.[8] Some sank to pitiful depths to earn the smallest amount of cash. One old man invented a 'waking-up' service for those anxious to get to their workplace on time. As well as making sure his customers were shaken from their sleep at the hour requested, he provided an updated weather forecast, enabling them to dress appropriately for the day ahead. Others went door-to-door, peddling whatever oddments came their way. Lisbeth knew of one who had found a child's pencil sharpener, and offered to sharpen pencils for a penny.[9]

Her best chance, she decided, was to use the leatherworking skills she had learnt at her Urania classes during those last months in Vienna. Good craftsmen could always find buyers. As she passed small workshops in shabby buildings, she peered in windows and saw shoemakers, tailors, hat makers or furniture restorers at wooden tables, engrossed in their craft. These two- or four-person operations could often compete with Chinese products for customers willing to pay a bit more for work of European quality.

The leather-making evening courses paid off; not long after she started looking, Lisbeth found a job with a small group of glove makers.

Her mother soon found work too, despite her lack of formal qualifications, taking a job as a part-time childminder for a family nearby. Every afternoon she went over to the room of a couple whose work hours coincided, and looked after their little daughter.

While Edith was content with this work, Lisbeth viewed her glove-making job as just a temporary measure. I can picture her in the tiny workshop, needle in hand and head bent over the soft leather, assuring herself she would not be there long; she would soon escape the stifling heat and the hides' pungent odour. The penetrating smell of tanning was foul – a mixture of decaying flesh and ammonia. She tried taking shallow breaths, but this only made her think of her father, whose breathing was becoming more laboured each day. She wished she could earn more, as if money could help ease his discomfort. Her head swam with the workshop's fumes, and with schemes to help the family.

17

Summer 1940: The Black and Gold Marbled Lobby

Lisbeth's chance to escape the leather workshop came sooner than she expected. Her mother's ear for gossip proved invaluable once again; one evening Edith came back from her work as their neighbour's childminder with important news.

'Somebody is looking for a secretary,' the neighbour had said to Edith. 'Can your daughter type? Can she take shorthand?'

Lisbeth had learnt both at the Urania, alongside her leather craft. It had even been the English shorthand that was commonly used in Shanghai, rather than German.[1] Her heart leapt at the news, especially when she heard where the job was. Not only was it in Frenchtown – the best part of the city – but in a prestigious tower block named Cathay Mansions. Lisbeth applied straightaway; somehow, she felt, the job was meant to be hers.

On a stifling day in the summer of 1940, Lisbeth set off towards leafy Frenchtown, to move up in the world. Knowing her leg would slow her down, she left in good time. Cathay Mansions was not too far to walk – less than two blocks away, south from Yang Terrace. And she wanted to savour the journey.

Frenchtown was *the* place to live, if you had money. As she approached the area's elegant streets, Lisbeth's spirits started to rise. She reached Avenue Foch, the boundary road separating her International Settlement area from its French neighbour. The avenue shared the unusual traffic rules of its extension, Avenue Édouard VII, its westbound traffic under French jurisdiction, while that going east following British law. As she crossed over into Frenchtown, she began looking out for the mansions of its wealthier residents. The former home of Dr Sun Yat-sen and his wife Soong Ching-ling was a large grey and red villa at 24 Rue Molière, overlooking Koukaza Park.

Koukaza Park, known simply as French Park, was one of Shanghai's most beautiful green spaces. In the 1920s it had epitomised the bureaucratic stance of the French Concession. Back then, its entry rules were harsh and specific, with those barred from its grounds including 'natives unless dressed in foreign clothes' (though this did 'not apply to servants in charge of foreign children'), 'persons wearing kimonos', and 'persons drunk or not dressed respectably'.[2] Now anyone could go in, for the Japanese had control of most of the city, and were more intent on monitoring the activities of Chinese Nationalists than controlling who dared enter a park.

Whenever Lisbeth came to Frenchtown, she recalled that this was an area favoured by the wealthy Sephardi families. She was not surprised that they chose to live here, their impressive villas set within high-walled gardens, often out of view of passers-by. The quiet streets were elegantly landscaped with lime and plane trees, whose shade sheltered pedestrians from the muggy summer heat. The Concession was smaller and felt more exclusive than the Anglophone settlement. And it was mainly residential, free from the factories and industrial units that marred the British and American sectors. But families like hers rarely lived here. Of the 18,000 or more Ashkenazi Jews in the city, only four thousand could afford to rent even a tiny room here in Frenchtown, while over double that number had to make do with Hongkew.[3]

Even the road names sounded better down here, Lisbeth thought. Once she had stepped south of Avenue Foch, Yates Road had metamorphosed into the romantic Route des Soeurs. It was named after two orders of nuns: the Soeurs Auxiliatrices du Purgatoire ran an orphanage, and the Filles de la Charité tended a garden. At number 100 Routes des Soeurs stood the self-proclaimed 'Leading Nightclub in Town' – Silk Hat – run by two immigrants named Sperber and Brumberger. Not far off at 146 was the

Figaro Beauty Parlour. Lisbeth paused at its window, thinking she might treat herself there when her wages allowed. Maybe it was now her turn to feel pretty.

Never one to doubt her own intelligence, Lisbeth was less sure of her looks. It was hard having confidence when both her sister and mother were known to outshine her. Even here in Shanghai, Edith still turned heads. Some said her dark hair and eyes brought to mind the romantic women of Vienna's high society immortalised by Klimt in swirls of purple and gold. Back home, it had been Ilse who had caught people's eye. But Ilse was far off in London; her passport had been stamped at British passport control in Paris back in May 1939, granting her entry to Britain.

Lisbeth felt sorry for her sister. She had learnt that Ilse's boyfriend had been moved from Kitchener Camp to a far less liberal place. The British government had hardened their attitude to refugees in the spring of 1940. The tabloid press was scaremongering about German-speaking 'saboteurs'; they wrote of potential fifth column 'aliens' lurking in society's midst. The real risk of a German invasion served to increase the pressure. And so that May, the government bowed to public demand and the internment of enemy aliens began.

Between May and June 1940, 30,000 German, Austrian and Italian refugees were arrested. Among them was my father. How could the nervous, slight nineteen-year-old have been viewed as a threat of any kind? But for society's protection, he was sent off to a camp and held behind barbed wire. Josef was first interned in Huyton, near Liverpool, and later in Mooragh Camp, in Ramsey on the Isle of Man. His parents, who had managed to leave Vienna in June 1939, were also interned on the Isle of Man. My grandmother, Liebe, was separated from her husband and housed in the women's camp, in Falcon's Nest Hotel, Port Erin. However, as Ilse was as-yet unmarried, she was not subject to internment.

I have no idea if my father ever saw or communicated with his own father during their time on the island. I know the two had never been close. Mendel – sometimes called Emil – Meller was a proud Orthodox Jew, whom we children knew as Opa. I never saw him show affection towards my father, and at some point the two completely fell out, with

Opa refusing to visit our home. Our Jewish identity – or the lack of it – was at the heart of the rift. Each man refused to give way, and after that we children met Opa on Sunday mornings on neutral territory. This was usually Kew Gardens, but sometimes we were lucky enough to be dropped off in Kensington Gardens to meet Opa beside the magical statue of Peter Pan.

Ours was a secular home, in which we three girls grew up learning nothing of Judaism. Opa was the only source of any sense of being Jewish that I picked up during childhood. It was in his Shepherd's Bush flat, when I was around five years old, that I first saw a menorah, which took centre stage on his mantelpiece.* And where I gaped at the strange accoutrements he strapped onto his forehead – a small black leather box pressed hard to his skin, with long winding tapes. I stood there, wide-eyed, as he explained that he needed these things to pray, a concept also foreign to me.† As he swayed, he muttered words in a strange language; afterwards, he would unwind the paraphernalia and put it away. Later he would peel me an apple and carefully slice it, and boast of his days as a cantor. The word meant nothing to me.‡ But when he started singing, there was something about his rich, mournful chanting that resonated deep within me. When Opa offered us granddaughters a Jewish prayer book, I was the only who wanted to accept it. I am sure I was drawn more to the book's shiny metallic cover, with its Stars of David set with fake turquoise, than to what lay inside. I have it still, in its protective case covered with Hebrew writing.

During my father's internment in the camp, he met many artists, scholars and intellectuals. I have a much-loved portrait of him, sketched in 1940 by a fellow internee, the painter Hugo 'Puck' Dachinger, a tangible record of this period of his life.

---

* The menorah is the Jewish seven-branch candelabrum used in worship.

† The *tefillin* are the small black leather boxes with leather straps worn by orthodox Jews on their head and arm during weekday morning prayers.

‡ The cantor is the official who sings liturgical music and leads prayer in a synagogue.

Josef's portrait painted while he was interned in 1940, and Ilse and Josef in 1941.

Lisbeth lingered as long as she dared at Frenchtown's many small boutiques' windows, admiring the lace-trimmed blouses, mink coats and fine-milled soaps on display. Like most young women, she longed to be able buy such frivolities, chosen for their beauty, scent or feel rather than items of coarse cotton or scratchy wool bought for their durability or warmth.

As she continued on her way, she noticed that many shop signs were in Russian as well as in English; clearly the Concession was more French in name than in nature. By 1937 only 1,200 of its million citizens held French passports, and the area was now home to almost 40,000 White Russians.[4] Many of them had settled there around the turn of the century; others had fled the Russian Revolution of October 1917. Their social status now spanned Shanghai's vastly differing demographics. The wealthiest were the Russian aristocrats escaping the Bolsheviks. Bringing their heirlooms and jewels, they now lived in the Concession's elegant villas alongside their successful Chinese and Sephardi neighbours.

At the other end of the scale were the penniless Jews, fleeing pogroms or poverty. Many Russians failed to thrive in Shanghai, and remained at the foot of the city's social ladder. Some of their women could be seen singing and dancing in risqué outfits in the Concession's bars and nightclubs, or laughing a little too gaily on the arm of a wealthy customer. Famed for their beauty, they were unkindly dubbed 'voluptuous vampires from Vladivostok', and held in low social regard.[5] Even more frowned upon by established Shanghailanders were those who had no choice but to become 'masseuses' or even prostitutes; such degradation of the 'white man' in the eyes of native Chinese was an unacceptable example of 'losing face'.[6] Many Russian men, unable to find work since the Japanese took over the city, could be seen on street corners, slumped semi-conscious beside the poorest Chinese. Having lost all self-respect, they spent any coins thrown their way on a 'concoction far worse than methylated spirits or even petrol', until the police dragged them off.[7]

Of course, between these extremes, many Russians – including some Ashkenazi Jews – had success, setting up small shops and businesses in Frenchtown. Avenue Joffre had so many corner restaurants serving blinis and borscht to homesick customers that it was nicknamed 'Moscow Boulevard' or 'Little Siberia'. Had Lisbeth walked that far, she would have been surrounded by the sounds of animated exchanges in Russian, mingling with balalaika music and violins from players strolling between café tables.

But today's journey did not take Lisbeth that far south, and instead, she turned west off Route des Soeurs onto Rue Bourgeat. A short walk to its corner with Rue Cardinal Mercier brought her to her destination. Before her rose the two massive towers of Cathay Mansions.

Lisbeth had to bend her neck back to view the top of the high-rise apartment building. Another of Sir Victor Sassoon's pioneering landmarks, Cathay Mansions offered both a residential hotel and a vast office block. One of its towers, a British Gothic construction in dark-brown brick, was eighteen storeys high. The other, a more elegant art deco building of only thirteen storeys, had a central tower fanning out to two stepped wings. Not for the first time did Lisbeth admire the ingenuity of the skyscraper-loving Sir Victor, whose Cathay Hotel had caught her eye the first day she had stepped onto the Bund. He had been the first person to dare build higher than ten storeys on Shanghai's watery soil, his engineers undaunted by the city's precarious location, poised barely above sea level.[8]

Checking her watch, Lisbeth glanced at the buildings around her before entering Cathay Mansions. She still had time. Diagonally opposite, on the other side of Rue Cardinal Mercier, was another art deco building with a sweeping, shady verandah: the Cercle Sportif Français, more simply known as 'the French Club'. It was a sophisticated gathering place for those high up in Shanghai's social and sporting recreational circles. Lisbeth had heard that the Cercle Sportif Français was the most cosmopolitan and welcoming club in Shanghai. When it was built in 1926, there were so few French nationals in the city that it had opened its doors to any foreigner willing to pay its membership fees.[9] On hot summer nights, couples waltzed high up on the roof terrace, or drank iced cocktails in the grill room.

While Lisbeth had reluctantly come to accept that her dancing days were over, her pulse still quickened at the idea of a sipping a glamorous drink, perhaps wearing a dress bought with her first wages. In later years, her favourite drink was a Dubonnet with a twist of lemon, a habit picked up during her time in Shanghai perhaps. And though she would never join the tennis players on court in the landscaped gardens, she smiled to herself as she imagined enjoying a swim in one of the club's two pools when her leg's scars had faded a little more. How much smarter than Hongkew's swimming pool complex! That one was open to people like Lisbeth; its Japanese management only banned the Chinese from using the facilities. A story about the pool had increased her fear of Shanghai's rulers. One of the lifeguards was a German Jew.[10] When a friend had gone to swim there, he had been astonished to see people leave their cash and gold watches unattended on the benches along the walls. On asking the German lifeguard if such valuables were ever stolen, the answer came: 'No. Because if they [the Japanese] catch them, they cut off their hands.'

Thinking of that story, Lisbeth checked her own watch and saw it was time for the interview. She entered the Mansions' lobby and stepped onto its black, cream and gold marbled floor. A large board ahead of her listed the names of the businesses housed there. She stepped into the ornate lift, its clock-face display of floor numbers circling from G for Ground, up to R for Roof Garden; I imagine her taking a deep breath and standing straighter, preparing to impress her potential employer.

The man was a German journalist, and although he was not Jewish, he was no Nazi sympathiser either. I do not know what the eighteen-year-old said to him that day, but she must have impressed him, although Lisbeth later declared that she had no idea how. Whatever his reasoning, when she walked out of Cathay Mansions that day, Lisbeth was no longer a glove maker. As she would soon delight in telling her neighbours and acquaintances, she was now a private personal secretary. (She may not have added that she would be working mornings only. They did not need to know that.)

Lisbeth's new boss was an intelligent man. And he was taking on a diligent young woman with a good eye for detail. She typed up the journalist's work quickly and efficiently. He had been tasked with a special assignment, which turned out to be to find out whether the Japanese were planning to enter the war now raging in Europe. Hitler seemed to be gaining the upper hand: that June, France had surrendered to Nazi forces. The importance of her boss's work made Lisbeth sit up even straighter at her desk. She found this new work both important and satisfying: at last she was in a position that suited her talents. She had 'arrived', as she put it; she was now 'a big lady, because [she was] paid very well ... better than the average person.'[11]

The journalist paid her in American dollars, at a salary Lisbeth had not even dared to hope for. She could buy her father a better brand of cigarette. And for the first time in her new city, she could hail a rickshaw puller whenever she chose. Her habit of riding around everywhere in a rickshaw, and her air of aloofness, led people in Lisbeth's community to call her 'Olympia'. She did not seem to object to this nickname, which she happily mentioned to others many years later.

Lisbeth Epstein had become part of the high life of Cathay Mansions, and suddenly life was full of promise. Although Arnold was looking thin, she could at least now bring more food home. And although she would soon discover that her employer was an alcoholic, what concern was this of hers?

18

Autumn 1940: Looking for Apricots

Her father was refusing to eat. Arnold looked as grey and gaunt as he had seven months earlier, when Lisbeth and Edith had barely recognised him on the Bund. He would smoke rather than take his share of food, encouraging the women not to waste what was on the table. He was not yet reduced to smoking the cheapest Chinese cigarettes. Everyone knew that these were 'remanufactured': rerolled from tobacco salvaged from discarded butts collected by impoverished men equipped with a bamboo rod and nail.[1] American brands like Camels or Lucky Strikes were more to his taste, which Lisbeth delighted in buying for him now she was earning good money. So, when Arnold let slip one evening that he had a hankering for some apricot dumplings, his daughter was eager to help, and quickly agreed to go to the market to look for the fruit.[2] Back in Vienna, her mother was known for her excellent *Marillenknödel*, balls of sugary dough in which tangy apricots lay hidden.

It was early autumn, a time when Shanghai's weather felt almost tolerable to Lisbeth. Summer, she now knew, was impossibly hot and humid; it easily reached the high thirties in the shade, with July temperatures even exceeding 40°C.[3] During the scorching summer that year, she had learnt the trick adopted by many Westerners: draping a small towel around one's neck to soak up the constant stream of sweat. Without this, the itchy rash of prickly heat was unbearable.[4]

Arnold Epstein in Shanghai, 1939 (referred
to as Prof. Epstein on the reverse)

People with money had an advantage when it came to dealing with the
city's stifling climate. They could go to the Wing On department store on
Nanking Road and take the lift to the seventh floor. Stepping through its
art nouveau doors they would be met by the welcoming breeze of the roof
garden restaurant. Once seated at a table, they could enjoy the respite of
the rooftop air drying the sweat from their brows. With iced drinks and
continental dishes set before them, they could listen to the resident band
or take a turn on the dance floor. Lisbeth knew that live music was played
there. The entertainment was often provided by a talented foursome from
Berlin led by Henry Rossetty, a saxophonist in his thirties. The band also
featured accordion, violin and drums, all brought over on the ship from
Europe. They had found work at Wing On within days of setting foot in
Shanghai, back in September 1939.[5]

The less wealthy simply had to be patient. By late August or early
September, torrential rains would arrive, cooling the city's subtropical

furnace. But these often brought flooding, filling the streets and buildings with filthy water from the Whangpoo. The Epsteins had soon learnt how to deal with the knee-high water, hitching up their trousers or skirts, and purchasing the high rubber boots essential for wading through the smelly floodwater.

As the months passed, January's cold would thicken the rain into sleet. Lisbeth and her mother had not yet experienced their first winter in Shanghai, but had been warned of the city's icy damp, whose chill fingers penetrated deep into one's bones. During that season, when temperatures could plummet to -12°C, she and Edith would be glad of their warm woollen clothing.

But on this early evening in autumn, the weather was pleasant enough for Lisbeth to start her journey on foot. She was headed for Die Markthalle on Chusan Road, in the hub of Little Vienna. She expected its stalls to be as crowded as ever, with those seeking Hongkew's low prices. She might even find rice there, a staple food that had become scarcer in recent weeks. In late September the Japanese had invaded French Indo-China,* meeting no resistance from the French. Since then, Tokyo controlled all supplies of rice entering Shanghai from those countries, prioritising it for their own troops or sending it on to Japan.[6]

Lisbeth walked towards Bubbling Well Road, planning to find a rickshaw to take her the rest of the way. As she turned northwards into Yates Road, she kept her eyes lowered. This was not for modesty's sake; that was not her nature. Nor was it to avoid the distraction of the road's tempting lingerie shops. She was simply taking care where she placed her feet. Although it was less common to see doll-sized bundles laid out among the pavements of this part of the International Settlement, habit forced her to take care.

Lisbeth's thoughts were on her quest for fresh apricots as she turned eastwards into Bubbling Well Road. A man was approaching. He stopped when he saw her. Had Lisbeth's eyes been raised she would have recognised the familiar figure. He had a distinctive lop-sided gait, and arms that seemed too long for his short height. He was their neighbour from Yang Terrace,

---

* Vietnam, Laos and Cambodia.

the Berliner who ran the library. As usual, he was dressed impeccably in a white shirt and dark jacket that emphasised his broad shoulders.

Sensing the presence of someone else, Lisbeth also stopped. The pair now stood face to face. They were around the same height, just a few inches over five feet. As usual, the man's brown eyes shone with humour.

'Where are you going?' he asked, his voice low.

She answered: 'I am trying to buy apricots, because my mother wants to cook apricot dumplings.'

He leant on his stick, musing, and then in his strong German accent said: '*Vell.*'

Lisbeth was suddenly aware of an awkward silence. To her own surprise, she heard herself inviting him to come to their place to sample her mother's famous dish.

'Why don't you come and try to taste some?' she asked the neighbour.

Did she think the man might enjoy talking to her parents? Or was there something about him that attracted her? Of course, he was hardly a stranger; she had seen him often enough before, in their terrace and his library.

He thought for a moment, and then smiled, saying yes, he would come to their home one day. He added: 'I will bring coffee. Whenever I go somewhere I'm afraid the coffee might not be good, so I always bring my own.'

Lisbeth noted the elegance of his old-fashioned German. She did not know if his answer was simply born out of politeness, or if he were genuinely interested in meeting her parents; Edith and Arnold were around his own age. After she and he parted ways, and Lisbeth continued her journey, she realised her attention had been drawn to the man's face and his voice rather than to his twisted back and short stature. As she considered their conversation, and the way he had looked at her, she felt her cheeks growing hot. She shook her head; she was not used to this feeling.

Lisbeth left no record of whether Arnold enjoyed eating his *marillen-knödel* that evening. But she would never forget that first conversation with her neighbour on the street near her home. Or that her journey to find apricots marked the start of a new chapter of her life.

19

Winter 1940:
The Destroyer of Dreams

Lisbeth knew very well that death was all around her here in Shanghai. She understood how serious a severe attack of typhoid could be and thought she had taken every hygiene precaution to avoid it. Did she let down her guard, forgetting one of the life-saving rules – eating chicken noodle broth from a risky street vendor, or shaking hands without care? She racked her brains trying to think what she had done wrong. However it happened, around nine months after her arrival, Lisbeth was struck down with typhoid. As soon as her mother felt her daughter's forehead, and heard her complaining of the crippling headache and stomach cramps, she had Lisbeth sent to Shanghai General Hospital. One of the two largest hospitals in the city, it belonged to the International Settlement, and was staffed by British doctors.

There, once the acute symptoms had passed, Lisbeth lay listless and wilting, sapped by the uncontrollable diarrhoea and the bacteria's effect on her muscles. All her strength had vanished; she could not even move an arm. If forced to choose, she thought, typhoid would be a good disease to die of: near the end, one feels no pain, merely weakness and exhaustion. She no longer cared about anything, and was ready to drift off into oblivion.

But the Western doctors would not let her. The staff at the hospital were already skilled in treating Shanghai's infectious diseases, and Lisbeth was relatively fit and had youth on her side. Although she soon discovered that she was 'great at picking up diseases', she eventually recovered fully from her bout of typhoid.

I was aware of my aunt's less than robust constitution when I first visited her in San Francisco. It was the summer of 1971, shortly after my eighteenth birthday; she was not yet fifty. I'm ashamed to admit that I was more excited about seeing the hippy city immortalised by Scott McKenzie's tribute ('Be Sure to Wear Flowers in Your Hair') than spending time with my rather staid and uncommunicative aunt. Lisbeth had never been physically strong, and her damaged leg slowed down her movement. This, together with her pallid face set against unnaturally black hair, emphasised her frailty.

I stayed in the basement of her 1940s home on Seal Rock Drive, separated from the main house. The guest room looked out on a small courtyard garden, bathed in San Francisco's damp and balmy air in which plants seemed to thrive. I was especially fascinated by a clump of dark purple fuchsia bushes. The huge bees I saw sucking at the bell-like flowers were, in fact, hummingbirds, darting dizzyingly from bloom to bloom.

Unable to walk far, Lisbeth took me everywhere in her old seatbelt-less Honda: to parks, museums and galleries; to 'eateries' for coffee and her favourite apple pie *à la mode* – with vanilla ice cream – or mountainous salads spiked with huge flavourless strawberries. If we neared a red light while descending one of the steeply sloping roads, Lisbeth would hold her arm limply in front of my chest to protect me. I shut my eyes and clung on to the cream faux-leather bench seat while the brakes slowly started to bite. I was grateful for her showing me the sights surrounding her gorgeous coastal home, but I would have preferred to explore more on foot.

Lisbeth often seemed a closed book to me, but a rare show of emotion hinted that her impassive façade hid strong feelings within. I discovered this when Claudia and I visited her together in 1993, when our aunt was 71. We were sitting at her kitchen table, where she was eating her usual breakfast of sloppy soft-boiled eggs in a bowl. She had been gazing blankly at the yellow and white mess, uninterested in and, we thought, deaf to our *sotto voce* conversation. Until our exchange included a remark that was less than complimentary towards her, the details of which now escape me. Lisbeth glanced up immediately, flashing a searing and malevolent look. No word was said, but the message was obvious. She was still alert as a hawk. And beneath that cool exterior seethed a tumult of anger. One that could erupt without warning, flaring up like a firework in a dark sky.

In the Shanghai winter of 1940, Lisbeth's employer, the German journalist, contracted typhoid. Perhaps the ice cubes in his whisky were made from contaminated water. Maybe he was simply unlucky. Well into his forties, with a body already weakened by excess liquor and a profligate lifestyle, he was unable to overcome the infection. As the year drew to a close, the illness took hold. Within weeks of the first rash appearing, he was dead.

When she learnt of her boss's death, Lisbeth was torn by conflicting emotions. She was devastated to lose her job, and her disappointment and frustration at this blow nearly overshadowed her sympathy for the man, whom she had grown to respect. A part of her almost blamed him for not taking care of himself, little knowing that alcoholics never see this as a priority. For a fleeting instant, before shame smothered it, she had the thought that even if he wouldn't look after himself, he should have considered her. Then the better part of her nature took over, and she grieved for the premature end of this interesting man.

But what work could she do next? She briefly considered teaching, like her father. Her wooden box contained a letter from the Shanghai Municipal Council, acknowledging her application to them for work as a supply teacher at one of the city's schools. It was dated 31 January 1941, a few weeks after Lisbeth turned nineteen. Although she may not have seriously wanted to be a teacher herself, Lisbeth was proud of Arnold's work, and impressed by his school. The Shanghai Jewish Youth Association (SJYA) School had been set up the previous year in Little Vienna's Kinchow Road.[1] The Kadoorie family had persuaded the SMC to permit the Jewish community to lease an old Chinese college, which had been standing empty since its students fled the fighting in 1937. In return, the SMC received a token rent of 100 Shanghai dollars per year.[2]

The school's curriculum was based on the respected Cambridge examination system, which was also taught in the Shanghai Jewish School for the city's Sephardi children. The high standards of the new school were achieved under the strict rule of its Jewish principal, Lucie Hartwich. A formidable, 'no-nonsense' Berliner, Mrs Hartwich was never seen without a full face of make-up. She had impressed Horace Kadoorie, the Sephardi philanthropist now living in Shanghai, when both were passengers on the same ship sailing from Europe to China. Kadoorie saw the language teacher giving English lessons to other German-speaking refugees on board; he immediately promised to build her a school in Shanghai for the émigrés' children.[3] By February 1940, the school had over 500 pupils, with 21 teachers; its monthly fee of $5 was waived for the poorest students.[4]

Lessons at the SJYA school were mainly secular, although because it was a Jewish school, Hebrew language and Bible classes were required. London-born Kadoorie insisted that the lessons be taught in English; the children could also study French and Chinese. He considered German unpatriotic, and forbade its use – a rule rigidly enforced, not just in class, but in the playground as well. Pupils soon became fluent in their new lingua franca. Those over fourteen were offered extension courses in subjects like carpentry and bookbinding.[5] However, most left by the age of thirteen or fourteen, considered old enough to join their parents in the struggle to earn money.

Lisbeth loved the photograph of her father in his dark jacket and bow tie, surrounded by his pupils, a dozen boys and twenty girls, aged from ten to fourteen. But she knew that competition was stiff: for each teaching post that came up, 30 well-educated European refugees would apply.[6]

Arnold with his class of children at the SJYA School, c. 1940.

Her boss's death robbed Lisbeth of her life-changing new status. Now she was just another of Shanghai's many thousands of jobless people, and was once again desperate for work. She would have to start all over again, thanks to *Salmonella typhi*, that tiny, invisible destroyer of dreams.

20

Spring 1941: Coffee at Yang Terrace

Some time after bumping into his young neighbour on her search for apricots, Bruno Loewenberg walked the few yards down the terrace where he lived to number 2 Yang Terrace. It was just three doors from the identical house where he rented a covered balcony. He studied the notice by the doorbell and rang the number of times specified under the name 'Epstein'. He always enjoyed meeting people, and looked forward to getting to know his Viennese neighbours better. It was a bright afternoon and, as he waited, the owner of the Lion Bookshop and library turned to admire the camellias and roses in the gardens opposite. The flowers and the green of the well-tended lawn lifted his spirits even further. His cane was in one hand, while in the other was a bag containing the promised coffee and some savoury crackers. He was also bearing information that would change Lisbeth's life.

The Epsteins welcomed Bruno. At 50, he was three years older than Edith, and only seven years younger than Arnold. They all knew the man from his library, but entertaining him in their home felt different. It turned out there was no need for nervousness. The room soon filled with chatter, spreading as fast as the unaccustomed aroma of the fresh-ground coffee. The family usually drank tea without milk; this was the first time Edith had made coffee since arriving in China. Even had the family wanted it, the drink was well beyond their income. Edith stood by the hotplate, her eyes on the polite, immaculately dressed guest, happy for this chance to get to know him better. The belt of her floral print dress emphasised her waist, as did the hand placed on her hip. She asked Bruno the best way to brew the coffee with her limited kitchen equipment. He did not hesitate to offer advice; he was a man who took his coffee very seriously.

Lisbeth looked on, staying silent. Although usually keen to impress, today she acknowledged the presence of someone more knowledgeable, maybe even more intelligent, than herself. She watched his eyes follow her mother as she boiled the water for the coffee. She recognised the same smile she had seen the last time they met as he leant forward, long-fingered hands folded across the top of his cane.

Coffee brewed; Edith passed the cups and the rare treat of pastries from Café Louis around. Lisbeth bit her lip as she wondered what her mother would chat about now the introductions were over. She hoped Edith would not regale their guest with tales of their comfortable life in those years before Hitler. It would not do to compare the light-filled apartment in Am Tabor with the poky room they were in now. Small talk would be easier, as they tiptoed around each other's sensitivities this early in their acquaintance. Safer to discuss their visitor's birthplace of Stettin, and the cities where his previous bookshops had been – Paris and Berlin.

Edith told him of their elder daughter, Ilse, who was embarking on a new life in London. They received few letters from her, so news was sporadic, but they knew that Ilse had been fighting for months to have her boyfriend, Josef, released from his internment camp on the Isle of Man. The relationship seemed to be quite serious; the couple had written to each other throughout the period of Josef's internment, although all their correspondence had been read and redacted by the censor. Her parents were glad that their daughter was not alone. More importantly, she was safe; Hitler would never dare to invade England.

Edith asked Bruno about the family he had left behind in Germany. His voice faltered slightly as he spoke of his stern but loving parents, his countless uncles, aunts and cousins. He saved his warmest words for his sister, the proud mother of his handsome young nephew, and whose gift of a ticket to Shanghai had saved his life. Then his voice trailed off into silence and he wiped his eyes. He had no idea where any of them were now.

Did the Epsteins know of their visitor's year in Buchenwald? If so, they would have steered clear of the subject. All the European refugees in

Shanghai knew it was better to stick to lighter topics, such as the cheapest places for sauerkraut or liver sausage, or how they filled any leisure time. Coming from Vienna and Berlin, the coffee drinkers in Yang Terrace shared a love of music and theatre. And, despite being so far from home, there was a surprising wealth of culture to critique. Since the arrival of the first refugees from the Reich lands and Poland, Shanghai had seen many forms of entertainment spring up.[1] There was a disproportionate supply of 'stage artists, singers, painters and authors, conductors and orchestra musicians' among the nearly 20,000 Jewish immigrants now in the city.[2] The need to escape life's dreariness drove many of these talented people to put on entertainment for their fellow refugees. Which meant that anyone who could afford the cheap tickets could go to plays, cabaret shows, light operas and comedy evenings, sometimes acted in Yiddish.[3]

The men in the room had arrived in Shanghai earlier than the two women, and compared notes about those first months. In the autumn of 1939, after that year's scorching summer, Arnold had gone to one of the original immigrant productions, staged in a makeshift set inside the *Heim*. Had Bruno seen it as well? It was a variety show called *Ein Bunter Abend;*[*] it had been directed by one of the community's most active stage producers, Walter Friedmann.[4] They also remembered another production, more controversial, put on in late 1940. Bruno knew one of its German writers, Max 'Mark' Siegelberg: the two had been in Buchenwald together. Like Bruno, Siegelberg had escaped the camp thanks to a ticket to China. Unlike Bruno, however, the writer remained consumed by rage at his treatment by the Nazis. His play, *Die Masken Fallen,*[†] was a vehemently anti-Nazi propaganda piece. It premiered, inside Shanghai's British legation, on 9 November 1940, exactly two years after *Kristallnacht*.

Such outspoken anti-German sentiment was unusual here in Shanghai. Most refugees like the Epsteins and Bruno focused their energy on surviving, turning a blind eye to the many Nazis whom they knew lurked within the city's long-established German community.[5] *Die Masken Fallen*

[*] 'A Colourful Evening'.
[†] 'The Masks Fall'.

provoked enormous resentment among these sympathisers of Hitler, and triggered a swift threat of reprisals against the Jewish community, both in Shanghai and back in Europe, from the German consulate. Although unspecified, these threats were taken seriously: after just two performances, Siegelberg and his co-author's play was cancelled.[6]

Lisbeth sat listening to the conversation, impatient to ask Bruno a question. She was becoming keenly aware of her need to find a new job. Some days she thought her father looked too weak to face his classroom duties. What if he were to lose his job? The other day she had heard a rumour that the girl who worked at the Lion Bookshop's library was about to leave. At last she spoke up, to ask Bruno if the rumour was true.

When Bruno confirmed it, she seized her chance. Without hesitation, or considering whether she was qualified for the work, Lisbeth asked if she could apply for the post. If their visitor had second thoughts, or wished to refuse, how could he? Perhaps he suddenly took a shine to the nineteen-year-old, or maybe saw in her the making of a good assistant, one young enough to mould to his way of working. Whatever influenced his decision, he encouraged her to apply. And within days she had been offered the job.

And so, from being a glove maker and personal secretary, Lisbeth Epstein was to become a librarian's assistant. She was to join Bruno Loewenberg at his bookshop on the corner of Bubbling Well Road.

21

8 December 1941:
The World Shifts Overnight

Lisbeth soon became a capable assistant to her new boss at the library. She learnt how to check books in and out with no mistakes. Her eye for numbers meant she never missed a late return or miscalculated any overdue fines. Having deciphered Bruno's way of running things, she was quick to suggest improvements. His record-keeping systems were occasionally, to her mind, over-casual. One of Lisbeth's strengths, she pointed out, was her attention to detail; another was her interest in figures and profit margins. Although Bruno paid her nothing like the journalist's rate, she found the work satisfying. And she found herself growing comfortable, almost relaxed, in his company.

In the summer of 2017, I started trying to locate Horst Eisfelder, whose parents had run Café Louis; I sent an email to an Eisfelder in Melbourne, Australia with little hope of a reply. The next day I was astounded to find a response to my message; to my delight, the man I knew from memoirs of Shanghai was still very much alive. We wrote to each other over the next few months. One of my sons was living in Sydney at the time, and so Horst and I arranged to meet.

I visited Horst on a warm afternoon; he now lived with his wife in a quiet residential road at the end of the Melbourne–Carnegie tram line in south-eastern Australia. Their home overflowed with memorabilia, including dozens of books, maps and, of course, Horst's photographs. I could hardly believe I was sitting opposite the man whose parents claimed to sell the best chocolates in wartime Shanghai, and whose images of the city provided such an invaluable record of its Jewish refugees.

I first showed Horst a photograph of Bruno, taken in 1940. 'Yes, I remember his face,' he replied, his accent still clearly marked by his German birthplace. 'His assistant I only remember as being so much younger, and with a very bad limp.'

Despite being aged 92, my host's memories were as sharp as his photographs. I listened as he described his experiences of almost 80 years earlier. Horst half closed his eyes as he recalled his often-told memories of the family's flight to Shanghai. Like so many others, the Eisfelders had held only vague notions of their Eastern destination. Expecting 'bamboo huts with rice paper', they had been stunned by the city's modernity: its high-rise buildings, trams, and double-decker buses, and its '50 radio stations and newspapers in every language'. They found themselves in a metropolis far more advanced than the city they had left; Berlin's tallest building was only five storeys.

The climate was the most trying aspect, Horst recalled: the summer humidity was awful, while the unaffordable cost of heating left the family freezing in bone-chilling winters. I listened, rapt, as this remarkable man described people from over seven decades earlier as if he had just seen them in the street. With great passion, he spoke of Richard Paulick, showing me a photograph of the architect's apartment block near Café Louis, where some of Bruno's library talks had been held. He also described the Czech journalist who helped run the discussion groups. Horst's words and his memories put flesh on the bones of the facts I'd researched, turning them into living reality.

Faced with this incredible opportunity to discover more details about Lisbeth's life in China, I probed Horst repeatedly for any personal memories of my aunt. But all he could remember was the 'very bad limp'.

Horst Eisfelder and the author in his Melbourne home, 2017.

Although Lisbeth's salary at the library was low in comparison to her previous one, she needed a regular income more than ever. Arnold had been off work since that summer. But it was not because of his health, as his daughter had feared. The SJYA School had been forced to close at the end of June and all staff were made redundant, including Arnold. Many of the Chinese who had fled the fighting in Hongkew in 1937 had returned, and wanted their old Kinchow Road college back.[1] The Municipal Council had bowed to the pressure, giving the teachers and pupils little notice to vacate the premises. The Speelman Committee (the CFA) had no funds to build a new school. Horace Kadoorie quickly set about raising money. He sent a begging telegram to his South African contacts, declaring: 'major calamity 1150 children literally thrown on streets.'[2]

Kadoorie's plea was successful. Work soon began on a replacement school in East Yuhang Road, just a few blocks from the old one on Kinchow Road. It was about to open in a few weeks, already known by all as the Kadoorie School in honour of its patron. The Epsteins were looking forward to Arnold's return to teaching. Lisbeth almost dared breathe again; life seemed to be settling into a pleasant new rhythm. They had even had good news from England. Ilse's boyfriend Josef had been released from the Isle of Man that April, so the couple had been able to marry at last. Their wedding had taken place on 12 July 1941.

But in December 1941, the whole city was shaken by events that none could have foreseen.

At 3am on Monday 8 December, sixteen-year-old Horst Eisfelder awoke to the boom of thunder. He was thrilled, rather than astonished, to hear the noise. He had recently taken up photography and the previous night he and a friend had been discussing how to capture a lightning strike on film. The unexpected storm offered the perfect opportunity. Grabbing his camera, he went to the window, only to see a clear starlit sky. There was no storm.[3]

Other sleepers were also shaken from their dreams, though memories differed as to the precise hour: some said 3, 4, even 5am. But everyone agreed that it was an explosion of sound that woke them. Quite a few were surprised, thunderstorms being unusual for Shanghai winters.

A few hours after Horst's awakening, another refugee looked up to the sky from a city roof garden. By now the pale winter sun had risen, and a light rain had started to fall, causing a rainbow to emerge. As she gazed at the rainbow, the woman saw above it a fleet of planes bearing the imperial red sunburst. From them fluttered thousands of leaflets, twisting and shining in the sunlight as they fell to the ground. She later described the sight as 'very beautiful, but also very terrible', for it marked the beginning of 'the most awful time of [their] lives'.[4]

It was not thunder that woke Shanghai residents early on 8 December. It was the heavy guns of a Japanese battle cruiser moored in the Whangpoo, beside the Japanese consulate. The *Idzumo* was a veteran of Japan's 1905 war with Russia. Since the 1937 conflict, she had loomed brazenly from her mooring, her grey bulk in plain sight of the shoppers over the creek on the Nanking Road and the guests passing through the doors of the Cathay Hotel. Now her provocative silence was over. Around 4.30am, the *Idzumo* rained shells on another craft moored on the river: the Royal Navy's gunboat, HMS *Peterel*.[5]

Though much smaller than the *Idzumo*, the British vessel had been moored on the Whangpoo for over a decade to deter any Japanese from entering the British settlement. This was now the only part of the city not in Japanese control. The French Concession was already in their hands: in June 1940, when France surrendered to the Germans and her Far East empire collapsed, Shanghai's invaders seized their chance.[6] Italy had also joined the Nazis that June, leading to a paradox in the International Settlement, which was meant to be defended by Italian and British soldiers together. Although they were now on opposite sides in the war, they still had to cooperate in this duty. The city's neutral US Marines were redeployed between the Italians' and British defence areas, to prevent any 'untoward incidents'.[7]

Until now, HMS *Peterel* had succeeded in keeping the peace in Shanghai. But overnight, everything shifted. On a Pacific island thousands of miles distant, five time zones to the east of Shanghai, it was still the morning of Sunday 7 December, a day that changed the course of history.

In Hawaii, the morning dawned no differently from any other quiet sunny Sunday. Few men were on active duty at the American naval base at Pearl Harbor. But at 7.48am local time, the Japanese launched their attack. There was no declaration of war; the raid came out of the blue. The result was devastating. Japanese bombs and torpedoes left a crippling proportion of the Americans' naval and air fleets destroyed. Almost 3,500 American service people and over 100 civilians lay dead or wounded.

An hour or so after the assault on Pearl Harbor, Japan declared war on both the United States and Britain. At around the same time, another band of their men set their sights on Japan's ancient foe, attacking the prized port of Shanghai.

At around 4am on 8 December, a group of Japanese marines boarded HMS *Peterel*. They ordered her crew to surrender. The gunboat's infuriated captain, Stephen Polkinghorn, refused with the words: 'Get off my bloody ship!'[8] The Japanese complied, but within minutes their battleship *Idzumo* opened fire on the *Peterel*, with the aid of an accompanying gunboat and shore batteries on the French Bund. Under such heavy bombardment at almost point-blank range, the British vessel exploded and capsized, though not before returning fire with small arms. Of the eighteen crew members on board, six were killed in the attack. All the others were wounded, as the Japanese machine-gunned any survivors – British and Chinese crewmen trying to help – who fell in the water.

Meanwhile, in the darkness, another group of marines was boarding the US Navy river gunboat, USS *Wake*, moored less than a kilometre from the *Peterel*. They had an easier time with the American crew, who knew nothing of the attack on their base in Pearl Harbor. Their captain was on shore, so the men, ignorant that the war in the Pacific had begun, surrendered without a shot being fired. The Japanese quickly hoisted their flag on the USS *Wake*'s deck.

Those woken by the gunfire were greeted by the sight of smoke and flames rising from Whangpoo harbour. When daylight came, onlookers saw that all the Western ships had left. Japanese troops were finishing what they had begun in 1937, quietly taking over the whole of the city. Their legging-clad soldiers seized all key sites not yet in their control.[9] They met no resistance from the Westerners, nor from the Chinese guerrillas operating nearby.[10] Apart from the sailors on HMS *Peterel*, the coup was bloodless; no more conventional fighting would be seen in Shanghai for the rest of the war.[11]

At around 4am, as the *Peterel* was being boarded, top British officials of the International Settlement received a telephone call telling them that war had broken out. At 6am, officials – including the SMC's chairman and the head of the Municipal Police – were called to a meeting with the Japanese consul general and other military and police representatives, to learn that the Japanese were in the process of occupying the whole Settlement area.[12]

Lisbeth and Edith slept deeply that night; neither woke at the noise in the small hours. But Lisbeth never forgot what she saw when she went out later that morning. The towering, turbaned Sikh policemen employed by the International Settlement's British authorities were gone. In their place stood fierce men loyal to Emperor Hirohito. In Lisbeth's words, 'one day there's war, the British are out, and the Japanese are in'.

Within hours of their attack on Pearl Harbor, the Japanese consolidated their hold on Shanghai. While troops arrested the surviving crew of HMS *Peterel* and USS *Wake*, police rounded up diplomats and consular officials of Allied nations. The officials were placed under house arrest at Cathay Mansions, or nearer the Bund in the Metropole and Cathay Hotels. By 10am Japanese forces had taken over that palatial symbol of British capitalism, the Hongkong and Shanghai Bank, quickly replacing its Union flag with their own Rising Sun. The bank was closed while staff handed over keys to safes and strongrooms, and their business was passed to the long-established Japanese Yokohama Specie Bank a little further down the Bund. When the city's British and American financial headquarters reopened on 11 December, they were besieged with customers desperate to take out their money. The Hongkong and Shanghai Bank dealt with 2,000 people in three hours.[13]

Within three days of Pearl Harbor, Japanese troops crossed Garden Bridge from their enclave in Hongkew and took over both the International Settlement and French Concession. The Japanese commandeered the city's most prestigious clubs and hotels and were ensconced there by the end of December. They evicted the Russian Jews from their Social Club on Bubbling Well Road, a magnificent building bought earlier that month when the US Marines Club had moved out.[14] The Japanese army's press office began operating out of the Metropole Hotel, while the imperial navy's intelligence unit took over the headquarters of Jardine Mathieson at number 27 the Bund.[15]

Lisbeth and her parents looked on in shock at the speed of events. Within one day their city had fallen into the hands of Hitler's allies. Until now, the Japanese had seemed to have no problem with Jews. There seemed to be no reason for the Epsteins to worry, at first; indeed the Japanese declared their wish that things should 'carry on as normal'.[16] They airdropped leaflets across the city with a message designed to generate calm. Printed well in advance, in a typeface meant to look handwritten and with only the date inserted by hand, they explained that Japan was now at war with Britain and the USA.

The Japanese also promised that law and order would be maintained. This might explain the ease with which their troops took over the city. The scarlet-turbaned Sikh police and the police answering to the leader of the Nanking puppet government, Wang Ching-wei, were no match for them.[17]

But Lisbeth's family were uneasy. The little security they thought they had won now felt shaky. They suddenly found themselves living in enemy territory, a city run by men on the side of the Nazis. It was impossible not to wonder how long it would be before their Japanese rulers, now allied with Hitler, turned on the Jews.

22

16 December 1941:
A Birthday in Darkness

The short, stony-faced men in steel helmets standing stiffly at the city's many checkpoints brought everyone out in a cold sweat. They patrolled in units of three or four, their bayonet-bearing rifles by their sides.

Lisbeth and her family looked on with sinking hearts as the Japanese paraded the streets, flexing their military muscles. The refugees watched the long columns of troops, accompanied by light tanks and other armoured vehicles, march down the main streets of their newly conquered city. These shows of power stretched all the way west to the External Roads area, reaching Amherst Avenue where James Graham Ballard and his family were living.*[1] The young schoolboy's first reaction – like that of many other children that day – was joy at the cancellation of classes. Another schoolboy, a twelve-year-old Jewish refugee, arrived at the Shanghai Jewish School as usual on the morning of Pearl Harbor, having heard nothing during the night. The principal called the children into the auditorium to deliver a serious lecture: he explained that the Japanese were starting to occupy the city. As the boy left for home a little later, he saw 'the Japanese marching past the school, occupying the American marine barracks across the street' with 'the American flag being lowered

---

* J.G. Ballard would later write the semi-autobiographical novel *Empire of the Sun*, which drew on his experiences as a schoolboy in wartime Shanghai, including his family's internment in the infamous Lunghua camp.

and the Japanese flag being raised in its place'. Horst Eisfelder and his friends viewed the day-long processions of Japanese machismo as just 'a bit of a joke'.[2]

Lisbeth and her parents saw nothing amusing in the replacement of the Western militia with these Japanese guards. A familiar dread swept through them as they watched the 'enemy nationals' disappear – soon the British, Americans and Dutch had all mysteriously gone from the streets. The Japanese ordered their new enemies to stay home, to await instructions about registering with the Gendarmerie, the Japanese police force; these Allied nationals would now need passes to move about the city.[3] They were forced to wear wide red armbands, and were warned of their likely internment. Many enemy nationals were arrested by the *Kempeitai*, the Japanese equivalent of the Gestapo, notorious for the brutality of its torture; some were later sent to hastily constructed camps at the edge of the city. Americans and British were thrown into the much-feared Bridge House, the *Kempeitai* headquarters, as political prisoners. Among those interned because of their British citizenship were some of the city's Sephardi community, as well as J.G. Ballard and his parents. Even German women with British husbands were interned.[4]

The Epsteins, like the rest of the Jewish immigrant community, were thrown into a state of shocked panic. Disturbing flashbacks of their last months in Europe, memories of police-run repression and the loss of basic human rights, shattered their daily routine. They heard rumours of antisemitic plans being devised by a Gestapo officer in the city, a man named Josef Meisinger. He had been posted to the city from Japan earlier that year, as Nazi Germany's chief representative; his remit was to spy on anti-German activity.[5] But many of Shanghai's Jews feared he was hatching a scheme to rid the city of its Jewish population. Some ridiculed the idea, considering him to be ineffectual and lacking influence.[6] Yet none could deny the new measures imposed by the Japanese authorities: they saw liberal newspapers being shut down, and anti-Japanese journalists thrown into detention. One such journalist who narrowly escaped this fate was the angry playwright, Mark Siegelberg; he was whisked away on an English ship bound for Australia.[7]

Meanwhile, Bruno Loewenberg was not intimidated. He kept his bookshop and library open, knowing that his customers, more than ever, needed their literary escape. He did his best to hide his own anxiety at being, once again, at the mercy of an authoritarian power. What he had witnessed at Buchenwald left him unable to look at men in uniform. The words the guard had spat at him as he left the camp now rang in his brain. Could the Gestapo's reach, which the man had threatened would find him wherever he went, really extend all the way to Shanghai?

If Bruno's terror did resurface when this unexpected darkness swept over Shanghai, only a few days afterwards he managed to banish such fears from his mind. On 16 December 1941, he awoke to his 51st birthday. And as a man who loved parties, he was not going to let a small detail like a foreign invasion get in the way of his celebrations.

In the carved wooden box I found a fragile sheet of paper dated '*Shanghai, den 16. Dezember 41*'. The sheet shows that among the well-wishers that day were four singers – two tenors, two basses – who performed a special birthday tribute to 'Herrn Bruno Loewenberg, Shanghai'. Their names were Marcus, Goldschmidt, Karp and Fraenkel. I had no idea who these men were, until a meeting with a professor of Chinese history brought these last two names to life.

In October 2016, I went to meet Professor Robert Bickers at Bristol University. His book, *Empire Made Me*, was the only one in which I had found a mention of Yang Terrace.[8] I had given him the names and addresses of the people whose lives I was researching, without expecting him to find much about them in Shanghai's archives. How wrong I was.

I followed Robert up a winding marble staircase to his office in the department of history. There, beams of sunshine streamed from large Victorian windows into a vast, high-ceilinged room, which exuded 1920s Sinophilia. One wall was lined with shelves filled with books and lever-arch files, black and white postcards showing photographs of intriguing Shanghai characters propped against them. I watched as the historian printed out the results of his research. The first sheet he gave me was a detailed street map of Yang Terrace in the 1930s, showing the eight houses in the terrace, located in the block bounded by Weihaiwei Road and Avenue Foch, and Yates and Moulmein Roads.[9]

Next Robert showed me reports in files of the Special Branch of the Shanghai Municipal Police, containing information I had never expected.[10] The subject of half a dozen of the files was Bruno Loewenberg. Dating from 11 November 1941 to 20 April 1942, they set out details of Bruno's business ventures. In those tempestuous months, around Pearl Harbor and the burgeoning war in the Pacific, all city enterprises were being vetted. The Shanghai Municipal

Police had to prove they were genuine businesses, and not fronts for Nationalist activism. The SMP were especially interested in potential 'political manifestoes'.[11]

The first sheet from the police files showed a 'Registration Form for Newspaper, Magazine or News Agency', submitted on 10 November 1941. It sought permission for the publication *Der Kreis* – 'The Circle' – a monthly German-language periodical on 'Literature, Music, Art'. The form showed a date of first issue was 15 December 1941, with a circulation of 400 copies. Its proprietor and publisher was Bruno Loewenberg.

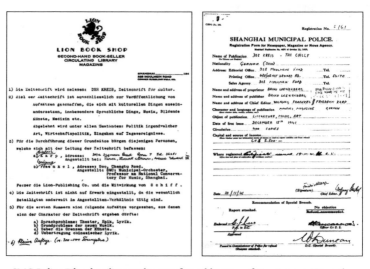

SMC Police Files detailing application for publication of *Der Kreis*, 10 November 1941 (Courtesy Robert Bickers)

The form had been attached to a second document, an SMC police report, dated the following day, giving more details:

> Attached herewith is the application for registration with the S.M.P. in respect of a German language publication to be called 'DER KREIS' (German for 'Circle'). The object of the journal is to awaken an interest in art in local refugee circles. The publication will only print articles dealing with art subjects and will have no political leanings and no editorial policy.

> The publisher of 'Der Kreis' will be Bruno Löwenberg, German Jewish refugee, born December 16, 1890 in Stettin and residing at 5 Yang Terrace. Bruno Löwenberg is the owner of the 'Lion Book Shop' at 238 Moulmein Road.* This store also conducts a lending library and seems to be a fairly sound business. He is the publication's main financial backer.

Seeing Bruno's name in black and white on a police file made my hands start to shake. I carried on reading.

> The editors of the 'Der Kreis' will be Wolfgang Fränkel, German Jewish refugee, born on October 10, 1897 in Berlin; arrived in Shanghai in May 1939.[12] He is a musician and is employed with the S.M.C. Municipal Orchestra, and Friedrich Karp, Austrian Jewish Refugee, born September 15, 1901 in Vienna; arrived in Shanghai on December 31, 1938. He is an accountant in the employ of Messrs. Turner, Sturrock & Brown at 9 Ave. Edward VII. Friedrich Karp is also a dillettante [sic] novelist and art critic.

The description of Herr Karp made me smile. But here was my answer! Karp and Fränkel were the editors of the arts magazine about to be launched by these German-speaking refugees.

My meeting with Robert Bickers had proved more valuable than I could have hoped. Before me was tangible proof of Bruno Loewenberg's presence in 1940s Shanghai. The signatures on each page, with their distinctive flourishes of fountain-pen ink, came from the hands of living people. I imagined the men facing each other across the bureaucrat's desk. On one side the SMC's burly policemen; on the other, the Jewish publishers, with no power at all.

I now also understood the handwritten lyrics on the flimsy sheet from the carved box, neatly lined up between treble and bass clefs marked in the

---

* This should read 328.

key of F major. When I read the words of the birthday tribute, they first shocked me, then made me laugh out loud:

> To be sung *'Maestosissimo con forza'*[*]
> Happy birthday to you
> happy birthday to you, happy birthday
> publisher of 'the circle'
> happy birthday, you Jew!

The sheet was signed by W. Fraenkel.

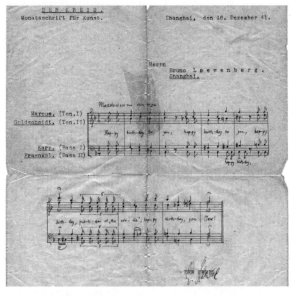

The birthday celebration sheet for Bruno, December 1941.

The previous day, a printing press at the New Star Printers on 685/10 East Seward Road had whirred into motion. The small office soon warmed up as 400 copies of *Der Kreis* rolled off the press.[13]

---

[*] Most majestically and strongly.

The celebration of the magazine's launch and the birthday of its owner may well have taken place in Bruno's library. Wherever the friends gathered, they would have been smiling and laughing as they raised glasses of cheap spirits to *Der Kreis* and to Bruno. For one evening the magazine's creators could put their worries aside. But as they made their way home, and contemplated a future under Japanese rule, perhaps a chill of foreboding replaced the warmth of the vodka. If so, the refugees' anxieties at what lay ahead would prove well founded.

23

February 1942: Bread with Burnt-Sugar Caramel

As 1941 slipped into 1942, it was becoming clear that the Japanese would not let things 'carry on as normal', despite their promises. Their hold was tightening over Shanghai and conditions for ordinary people, like Lisbeth and her parents, were becoming harsher each day.

Within days of Pearl Harbor, American aid to the city was blocked. Neither the large donations from New York's Joint Distribution Committee, nor the smaller sums sent regularly from friends or relatives in the US, could get through to Shanghai.[1] Those still dependent on the charity of the *Heime* suffered most: their daily ration of bread shrank from sixteen ounces to twelve.[2] Like everyone else, the Epsteins found food scarcer and more costly. No goods were allowed to enter the port; the city's merchants could only trade with each other. Although tea was still abundant and cheap – no longer being exported to Europe or America – coffee imports were stopped; the price of Bruno's favourite non-alcoholic beverage sky-rocketed. Others took their caffeine more directly. Both Japanese and German troops used the stimulant in the form of white powder, and by late 1941 demand for the drug had grown dramatically.[3] Since it could no longer be imported, people put their minds to new manufacturing methods. While everyone knew caffeine could be extracted from the city's plentiful tea, the usual solvents – chloroform or carbon tetrachloride – were now hard to get hold of.

A Jewish refugee called Mr Marcuse solved the problem. He discovered a new way to extract the drug from tea without using chloroform, and used his 'secret process' to set up Hongkew's first, and highly successful, caffeine factory.

Flour was in such short supply that bakers were banned from using wheat to make anything other than bread, forcing even Café Louis to stop selling cakes for a while. Horst Eisfelder watched his father switch to baking bread; as rice supplies grew ever scarcer, there was growing demand for it from the Chinese. Eisfelder senior created two sorts of loaf, white and 'wholemeal' black bread. No one guessed that the 'wholemeal' was simply white bread with burnt-sugar caramel mixed in. Horst was amused that his father's customers seemed to prefer this black bread. They thought it looked healthier, and believed it less likely to rot their teeth. But Louis Eisfelder soon started baking his famous cakes once again. He first used potato flour, and then – once he realised there were no repercussions for flouting the ban – went back to wheat.[4] He even managed to find the ingredients for chocolates from the city's warehouses' rich stockpiles, although these were solely available to those who had money. As ever, people with deep enough pockets could still buy almost anything.

There are always those who find ways to turn the misfortune of war to their advantage. Shanghai had more than its fair share of wheeler-dealers, who soon ran a thriving black market. Lisbeth's family knew of many people suddenly flaunting more cash than before. But not even the wealthiest could buy petrol; there was none to be found. The city's buses stopped running. Bicycles were now *the* mode of transport, socially acceptable for even the richest Westerners.

It was not just goods that were barred from the city, but also news, which for many immigrants was even worse. Before Pearl Harbor, Lisbeth's father had been an avid reader, spoilt for choice with three German-language papers set up by Jewish refugees. Like other émigrés, once war began in Europe, he was eager to keep abreast of events back home, and the newspapers did their best to keep their readers informed. His favourite was the *Shanghaier Morgenpost*, 'the high point of refugee journalism in Shanghai'.[5] The refugees refused to buy Shanghai's existing German-language paper, as it was sponsored by the Nazi government in Berlin. A refugee named Egon Varo also put out a weekly gossip paper, or 'scandal sheet', *Der Querschnitt*,* which Bruno very much enjoyed reading.

But once the Japanese took over, they closed down almost every channel of communication. Only a single German paper remained: the daily *Shanghai Jewish Chronicle*. Ferdi Eisfelder, Horst's cousin, was one of its manual typesetters; its editor was Ossi (Osias) Lewin, a Viennese Jew. The *Chronicle* was possibly not the city's best publication, but it was the longest lasting, as it was tolerated by the Japanese. While this raised some suspicions about Lewin, the paper was still highly censored.[6] The refugees now gleaned even less about the plight of relatives back home. For news of what was going in Europe, they had to rely on letters from contacts overseas. Occasionally, someone managed to get a paper from abroad – from Germany, or Britain, or America – but the stories they relayed were already out of date.

Bruno and his friends' art magazine *Der Kreis* also folded. Its first edition turned out to be its last. On 17 January 1942 the editors wrote to the SMP to 'beg' for the renewal of their publication's certificate. Then, just three months later, the men returned the certificate, unused. *Der Kreis*, they told the police, 'owing to present difficulties, has ceased to be published.'

Free speech was gone along with freedom of the press. Communication by wireless was censored or blocked altogether. Shortwave radios were banned, preventing broadcasts from Europe reaching the news-hungry refugees. Like everyone else, Lisbeth's parents had to register the family's radio set with the Japanese police, and were only allowed to keep it if they taped over its shortwave switch or 'cut off the tubes'.[7] One refugee managed to trick the authorities into keeping his set with all its functions, pretending it had special 'pro-Japanese' speakers. Henry Rossetty, the band leader from Berlin, declared his radio to the authorities for possible confiscation. But he explained: 'Look, I am a musician and I love Japanese music, and this set is made with special loudspeakers to bring out the Japanese music.' He was permitted to keep his radio.[8]

The Epsteins found the loss of German-language radio a cruel blow. To listen to their mother tongue or hear a well-loved piece of music had been

* 'The Cross Section'.

one of their few ways of reconnecting with their lost life in Vienna. Familiar songs and German conversation brought a fragment of home to these alien surroundings. Memories of gatherings with old friends, and operas they had gone to years back, swathed them in a temporary cocoon from reality. Some refugees depended on the radio for their sanity.[9] But the Epsteins were no risk takers. The consequences of disobeying the new laws were too terrifying. They had heard people talk of a field in Hongkew, where they saw the flash of a Japanese blade removing a miscreant's head, or a bayonet used to stab a victim to death for no reason. Until now the targets had always been Chinese, but who knew when the Jews' immunity might end? Only the refugees' underground movement – who were trying to provide intelligence to the Allies, and aiding downed pilots – risked defying the ban. They hid their radio sets and continued broadcasting to their comrades.

Lisbeth and her parents were shocked by other changes going on within the Jewish community around them too. Jews with British connections – like those Sephardim born in London – were in danger, and most of the wealthy Jews of Baghdadi origin had disappeared from the streets. In January, Paul Komor, the IC charity executive, was dragged to Bridge House by the *Kempeitai*, on suspicion of spying for Britain. Other Jewish charity workers now looked to their own interests first. Reuben David Abraham was honorary president of the Juedische Gemeinde, the city's largest Jewish aid organisation. Until now, both he and his wife had contributed generously to its women's branch.[10] But they were also British subjects. When Laura Margolis, the JDC aid worker, asked Abraham for funds for the *Heime*, he refused, reasoning that 'since the Japanese took Shanghai they could also worry about the refugees'.[11]

As fast as the Sephardim were disappearing, so the city's Russian Jews were rising in prominence. The long-established community had resented the arrival of Central European Jews fleeing Hitler, whom they saw as competitors for jobs and cheap housing. Margolis criticised their attitude as lacking any social conscience.[12] When she turned to them for assistance, they were unhelpful. It would not be long before their resentment would show itself in more sinister ways.

Luckily for Lisbeth, the library continued to thrive. The Japanese had no cause to close it, since Bruno was neither British nor American. His customers needed the solace of books more than ever, and borrowing from the library was still within most people's means. Just turned twenty, Lisbeth felt secure in her job; she had been Bruno's assistant for almost a year. But when she returned to the family's room in Yang Terrace, she was enveloped with deep gloom. Her father was still not working, although the new school for Jewish refugees had been open for over a month.

Horace Kadoorie's fundraising efforts to find new premises for the school had paid off. The facilities were impressive, with airy rooms and green space for the pupils to run around in. The school also offered the children some much-needed stability, a return to near 'normal life', which their parents were finding harder to provide as their situation worsened.

But the influence of the Japanese extended as far as the new refugee school. They saw its benefactor, the London-born Kadoorie, as an enemy alien, and stripped him of any influence over its management. Instead, they placed the school under the control of the city's Jewish community, the Juedische Gemeinde. They also insisted that, although lessons would still be taught in English, pupils now had to learn German, and Japanese too. The school's principal, Mrs Hartwich, was summoned to the Japanese Naval Bureau. There the indomitable woman was asked in perfect and polite English whether Japanese was taught in her school, to which she replied, 'Not yet', as she had not found a qualified teacher. The commander promised he would 'send someone over. That is all.' And he did.[13]

But Lisbeth's father did not return to the reopened school. Lisbeth sighed as she looked at the man sitting opposite her at the table in Yang Terrace. His face was gaunter and more yellow, and his constant coughing terrified her. Arnold was too sick to teach. No matter how much food his wife offered him, or his daughter cajoled him to eat, he couldn't put on weight. He was fading away before their eyes.

Lisbeth watched her father draw what comfort he could from his cheap cigarettes. She tried to cheer him by talking of Ilse. She hoped the prospect of his becoming a grandfather might raise his spirits, now that Ilse and Josef had been married for over six months. But his smile at the mention of Ilse's name soon faded as a new bout of coughing began.

Lisbeth thoughts turned instead to his birthday, which was only a few days away, on 1 March. She was determined to find him a gift. She had abandoned the idea of making or buying a cake, as she could not afford to buy one, or even the ingredients had she had the skill to bake one. But there was an obvious alternative. Now that his favourite newspaper was no longer being printed, she would find her father a book. There were plenty to choose from at her workplace. And Bruno was sure to give her a good price.

But a catastrophic event stopped Lisbeth ever buying her father that gift. Her worst nightmare came true.

Towards the end of February, Arnold Epstein collapsed. Lisbeth's own heart was pounding as she felt the weak pulse in his wrist, while her mother ran for the house phone. She almost never prayed, but found herself begging some higher power to save his life. After what felt like an eternity, she heard the house bell ring and ran to open the front door. She stood at the foot of the banister, clutching the wooden handrail as she watched in tears the two white-jacketed men climb the stairs to the Epsteins' room. There the men gently lifted Arnold, with as little effort as if they had been lifting a child, and placed him on their stretcher. They manoeuvred him down the stairs and across the path to the ambulance waiting on Weihaiwei Road. They then drove him to the only hospital that the family could now afford: the Emigrant Hospital and polyclinic, attached to the *Heim* on Ward Road.

Back in the silent room, neither Lisbeth nor her mother dared voice their thoughts.

Over the next few days, Edith and Lisbeth hoped for a miracle, knowing the hospital staff would do all they could to save Arnold. Lisbeth managed to visit her father just once more. She and Edith could see the nurses were doing their best to keep things clean, but the hospital's funding was minimal. Instead of mattresses, its hundred beds were padded with lice-infested straw.[14]

The cancer destroying Arnold's lungs was far too advanced. No nursing care – either in Shanghai or back home – could have saved him. On 26 February 1942, three days before his 58th birthday, Lisbeth's father died in the hospital on Ward Road.

Over the next few hours, the two women distracted themselves with the arrangements for Arnold's burial. I have no knowledge of where my grandfather was laid to rest, but they may have turned to the Jewish burial society – the Chevra Kadisha – for help.[15] After going through these practical motions, each had to face the desolation left by this new loss. Edith, not yet 50 and thousands of miles apart from her elder daughter, felt enveloped in another blanket of darkness. To whom could she now turn with her fears, the anxieties so far hidden from her children? As for Lisbeth, her closest ally was gone – the only man who truly understood her, whose comforting hands had always smoothed the hair from her brow. Never again would she breathe in her father's familiar smell, or bury her face in the warmth of his chest, his arms tight around her. Even the pain from her shattering fall down the lift shaft seemed more bearable than the emptiness she felt now.

By the summer of 1942, the women were resigned to their lives without Arnold. And then a new blow hit their community. All Jewish refugees who had recently fled Europe were summoned to the Office of Stateless Refugee Affairs in Hongkew. There, in the cramped offices at 70 Muirhead Road, they were forced to exchange their usual identity cards for new ones, issued by the Juedische Gemeinde on behalf of the Japanese authorities. While the identity cards of non-Chinese residents bore a green stripe across the top, the Jews' new cards – or 'resident certificates' – bore a broad yellow stripe, and the words 'German refugee' overprinted in both English and Japanese.[16] The city's established Russian Ashkenazi Jews were exempt from the yellow-stripe identity card law. The Japanese were already treating these Jews differently from their recently-arrived neighbours, the Jews who had escaped Europe's Nazis.

As the women returned home from Muirhead Road, Lisbeth tried to ignore the shudder of fear and the sickening feeling of déjà vu that this edict sent through her. She and her mother made light of the new cards. But both knew that once again, the colour yellow was being used to warn others that the bearers were Jews. At least Arnold had been spared this ominous resurgence of antisemitic persecution. A small silver lining to a dark cloud looming ahead.

24

February 1943: The Ghetto

In the months after Arnold's death, Lisbeth and Edith supported one another as best they could: the mother offering comfort through her cooking, while the daughter supported them financially with her wage from the library. Lisbeth forced herself to keep going. Work helped to distract from her grief, and stretched her intellectually. With money so tight and food scarcer than ever, the women were preoccupied with survival. Only at night, before sleep swept her away, could Lisbeth face up to the devastation of her loss. She would silently try to recall Arnold's voice and picture his smile.

Edith was also becoming worried about Ilse. As she prepared their daily meal, her conversation with Lisbeth now focused on what life must be like on the other side of the world. They were desperately short of news from England. Reports of the war in Europe were impossible to get, thanks to Japanese censors; even worse – they hadn't received word from Ilse in months. There were rumours of German bombs falling on London; were Ilse and her new husband still safe there? The uncertainty was as sapping as their meagre diet.

Lisbeth's job at the library provided refuge from these concerns, and she found herself looking forward to seeing Bruno every day. The pair were, in her words, 'getting acquainted'. By now she had learnt of Bruno's marriage back in Germany to his Aryan bride. Clara and Bruno had married the same year that Lisbeth was born, 1922: Bruno had been thirty-two and his bride ten years younger. The couple separated only seven years later. Bruno had shown

Lisbeth a photograph of Clara. To her surprise, she felt a flicker of jealousy at the singer's fine features and high cheekbones. Nothing adds more to a man's attractiveness than seeing his ability to win the attention of a beautiful woman. Lisbeth felt something shifting within her, unsettling both her and her view of the man she worked with. Although she kept her focus on her duties, she tried to stand beside him more often, to lean in more closely as he showed her a particularly rare book. Somehow, he could still afford a rich cologne, whose masculine scent she found intriguing. She gradually sought out more contact with this man in whose company she felt strangely at home.

The customers at the library also stopped Lisbeth brooding. She especially liked to attend the discussion groups that took place after the library's lectures. She and her mother were turning more and more to the Jewish community around them to fill the void left by Arnold's death. There was no shortage of gossip from that quarter, and Lisbeth never knew what stories and rumours she might hear. She had once found idle chatter beneath her, but now welcomed the distraction from her thoughts. And ever since the Jews fleeing Hitler had first arrived in the city, one thing that kept their community going was the spread of rumours. The Germans called these *Bonkes*. The refugees joked of 'a stock-exchange, where you can exchange one new rumour against two old ones'.[1] In the spring of 1943 this was truer than ever.

But the rumour that came on 17 February was quite unexpected. It sank the immigrants' hearts to new depths.

On that February evening in 1943, a group of young adults gathered at the Café Louis after a talk at the Lion Bookshop. Lisbeth and Bruno may well have been there; Horst Eisfelder, the café owner's son, certainly was. He would never forget what happened.

At some point during the meeting, a rumour began to buzz around the room that the Japanese were concocting a sinister plan.[2] They were going to eject all the Jews from their homes and workplaces, and force them to live in one small part of the city. This confinement was to be inside a square mile within the dreary district of Hongkew. Everyone shook their heads in disbelief; surely it couldn't be true. But as the meeting was drawing to a close, Horst Eisfelder was shocked to see his cousin Ferdi burst in. The young man had rushed straight from work at the *Shanghai Jewish Chronicle*. The room went silent as he told them the rumours were true. The front page of the next day's edition of the *Chronicle* would carry a proclamation, setting out the fate of the Jews.

The gathering dispersed amid mutterings of dismay, to await what the morning would bring.

On Thursday, 18 February 1943, when Lisbeth awoke to the radio, she and her mother heard the news. The same chilling message from the Imperial Japanese Government was printed over all the city's remaining newspapers. On the centre of each front page, signed by the commanders-in-chief of the Imperial Japanese Army and Navy in the Shanghai area, was the following text:

PROCLAMATION
Concerning Restriction of Residence and Business of Stateless Refugees

I. Due to military necessity places of residence and business of the stateless refugees in the Shanghai area shall hereafter be restricted to the undermentioned area in the International Settlement.

East of the line connecting Chaoufoong Road, Muirhead Road and Dent Road; West of Yangtzepoo Creek; North of the line connecting East Seward Road, Muirhead Road and Wayside Road; and South of the boundary of the International Settlement.

II. The stateless refugees at present residing and/or carrying on business in the districts other than the above area shall remove their places of residence and/or business into the area designated above by May 18, 1943.

Permission must be obtained from the Japanese authorities for the transfer, sale, purchase or lease of the rooms, houses, shops or any other establishments, which are situated outside the designated area and now being occupied or used by the stateless refugees.

III. Persons other than the stateless refugees shall not remove into the area mentioned in Article I without permission of the Japanese authorities.

IV. Persons who will have violated this Proclamation or obstructed its enforcement shall be liable to severe punishment.[3]

The Proclamation confirmed the rumour: the refugees were being forcibly moved. Yet no one could call it antisemitic: its text never once mentioned the word 'Jew'. Some thought that the Proclamation's euphemistic language stemmed from Japanese sensitivity. Everyone knew, though, that its contents – 'Concerning Restriction of Residence and Business of Stateless Refugees' – applied only to Jews; specifically, to those who had recently fled Hitler.

An explanatory article in the English-language *Shanghai Herald*, printed alongside the proclamation, made this plain. 'Stateless refugees' were those who had 'arrived in Shanghai since 1937 from Germany (including former Austria, Czecho-Slovakia), Hungary, former Poland, Latvia, Lithuania and Estonia etc. and who have no nationality at present'.[4] The proclamation applied only to the European Jews whose citizenship had been stolen by the Nazis, while sparing the stateless Jews from Russia who had settled decades before.

Not once did the proclamation ever use the word 'ghetto'. Instead, it preferred the less emotive 'designated area'. The accompanying article was at pains to explain that this 'was not an arbitrary action intended to oppress', but rather aimed to 'safeguard so far as possible their place of residence as well as their livelihood in the designated area'. The Japanese intention to 'safeguard' was of course to 'control'.[5]

Lisbeth and Edith hurried out of their house to discuss the news with their neighbours. Everywhere they looked, they saw the proclamation on display: on posters nailed to trees, on telephone poles and kiosks. They met small groups of men and women, anxiously gathered at street corners and in cafés, loudly debating what it all meant. Some argued for immediate resistance to the proposed relocation; the less pessimistic preferred a more passive approach, to just 'wait and see'.

The proclamation's significance began to sink in. The long arm of the Gestapo had at last reached Shanghai. But who had master-minded the imperial edict? People speculated on the authority behind it. Were the Japanese yielding to pressure from the Germans, or was the idea their own? Some said the latter, the proclamation appearing to have taken Shanghai's German consul general, Martin Fischer, by surprise. On 20 February, Fischer sent an encrypted cable to his superiors at the

German Foreign Office, notifying them of the 'unexpected Japanese action'.[6]

Then again, another official wrote of having 'no doubt' that it was the German authorities who had instigated the internment of the Jews. According to Fritz Wiedemann, the wartime chief German consul of the coastal city Tientsin in Northern China and an open Nazi supporter: 'The Japanese themselves were not antisemitic, and we were under orders to instruct the Japanese authorities about the racial policies of Germany and to suggest appropriate measures.'[7] There were even rumours that another German official in Shanghai had such measures in mind. By now, SS Colonel Josef Meisinger was said to be making elaborate plans to exterminate all the Jews under Japanese control. These included isolating them in a Nazi-style concentration camp on an island in the Yangtze delta, there starving or gassing them to death, or sending them off to the South China Sea in freighters without water or food.[8] No proof was ever found of such plans.

Lisbeth and Edith were stunned by the announcement. Since settling in Shanghai, the Jewish immigrants had felt tolerated, almost supported, by the Japanese.[9] Even after Pearl Harbor, the city's new rulers did not single them out, directing their strictures instead towards the Americans, British and Dutch. The Epsteins, along with other Jews in their circle, had begun to relax, their suspicions about Japanese intentions for their community gradually fading.[10]

The proclamation changed everything. It shattered any sense of security the German-speaking Jews had dared wrap around themselves. Their movements were again to be controlled by uniformed men, under threat of 'severe punishment'. And everyone knew the Japanese capability there: they had seen the cruelty meted out to Chinese dissidents, and heard of the brutal tortures devised by those running Bridge House. Even the wealthiest European Jews, who had concealed their refugee status until now, would have to move from Frenchtown to Hongkew.

However, there were exemptions for one Jewish community. It had been obvious since the previous summer, when the Epsteins collected their new yellow-striped identity cards, that the Japanese did not view all the city's Jews equally. Shanghai's Russian Ashkenazi Jews had been permitted to keep their old identity cards. And now this group was again exempt, this time from the restrictions of the ghetto.

Lisbeth and Edith were not alone in noticing this preferential treatment. The long-standing rivalry between the Russian- and German-speaking Jews – which had often erupted into street brawls – grew even fiercer.[11] Many of the Jews who had fled Hitler even believed the proclamation had come out of a conspiracy between the Russian Jews and the Japanese. They suspected it had been on Russian advice that the Japanese never used the word 'Jew' in their text, only 'stateless refugee'.[12] Worst of all, they now believed the Russians already knew of the plans for what was, in practice, a ghetto.

A meeting five days later strengthened such suspicions.

The Office of Stateless Refugee Affairs was run by a naval officer named Tsutomu Kubota. On 23 February, Kubota met with hundreds of Russian Jews at their club to explain the proclamation's rationale. It was not antisemitic, Kubota said, but an attempt to deal with the problem of housing and feeding the thousands of stateless refugees.[13] In the *Heime*, many refugees were dying of hunger and heat exhaustion, as well as typhus and beriberi. Others were resorting to begging or petty crime. Kubota now needed the Russians' cooperation in overseeing the Europeans' relocation to Hongkew, and in making the Designated Area habitable. If they refused the 'request', the Japanese would 'take matters into their own hands and do it their own way'.

Had the Russian Ashkenazi Jews declined Kubota's 'gentle' ultimatum, they too would be sent to the ghetto. And so they became – unwillingly or not – the tools of the Japanese.

A few days later, a new relief organisation was born: the Shanghai Ashkenazi Collaborating Relief Association, known as SACRA. Its task was to put the proclamation into practice and move all the stateless refugees to Hongkew. To the fury of these recent immigrants this 'authoritative Jewish body for all Refugee affairs' was to be run by the Russians on the behalf of the Japanese, widening the rift between the two Jewish groups. A week after the proclamation, the Japanese interned the JDC's Laura Margolis, leaving Shanghai's German Jews with no support other than SACRA.

No air strike could have shaken Lisbeth and her mother's lives more violently than this unexpected proclamation. After years spent recreating a semblance of home, they were being uprooted again, and forced to start all over once more – this time in shabby Hongkew. The Designated Area covered less than a single square mile: 40 square blocks of dilapidated lane buildings, already packed with 100,000 Chinese people and 8,000 of the poorest refugees.[14] Everyone soon called it the ghetto.

They had no choice but to move, and quickly. The proclamation's deadline of 18 May left only three months to arrange everything. Lisbeth and Edith were forced to sell most of their belongings to pay for the unwanted relocation. They were close to panic; thousands of refugees were suddenly scrambling to find rooms, all desperate to rent somewhere to live across Garden Bridge. It felt even worse knowing they depended on SACRA's agents for help with the logistics of moving. Rather than easing their financial worries, the agents were charging inflated rents for the tiniest rooms. The costs of even the filthiest premises, which had to be deloused and disinfected, were ballooning by the day. To make things worse, the Russians were demanding 'key money' on top of rents – illegal bonuses given to landlords for transferring a lease.[15]

But Lisbeth and Edith turned out to be doubly fortunate. Firstly, they had only rented their room in Yang Terrace. Secondly, despite Arnold's death a year earlier, they were still able to benefit from his Czechoslovakian birthplace. This entitled them to lodgings in what Lisbeth later called 'the special club for people who were one way or another connected with Czechoslovakia'. The Czech Club was at 43 Chusan Road, the vibrant street in Little Vienna they already knew very well. Others were not as lucky. They saw friends being offered a pittance for the purchase of their homes; these often went to Japanese buyers, who could hardly believe their luck at the one-sided bargain. To the horror of his family, Louis Eisfelder was summoned to Bridge House to discuss the price of his café. At the *Kempeitai*'s headquarters, he was persuaded to hand it over for a 'nominal sum'. The buyer was ostensibly a Jewish doctor, but everyone knew the business was destined for Japanese hands.[16] There could be no discussion on price; SACRA's decision was final.[17]

The edict's effect on Bruno was more complicated. Not only was he forced to leave his balcony room in Yang Terrace, but he also had to give up his work premises in Moulmein Road. Bruno put the bookshop and library in the hands of his business partners, the German Jewish woman and her husband who had helped him set up the library. Because they had been in the city since long before 1937, they were exempt from the proclamation, and could continue living in the International Settlement. Bruno trusted the couple, and they divided all the stock up between them. He took his half of the books to Hongkew to start a new business there. He and the Epstein women met the May deadline for moving.

For Bruno, who loved nature, one of the worst things about the move was Hongkew's drabness: the square mile of the ghetto was unrelieved by any greenery. The nearest suggestion of foliage was said to be a green-painted bench. But he soon found new premises for his library, on Ward Road, the main road through the ghetto. Number 381 Ward Road was three blocks from the Municipal Gaol, on the opposite side of the road. The building was a substantial villa with a huge hallway: a beautiful old Mandarin house, full of carved wood and with two large glass doors. It had three floors, each room serving as home for a refugee family. Bruno rented just the hallway for his business. At the front of this hall he set up his new bookshop and library, putting a partition up at the far end. Behind the screen he placed his mattress and other things. This was where he ate and slept. It was a tiny living space, but good enough.

Lisbeth and her mother prepared to adapt to yet another new life. For the first time Lisbeth realised how much of what life had once offered she had taken for granted. The spaciousness of her home in Vienna, and her freedom to walk through its streets and parks; even Yang Terrace had its gardens. Now a simple stroll to Frenchtown with its shop windows and restaurants was denied her. She was confined to a dozen or so of Hongkew's crowded streets and grimy alleys, where half-naked Chinese infants ran around with 'cotton tails' – wads of rag hanging from their backsides to stem their constant diarrhoea – and men urinated against walls. The ghetto's boundaries did not even let her walk as far as Hongkew's Whangpoo waterfront just south of Yangtszepoo Road. Although the view there was nowhere near as glamorous as the Bund's, how Lisbeth longed for different air to breathe, and the chance to watch the boats move along the river. But yet again, she was being punished for simply being a Jew.

When my sister and I retraced our relatives' footsteps in 2004, we went in search of the old Czech Club, and walked to number 43 Zhoushan Road, which Lisbeth would have known as Chusan Road. We found a lane house with tall grey shutters protecting a heavy inner wooden door. A crude mop hung on the brick wall outside. As Claudia and I peered in through one half-open shutter, as close as we dared, a man emerged from the dark interior, and waved us fiercely away before slamming the door. As it closed, we glimpsed a large decorative wall hanging, a crimson square with Chinese characters in gold.

That evening, as I tried to imagine how my relatives must have felt, I found myself remembering my visit round the part of Venice where that city first confined its Jews. In the sixteenth century, Venice was one of the earliest places to treat its Jewish population in this way, giving us the notorious word 'ghetto'. The two bridges leading to its ghetto were locked each night, with punishments for any Jews found outside during the hours of curfew. I remembered walking through those streets, hoping to catch a glimpse of sky. Strangely, unlike elsewhere in Venice, the sun and sky were obscured. I learnt that the reason for this oppressive feeling was because the ghetto was the only place where buildings could reach six storeys. Built high, and close together, its tenements could cram in so many more Jews. I felt sick when I understood in what contempt these people – my people – were held. And I am saddened to think that such dehumanising of 'others' still flourishes today.

I have a vivid memory of my own first encounter with antisemitism. When I was seven or eight, a child in the playground told me quite forcefully that I should go home to Israel. I have no idea what prompted his jibe, maybe my unusually black hair, or my parents' marked foreign accents. That evening I asked them what he had meant. I don't remember their answer. But I do know it was the first moment I realised that I was 'different'.

This difference was reinforced a few years later. During an English lesson at my all-girls grammar school, the teacher picked me out to read the part of Shylock in *The Merchant of Venice*. Nothing was said, but my cheeks burned with embarrassment at her choice: I was the only Jewish girl in the class. I usually loved reading aloud, but my mouth suddenly went dry, and I had to swallow hard before I could begin.

Looking back now, I feel ashamed at how upset I was by this trivial incident. How can I compare my mortification to what my relatives went through? And yet I cannot help but feel that a teacher's singling out a child for any 'racial' physical characteristic must always be wrong.

My aunt could not leave the ghetto, or escape the hard eyes of its guards. Nor could she or anyone else guess how long the men in uniform planned to confine them, or whether the Japanese might be hatching even deadlier plans.

25

Summer 1943: A Body in the Yangtze

Most of Shanghai's Jews knew nothing of the conditions inside the ghettos of Nazi-occupied Europe. If they had, they might have used a different name for their own place of detention. Their 'ghetto' was quite different from those run by Hitler's henchmen. It was not isolated from the rest of the city by high walls or fences, or continuous barbed wire; its borders were just lines on a map.[1] Nor were its inmates separated from non-Jews. Although the Japanese tried to bribe some of Hongkew's Chinese residents to move out and make way for the 8,000 Jewish newcomers, most would not leave their homes. The scant square mile of the Designated Area now had Chinese and Europeans packed cheek by jowl, neighbours in poverty. For the most part, the population of around 100,000 Chinese tolerated their uninvited neighbours (now totalling at least 18,000 Jews), and some friendships were formed between the communities; there were even some marriages.[2] The Jews who had been forced to swap leafy Frenchtown for dank lanes strewn with fish heads and human excrement may have had cause for revulsion, but the close presence of Chinese neighbours offered a little comfort.

There was another difference between the ghettos of Europe and Hongkew: under certain conditions Shanghai's ghetto inmates could come and go. The Japanese had no wish for the stateless refugees to lose their means of earning a living, nor for their children to stop their education. Those with jobs or who attended schools outside the Designated Area were able to apply for permits to leave the ghetto during working hours. At regular points along its boundary the area had portals to the streets just outside, marked with an unambiguous sign: STATELESS REFUGEES ARE PROHIBITED TO PASS HERE WITHOUT PERMISSION. But 'permission' was possible. It came in the form of an officially stamped pass, granted to those with a temporary need to leave. As well as for schools or work, passes were also granted for visits to doctors or clinics outside the area.

Outsiders could visit the ghetto too. Any 'enemy nationals' wishing to do so had to show an officially stamped pass. Among those wanting to enter the ghetto were some German Christian women, who had been married to stateless refugees but divorced their husbands after the proclamation was announced. They had been encouraged by the Nazis to renounce their Jewishness; in doing so, they were free of the yellow stripe on their identity cards, and given a green striped card instead. This meant they could stay in their homes and, in return for re-embracing their Aryan race, they were rewarded with financial aid and support from the German consulate. The women spent the extra money on food, which they brought to their ex-husbands when they visited each evening.[3]

Lisbeth and her mother had little need to leave the ghetto. But Bruno Loewenberg was obliged to leave every time he needed to purchase new stock for the bookshop. Uniformed guards blocked every exit, making sure each pass was in order; only the area's more remote parts had its borders unchecked.[4] Many of the guards were Japanese sentries, or White Russian police. But others were ghetto inmates themselves, stateless Jews who had been co-opted into performing guard duty. The Japanese conscripted all males between 20 and 45 into this auxiliary force, making them 'volunteer' for duty for several hours each week.

The Japanese had been using non-Chinese residents to maintain law and order in Hongkew since September 1942. That month they set up a foreign branch of the *Pao Chia*, China's system of community protection.[5] *Pao Chia*[*]

---

[*] 'Protect the Home'.

was centuries old; it divided residential areas into districts and blocks, with guards assigned to patrol specific areas.[6] Each man was equipped with a whistle and a rope, to help apprehend any wrongdoers, or at least rope off their intersection if a crime was committed. The Foreign *Pao Chia* began with 2,000 European Jews and Russian immigrants.[7] Within less than two years, Hongkew's Jewish *Pao Chia* expanded to 3,600 European Jews, around 20 per cent of the total number of Jews in Hongkew.[8] They were led by a Viennese lawyer, Dr Felix Kardegg – a much-liked man who was also president of the Juedische Gemeinde.[9]

Many of the refugees forced to guard their own ghetto would gladly have overlooked their compatriots' misdemeanours. They would have let them sneak out with no pass, or return a few minutes after curfew. They might even have ignored an incorrect name or date on a pass, had they not known that the sharp unforgiving eyes of the Japanese or White Russians were always on them. But for others, the badge of authority brought out their worst militarism, and it was clear they took pleasure in reporting the offences of their fellow inmates.[10]

At 53, Bruno was exempt from joining the Foreign *Pao Chia*. He had seen first-hand how men could be affected by the weight of a uniform; now he saw again, to a lesser degree, how some puffed up the instant their sleeves bore insignia, how even the scrappiest emblem of power could turn a man's head. The *Pao Chia*'s badge was a white armband, with stripes showing the officer's rank; its Chinese characters declared the wearer a member of the 'International Settlement Foreign Pao Vigilance Corps'. For those who had been rendered stateless, rejected by their homeland, this sudden gift of authority in Shanghai displaced all sense of reason. He saw neighbours become overbearing and obnoxious, nit-picking over a pass's illegible stamp, or the fact that an inmate had forgotten his or her resident's certificate. Others forgot their true status, and the vulnerability that went with it. One Austrian refugee, Fred Schrantz, became the subject of whispers in Bruno's bookshop.

While patrolling the ghetto on *Pao Chia* duty one day, Schrantz was accidentally hit by a truck. Its drivers said they were working for the Japanese army. Although he was unhurt, Schrantz's precious bike was destroyed. He yelled at the soldiers, demanding compensation, and pointing out the three stripes on his armband showing his status as a *Pao Chia* captain. Onlookers urged Schrantz to be quiet, shouting, 'Stop it, be glad you didn't get hurt. Forget it!' But he demanded to be taken to the soldiers' superior. Eventually the driver of the Japanese-owned truck agreed, and drove Schrantz away.

He never returned. A week or so later, Schrantz's body was fished out of the Yangtze.[11]

The 'soldiers' turned out to be Korean staff working for the Japanese army. They had stolen the truck, and murdered Schrantz to cover up their mistake. The murderers were forced to confess by the Japanese, who delivered a load of valuable coal to the man's widow as compensation. No one learnt the fate of the Koreans.

Little by little the refugee community rebuilt itself within the confines of the ghetto. Not far down from Bruno's library a familiar business reopened its doors. The Eisfelders soon set up an elegant new Café Louis, on the ground floor of a three-storey house at 25 Ward Road. The business soon flourished. Horst had a friend with a non-Jewish German mother, which meant he was not stateless and so could travel throughout the city. The friend would cycle across Shanghai to deliver Café Louis' chocolates and cakes to their many customers living on the other side of town.

If only things had been as simple for Bruno. But he and Lisbeth were still stateless. Not only had they lost all links to their homelands; they had lost the right to move freely through Shanghai. Bruno was forced to apply for a pass whenever he wished to leave Hongkew. Each pass was valid only for a few weeks, and each time it expired he would brace himself for the ordeal of renewing it. He would join the long queue outside the Office of Stateless Refugee Affairs. In the days before each visit, he would vomit with fear. For, like others in the line that snaked down Muirhead Road, he was about to face the man the ghetto loathed most.

The Japanese official, Kanoh Ghoya.

26

'The King of the Jews'

Of the two officials who issued passes out of the ghetto, it was the smiling Sub-Inspector Okura who was the more dangerous. He was a known killer – a man with refugees' blood on his hands. Yet despite this, the Jews feared and detested his colleague, Kanoh Ghoya, far more. The refugees hated his capriciousness and foul mouth; no one could predict his reactions.

Tsutomu Kubota, who ran the Office of Stateless Refugee Affairs, had chosen his underlings well. Both men relished carrying out their boss's dirty work for him. Okura was unusually tall for a Japanese in those days, and powerfully built, while Ghoya was plain and ungainly: at only four feet, he was often described as a dwarf.[1] Bruno rarely crossed paths with Okura, who had overseen the relocation of the stateless refugees to Hongkew. But moving nearly 8,000 people in just thirteen weeks had proved impossible, even for the powerful Okura.

SACRA had failed in the job the Japanese had assigned them. Three weeks before the 18 May deadline, 5,000 refugees still had nowhere to live.[2] Even worse, some people were making no effort whatsoever to comply with the proclamation. Kubota was growing impatient. Along with communism, anarchy and crime, the Japanese would not tolerate insubordination. Okura responded by meting out punishment to anyone caught violating the ghetto regulations, and arresting those who refused to move to the Designated Area. For each day the refugees stayed in their homes past the deadline, they would be detained in the 'death cell' of Wayside Police Station, a place 'dirty and filthy beyond description'.[3] Okura made an example of a Mr Michaelis. His refusal to move cost him a few days in the police bunker, which seemed harmless enough. But soon after he was let out, he fell ill with typhus and died in agony a few days later. The threat worked: by the spring of 1944, only 250 stateless refugees remained outside the Designated Area.

These duties brought out Okura's natural sadism. On one occasion, he threw nearly 90 dissenters into the cell, cruelly slapping and beating them first – and his build made his slaps truly devastating. If someone fainted, he would revive them by pouring cold water on their heads, before continuing the assault. At least seven refugees, mostly Poles, lost their lives after spending time inside the Wayside station.[4] Among them were yeshiva students, Orthodox Jews who made no secret of defying Japanese orders.[*] Easily recognised by their beards, hats and sidelocks, they – along with other Poles in the city – were refusing to move. They had seen people rounded up back in Poland, and the memory filled them with dread. They also considered themselves exempted from the terms of the proclamation: they were not stateless, as Poland had a government in exile in London. Nor did they recognise SACRA.[5]

Although Bruno Loewenberg was never outwardly religious, he respected others who were. He admired the rebellious nature of the Orthodox Poles. When they were assigned lodgings in the Salvation Army compound at 630 Muirhead Road, they would not go. How could they live in a place 'still partially occupied by the dregs of Shanghai's society – former prison inmates, drunks, etc.'? Instead they marched to SACRA's office, where they rioted, smashing up the furniture before throwing it out of the window, 'demanding to be accommodated in private houses in the designated area.'[6] Eventually they won the argument, a victory that would later save their lives.

Within a year of the proclamation, the relocation was complete. Now the stateless Jews had been moved into the ghetto, Mr Okura's work changed to granting passes out of the Designated Area. He was responsible for the short-term passes, valid for a few hours or up to two weeks, for medical examinations, including X-rays, or for attending a funeral. By now Lisbeth

[*] A yeshiva is a school where Orthodox Jews study Jewish religious texts (notably the Talmud and the Torah). The original Mir Yeshiva was in the town of Mir, in modern-day Belarus.

and Edith were accustomed to their room in the Czech Club, while Bruno's new business was flourishing, although he still dreaded applying for 'seasonal' passes to leave the ghetto in search of more books for his shop. During the ghetto's first year, the Japanese were fairly lenient; they even gave out short-term passes to groups, such as a whole audience with concert tickets, or the black-hatted yeshiva students granted daily leave for their studies at a synagogue outside the Designated Area. And Bruno's seasonal passes were valid for a full three months. But then the policy changed and seasonal passes were scrapped, to encourage people to work within the confines of the ghetto. Bruno now had to get the buff-coloured pass – which showed which parts of Shanghai he was able to access, and when – renewed every four weeks.

Every month Bruno had to go to the office that ran the ghetto, within Wayside Police Station. In the days leading up to the meeting, he would sink into 'a complete state of nervous collapse'. For the man in charge of granting or denying the renewals of monthly passes was Kanoh Ghoya.

Above and overleaf: Bruno's pass out of the
Designated Area, showing WHOLE TOWN.

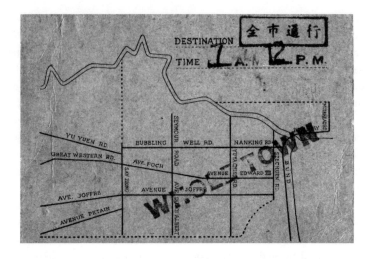

Bruno was not alone in his terror of Ghoya. Although physically weaker and less dangerous than Okura, Ghoya would leave a lasting trauma on the refugees who encountered him. An ex-chief of the Japanese police, by 1944 he was said to have had a complete personality change. He had once been friendly, a lover of music; now he was a screaming tyrant.

Each month, when Bruno joined those queuing up in freezing rain or under a broiling sun outside the Stateless Refugee Affairs headquarters, he succumbed to the line's collective anxiety. Although a *Pao Chia* guard stood there to stop them talking, the Jews sent whispers up the line. In their best suits and polished shoes, they tried to gauge Ghoya's mood. Inside the station, the procession inched forward through the dark hall leading up to his second-floor offices. People would ask those returning: 'Is he beating people today?'[7] Or, as they approached the official's outer room, they would watch for warnings from Ghoya's Jewish assistants that their boss was in a particularly bad temper. Once they were within earshot of the office, they could hear Ghoya ranting and raving in his heavily accented English. This often so unnerved people that they turned back and left rather than face the despot inside, no matter how long they had been queuing.[8]

Although Bruno knew of Ghoya's extreme volatility, it never became any easier to face him. Sometimes the bully would make people wait in line for twelve hours or more, only to make them come back each day for two or three weeks before deciding on their application. Ghoya's desire to humiliate was quite arbitrary. He might work himself into a frenzy before screaming abuse, causing some women to weep or faint at his insults, though others found him ridiculous, and could barely hide their laughter.[9] Sometimes he agreed to nearly every request for a pass, other days none. Bruno knew of men whom Ghoya had accused of being spies, liars or gangsters, before slapping them hard around the face. The next moment, as if on a whim, he would hand the bewildered refugee a pass for a wider area than he had requested. Just hours later, he might drag another to his office window in a fury, threatening to throw him off the balcony. The refugees' deep resentment was triggered by the total powerlessness they felt in front of this irrational bully; it brought back dreadful memories of all they had fled from.

Ghoya's cruelty and rage bore all the hallmarks of a psychopathic tyrant, who demanded both love and fear simultaneously.[10] The man tried hard to be liked; he would engage with the ghetto residents' children, asking if they knew who was the 'King of the Jews'. If they answered with the name Kanoh Ghoya, he would reward them with sweets. Other times he would beat refugees in the ghetto's streets or in cafés for not wearing the metal badge that denoted their permission to leave, even though the rules only required these to be worn outside the ghetto. He liked being seen at Jewish services, as well as football matches, concerts and plays, although he would then decide to ban other performances for no reason.

Little did the self-styled King of the Jews know that his 'subjects', over whom he held so much power, hated him above all other Japanese. They ridiculed his unfortunate looks, calling him 'the Monkey' in private, and would later depict him as ape-like in cartoons.[11] An amateur violinist, he often invited European musicians to accompany him. A caricature later showed Ghoya playing his violin with Alfred Wittenberg, Shanghai's most noted refugee musician, one of the greatest in China. Ghoya disagreed with the professor's interpretation of the piece. 'If you don't beat proper rhythm, Professor,' the dictator screams, 'I'll kill you, you dirty swine.'[12]

Although Bruno was sick with fear before each meeting with Ghoya, he was never a target of the official's abuse. The reason was most probably because Bruno was short. Ghoya's violence was always directed at anyone much taller than himself – which was almost everybody. He would jump on his desk, screaming and slapping their faces, hitting their heads with his ruler, or making them kneel at his feet as they awaited his decision. But he never hit Bruno, nor refused him a pass. Every month, Ghoya stamped it with access to 'WHOLE TOWN', allowing Bruno to go in search of new books.

Before leaving the ghetto, Bruno had to pin a round blue metal badge to his right lapel. Blue showed that he was allowed out of the ghetto for one month; a red (or pink) one signalled validity for only a week. The Chinese characters on it read 'May Pass', leaving no doubt of Bruno's refugee status.[13] As soon as he set foot outside the ghetto, he would have his pass ready for inspection at any time.

Bruno's memories of Buchenwald were never far from his consciousness, and flashed back without warning. He still shook when near uniformed guards, or anyone who looked like police. One evening he was walking on Chusan Road when his paranoia proved justified: a passing soldier struck him hard on the cheek. It took him days to recover. Whenever Japanese customers entered his shop in Hongkew, he would force his breathing to slow down. Since the Japanese were fascinated by German culture, this happened often. One day, a Japanese customer selected a large number of German books from Bruno's shelves, including a copy of Marx's *Communist Manifesto*. Shocked, the man confronted Bruno: 'Why do you have that book here?' Bruno tried to stay calm as he explained that it was a historical document, and in bookstores 'one doesn't ask about things like that'. The man picked up the *Manifesto*. He added it to his purchases, saying he was buying it 'so that it's in a safe place and other people won't see it'. He then asked Bruno to deliver all the books to his house. To the refugee who had fled Hitler, the words rang out as a death sentence. He was convinced that the buyer planned to have him thrown into jail or a concentration camp. But he dared not refuse.

When Bruno arrived at the Japanese customer's home, barely disguising his terror, the man called his son to the room. He told the boy: 'Now this is the book you should not read,' and proceeded to explain the supposedly repellent concepts the *Manifesto* contained. After the speech, he let Bruno return home, unnerved but unharmed.

The bookseller never overcame his fear of those meetings with Ghoya; he would recall them for decades to come. But life went on, despite its degradation and hardships. Bruno and Lisbeth continued to work side by side. Until, in their second spring in the ghetto, an unexpected event altered everything.

27

Spring 1944: A Lifeline Split Twice

Chusan Road had been the heart of the European refugee community since long before the birth of the ghetto. Now it was even more densely packed with people conversing in German and Yiddish, as the stateless Jews could live nowhere else. Each day that Lisbeth and Edith awoke in their new home, they silently thanked Arnold for his Bohemian birthplace. Without it they would never have won their lodgings at the Czech Club at number 43. They had the luxury of decent sanitation, and when they stepped from their front door, the commercial buzz of Little Vienna lifted their spirits. It almost felt like being back home, except they could not travel further than their designated square mile.

The Epstein women still shopped at Die Markthalle, which was now on their doorstep. They bought vegetables and the cheapest cuts of meat: scrawny chickens, various types of offal, or preferably a nice piece of salami. If cash was especially tight, the shopkeepers let them buy liver sausage by the half-ounce. As always, Edith prepared the meals. The club had a modern electric cooker, sparing her the struggle of using a traditional Japanese stove, or *hibachi*. She and Lisbeth had seen many friends trying to use these, which looked like earthenware flowerpots with a hole in one side. When out walking, they often passed people wreathed in clouds of choking grey fumes. Unable to afford charcoal, the cook was using briquettes made by street vendors – blocks of coal dust, ashes and sand held together with damp straw. These produced so much smoke that they could only be used outdoors, in the ghetto's narrow lanes or on a building's flat rooftop.

Although Lisbeth missed Yang Terrace, she knew others were far worse off than she was. Some who couldn't find work were forced to move into one of the *Heime*, which were now barely funded. She saw people from her community begging, a situation that depressed her, and made many refugees feel shame at their countrymen's plight. To avoid this humiliation, the Juedische Gemeinde started issuing 'beggar tickets', for the poorest to exchange for clothing and food.[1] But most refugees remained hopeful, powered by the same spirit of determination that a few years earlier had rebuilt Hongkew's streets out of rubble. Few gave in to despair; the suicide rate was no higher than normal.[2] They still had their creativity to draw on, and their talent for gossip.

Gossip was still the cheapest leisure activity, and was now, in the tightly packed ghetto, valued more highly than ever. Egon Varo's weekly scandal sheet, *Der Querschnitt*, was gone, and the *Shanghai Jewish Chronicle* – the only remaining German-language daily – was stripped of any news from abroad by Japanese censors.[3] People turned inwards for stories. Like that of the destitute neighbour whose daughter had resorted to selling her body, or the former journalist, his shoes lined with cardboard, now begging for small change. And there was never-ending speculation about the course of the war. The telling and retelling of such tales 'was the major indoor sport' in the ghetto.[4] Lisbeth joined in with enthusiasm; she knew that rumours were vital for sanity, that they kept people alive. The 'stock exchange' of the refugees' rumour mill was kept busier than ever.

Her work at the Lion Bookshop kept her occupied as well. The ghetto offered the refugees much less entertainment than the whole city had done, so Bruno's library was even more popular than it had been previously. With the books from his original shop, and his purchases from the streets outside Hongkew, his business was thriving. He started looking for sites to open new branches. He also gained a band of unexpected helpers.

The large Mandarin villa which housed the library was reached through a narrow entrance, leading to two courtyards connected by one of its large glass doors. A band of Chinese street children lived in the narrow entrance, skinny orphans in rags who had no one to look after them. Bruno walked past them each time he entered or left the building. They survived by begging, but as few of the other Hongkew residents had money to spare, the young beggars were more likely to receive a kicking than be given any cash. One winter's day, Bruno gave them an old overcoat he no longer needed, to use as a blanket. From that day on, they were utterly devoted to him. Free to roam throughout the city, the skinny youngsters would transfer books from one place to another, in return for a few pennies or just one of his smiles. Lisbeth found her boss's act surprisingly moving.

They had now worked together for almost three years. Bruno always loved theatre, and sometimes asked Lisbeth to join him at one of the plays and operas put on by the ghetto's artistes. She agreed, for what other fun was to be had? The performers were doing their best to continue to provide some diversion. Despite Kubota's tightening grip over their activities, and funds being scarcer than ever, they 'remained steadfast to their belief in the morale and inviolability of art'.[5] The cultural life of the community was remarkable for such a small population.[6] Against all the odds, they staged concerts, operettas and plays inside the Designated Area. They did not seem to mind that their performances were patronised largely by Nazis. Since the war reached Shanghai, the city's long-standing German residents had quickly formed their own Nazi Party, Gestapo and even a Hitler Youth Movement.[7]

The refugees set up a new group to support their cultural endeavours: the European Jewish Artists Society. EJAS staged productions of *The Bat* (a popular comedy-mystery premiered in 1920, adapted by Mary Roberts Rinehart from her own novel), *The Merry Widow, The Beggar's Opera, The Count of Luxemburg* (an English operetta with music by Franz Lehár) and even a successful *Charlie's Aunt*. More ambitious efforts, such as *Carmen* and *Cavalleria rusticana*, were over-challenging; these were panned by harsher members of the audience, who unjustly judged them against professional performances back home.[8] In their laughter-deprived lives, comedy acts offered the greatest relief. However materially dispossessed the Jews were, they refused to lose their sense of humour. Despite their grumbling bellies and depressing surroundings, storms of applause were still raised by cabarets and shows like the *Laugh-Sanatories*.

Bruno's other great love remained art, and he counted many artists among his friends. Back in the early days of the ghetto, he had taken Lisbeth along to an art show held in the Kadoorie School. It had been put on by the Association of Jewish Artists and Lovers of Fine Art (ARTA), which had been formed the previous year to raise awareness of the refugees' work. [9] Bruno enjoyed introducing Lisbeth to two of the exhibitors, both fellow Germans. One was the talented David Ludwig Bloch, the other a self-taught painter and print maker, Fred Fredden Goldberg. Bruno's friendship with Fredden Goldberg dated from their Berlin days; he and Fred were the same age, and they would joke and reminisce together as if they were in a café on the Kurfürstendamm.

Bruno had other experiences in common with Bloch. The German had spent four weeks in Dachau before escaping Germany, when he boarded the *Conte Rosso* for Shanghai on what was reputed to be her last voyage in April 1940, only a month after Lisbeth and Edith.

If sales were good, Bruno would sometimes take Lisbeth for a coffee or a snack at one of the Designated Area's cafés or restaurants. He occasionally invited her mother as well, but Lisbeth preferred to have him to herself. She was growing increasingly fond of his company. Her favourite place was the Roy Roof Garden, the biggest coffee house in the ghetto; its scores of tables, separated by tall potted plants, seated hundreds high above the streets of Hongkew. At 57 Wayside Road, not far from the White Horse Inn, it was almost next door to the much smaller Café Louis.

In 2017, I returned to Shanghai, this time without Claudia. I was more focused and better informed of the city's history than on my first visit. Hongkou's local council was taking a renewed interest in the streets that had been home to my aunt and grandparents, so I hoped to discover more about the places where they had lived.

It was December, and the sky was an unusually clear blue for a Shanghai winter. I was back at Waibaidu Bridge, about to cross over to Hongkou. To my left, where the Bund ended, vermilion and yellow flowers carpeted the lawns of Huangpu Park, the old British Public Gardens. Above the blossoms hovered giant topiary humming birds, suspended beside sculpted evergreen arches. Across the bridge, I saw the familiar sight of Broadway Mansions, its stepped bulk soaring up to greet me like an old friend.

In my hands were two maps. One I knew as well as I knew my own home, Cambridge. It showed 1940s Shanghai, when 'only' 5 million people lived there; by the time of my visit, the population was five times that number. The old English and French names made me think of my aunt, and I could not help smiling as I pictured her walking here. The other map had Shanghai's current Chinese road names, which meant little to me. I had marked on both maps the places I wanted to see, starting with what had once been Ward Road, and the ghetto's principal road through Little Vienna.

I crossed over the bridge to meet my friend, Yun Ye. I was heading for Astor House, Shanghai's first British-built hotel, and the best place to stay before the Cathay stole its crown in the late 1920s. The cream-coloured hotel spanned a whole block beside the river; entering it was like stepping back in time. It reminded me of a British gentlemen's club. Its walls were covered with dark wood panelling; its floors were parquet, or cream and ochre tiles. Plaques and sepia photographs displayed its colonial past. I found them all fascinating, but my favourite one read:

> The Color of History
> In Britain's Neoclassical architectural style, colorful inlaid glass is used. The daylight shines in through the glazing, which is mysterious and splendid, just like a beautiful and fetching expression in a ladies eyes.

Yun was already in the hall when I arrived. She seemed as keen to visit the Ward Road *Heim* where my grandfather had once lived as I was. In her school days, she told me, this aspect of Chinese history was never taught.

The old *Heim* was within walking distance, and we soon reached the gate of number 138 Changyang Lu. There we saw a distinctive white plaque, which hadn't been there on my previous visit. In Chinese and English text, it named the site as the:

> First Refugee Camp (Asylum at Ward Road) ... Originally the Russian merchants' rest house, the Asylum was converted to barracks in 1939. It was the largest Asylum in the Jewish isolated zone of Shanghai in the World War II.

Peering through the gate, I gazed at the ex-barracks. Hongkou's ubiquitous washing lines stretched beneath red-brick balconies. Trailing house plants and vines with crinkly round orange fruits grew along black rubber cables. There were new air-conditioning units fixed to the building's white-painted walls. Once again, I felt thankful that this utilitarian block had not been Arnold's home for too long.

Our next stop was number 67 Changyang Road, the famous White Horse Inn. The building looked just as it had in old pictures, except the black and white was now bright in pretty pale-pink and tangerine, with red and cream stonework. On a lawn in front of the building stood tables with parasols, white and salmon against the deep azure sky.

Ward Road sign and White Horse Inn, Shanghai, photographed in 2017.

I thought we were about to enter the original building rented by the Mosbergs in 1939. But once inside, I discovered that the inn was only a replica, painstakingly reconstructed from blueprints of the original White Horse Inn. The real building had stood 100 metres down the road, but had been destroyed in 2009, when the council bulldozed it to widen a road. A few authentic tables and chairs were roped off in front of walls hung with candelabra and framed Austrian scenes. Photographs of the broadly smiling owners recalled the liveliness of Hongkew's popular hotspot. It was not hard to imagine how Lisbeth must have felt when taken there in the 1940s, and to the nearby Roof Garden.

The 22-year-old Lisbeth loved the Roof Garden's live music. Talented three- or four-piece bands were mostly made up of Jewish musicians, including the quartet who had come from Berlin, led by the saxophone-accordion player, Henry Rossetty. The proclamation had put an end to their work at the Wing On's roof garden that looked down on the Bund.[10] But they had been happy to take work at this new rooftop venue on the other side of Garden Bridge. Now they played for Japanese and Chinese, and members of the affluent international class; many Europeans from the ghetto also sat at the tables, since the café's prices were not high. As well as playing old favourites from home, the band learnt new pieces asked for by the Chinese and Japanese; they worked day and night to translate the East Asian music notation into a form they could read. But music from America – Japan's enemy – was forbidden. The band played for a minimum wage of two bottles of beer each evening, but requests cost a little more. Their violinist even earned some extra cash giving lessons to the music-loving but tyrannical ghetto official, Kanoh Ghoya.

Lisbeth enjoyed sitting opposite her boss, listening to the café's sultry jazz. She might have noticed his unusually long eyelashes for the first time as they sat alone together. And if he caught her staring, I imagine her quickly turning her head to discuss the view over the ghetto. Look – there's our library, she would say, for it could just be made out, three blocks up from the grey mass of Ward Road's Municipal Gaol. The pair would sit in the cool breeze of the evening, the smells of sauerkraut and paprika-laced goulash soup wafting by as the servers wove skilfully between the many tables. Lisbeth could have listened to Bruno for ever; he always had something interesting to say. Perhaps they both smiled at the Chinese waiters, whose astute grasp of key German words proved quite sufficient to deal with all their customers' orders.

It made sense that Rossetty's band were paid in beer in those years after Pearl Harbor. Inflation continued to soar – slowly at first, but soon the rates were changing daily. Meat that had cost 30 cents a pound in 1938 was now impossible to buy: a small chicken could fetch $300.[11] Not even the book world was immune. Lisbeth and Bruno had to invent a new system for recording borrowing fees, which now had to be charged on a daily – not weekly – rate to keep up with inflation.[12]

The pair worked together smoothly, with few disagreements. They were getting to understand each other's nature, so different from their own. Bruno found people fascinating, and would effortlessly draw them in, gaining their friendship and trust. He made people laugh, a thing his assistant was rarely able to do. He could empathise with others, which reserved Lisbeth found hard. He told people he could see into their hearts, understanding their characters – even predicting their future. He delighted in demonstrating his skill in analysing handwriting, as well as reading people's palms.

Maybe it was during a quiet period at work, or one evening over a glass of his favourite vodka, that Bruno took Lisbeth's palm in his own. He looked down to discover what lay there, and then back at her wide eyes. The liquor may have sharpened his understanding; it likely strengthened the growing warmth that Lisbeth felt towards him. What is certain is that Bruno took Lisbeth's hand to study her fate. Her lifeline was split twice, he told her, once when she was fifteen and again when she fled Vienna three years later. Her pulse quickened under his gaze. And when he spoke of the great intellect and sensitivity he read from her palm, she felt the joy of being truly understood. Bruno even offered her sympathy. He said he recognised how thwarted, how frustrated she felt by having her chance of attending university snatched away.

Something shifted. Lisbeth still enjoyed working with the man whose rich voice so intrigued her. And their relationship did alter; as often happens with colleagues, it grew much closer than friendship. Whatever intuition Bruno had used to divine the young woman's life from the lines on her hand, he had missed a significant milestone ahead. One that would prove momentous for them both.

In the spring of 1944, a year after the Jews were forced into the ghetto, Lisbeth discovered she was expecting Bruno Loewenberg's child.

28

August 1944: Birds, Flowers and Good Luck Symbols

So, at 22 years old, Lisbeth found herself pregnant and unmarried. A predicament she might never have imagined back home, but now she was living in a topsy-turvy world without rules. I imagine these rules would have been swept aside anyway, by the unfamiliar hormones surging through her body. Her breasts were already feeling different, and the emotions swirling inside her head – a joyful excitement at the new life growing within her, mixed with terror at the thought of childbirth – were completely new to her.

I find it hard to believe that Edith never discussed sex and contraception with her daughter. During the lean times of the ghetto, few wished to start a family, or increase its size, and being an unmarried mother may have still been the subject of gossip. Every pharmacy window displayed its large stock of condoms. And for those women who became pregnant, there were always ways out. One doctor in Hongkew offered a regime of vodka and quinine, which proved unpleasant but effective.[1]

Lisbeth had no wish to take what she saw as such a merciless step. Having seen so much death in her short life, to end a new one before it had the chance to begin felt almost criminal. As for Edith, after her initial shock at her daughter's situation – who knows how much she even knew of her daughter's involvement with Bruno? – she may also have welcomed the news: it would give both women something positive on which to focus, a small ray of light in the gloom of the ghetto. Or might she have had misgivings about her daughter bringing another child into their confined square mile? I would rather imagine that Edith was supportive. That she reassured Lisbeth that however tight their finances were, they would manage. And that the shared experience of a pregnancy brought a new closeness between the women.

To my own deep regret, I shall never know how my birth mother would have reacted to my own pregnancies, or what support Ilse might have offered. Although I had a loving stepmother, Ruth lived 70 miles away; besides, her main focus was on my father. When I was expecting my first child I had no close friends who had gone through pregnancy, although my sister did send me congratulations, and a book illustrating the stages a foetus goes through. I was 28 years old, and felt quite isolated, with no one to talk to about the overwhelming challenge of becoming a mother myself.

I believe that Lisbeth had now fallen in love with her boss, and that her heart would have quickened with joy at the thought of a deeper tie between herself and Bruno. It has crossed my mind, perhaps unfairly, that she planned her condition, as part of a strategy to anchor her unpredictable life. With her father gone, she may have welcomed the security – both financial as well as emotional – offered by this successful and charismatic older man. But this is pure speculation. More likely she would have been preoccupied by practical questions: would Bruno make a good father? Would he be prepared to take her on, and look after her and their child? Where would the new family live? Uncertainty as well as happiness must have filled Lisbeth's head during those early weeks of her pregnancy.

Where or when she told Bruno the news is something I shall never know. Was it at work one morning, or over a drink towards the end of the day? I would like to think they both shared delight at the thought of a child. For Lisbeth, it would allow the awakening of a new side of her nature: the chance to care for another. And, at the age of 53, Bruno may well have welcomed this late chance to become a father. By now he too may have fallen in love with the intelligent young woman from Vienna, and rejoiced at the idea of her becoming the mother of his son or daughter.

However unlikely the match might have appeared to outsiders, the momentous news of a shared pregnancy marked a turning-point in their lives. Lisbeth and Bruno decided to get married. I am sure this reflected their mutual feelings; I have no reason to believe that Bruno only married Lisbeth out of chivalry, to spare her the stigma of being an unmarried mother. As neither was outwardly religious, they chose a civil ceremony. Chinese law required such events to be held in a public place, 'with the doors open' for anyone to be present. They picked the Café International at 81 Chusan Road for the occasion, which the owners described as 'the oldest and most spacious establishment since the beginning of the immigration'.[2]

And so, on 6 August 1944, Lisbeth and Bruno were pronounced man and wife by one Morus Ehrlich, LLD, Attorney-at-Law. The bride's mother was present, as were the two official witnesses – Ernst Zander, bookseller, and Joseph Sachs, merchant – as well as a small circle of friends and the

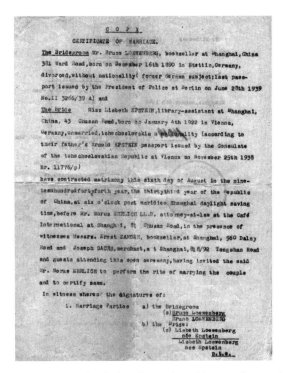

Above and overleaf: Copy of Lisbeth and Bruno's wedding certificate (July 1947).

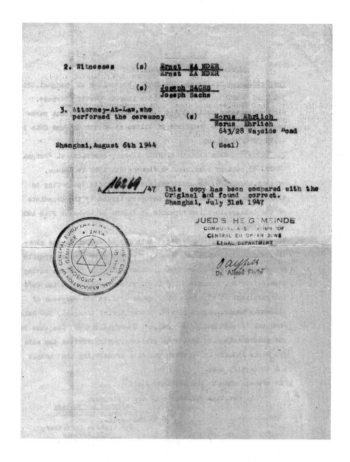

onlookers who happened to be dining at the Café International that day. The meal was good, Bruno spending generously on the best German-style dishes they could afford. The bride was also delighted with the Chinese marriage certificate the lawyer presented to them. It was beautifully decorated 'with all kinds of birds, flowers, and symbols for health, good luck, and money'.

A few days later, Lisbeth typed out a letter, addressed to the Refugee Affairs Bureau on Muirhead Road, and delivered by hand. It was for the attention of Kanoh Ghoya, and read:

Shanghai, August 11th 1944
To the Shanghai Stateless Refugee Affairs Bureau,
Muirhead Road

Dear Sir,
I herewith beg to apply for the changing of my name on account of
marriage, which took place on August 6, 1944.

My former name was: Lisbeth Epstein.

My new name will be with your kind permission: Lisbeth
Loewenberg.

A rectangle stamped in red ink aslant across the top of the page bore the
word 'APPROVED' in block capitals. Two handwritten lines of Japanese
characters in a clerk's scarlet pencil ran down the page, translating Lisbeth's
application from its original English.[*] I was disappointed not to see the
approval given in the actual handwriting of the 'King of the Jews'.

After the wedding, Lisbeth packed her suitcase, said goodbye to Edith,
and left the Czech Club. Her new home was to be with Bruno in
the Mandarin house on Ward Road. Although just a few streets away,
emotionally it was a huge distance to travel. She was leaving the mother
who had always been by her side, from the agony of her fall, the terror of
the November Pogroms and their escape from Vienna. But a new life was
about to begin – one as an independent adult, to be shared with the man she
loved. Would the transition to being his wife – and, she hoped, equal – come
naturally? A tinge of anxiety at this new role must have tempered her joy.

Bruno had wisely removed his belongings from 'his tiny spot behind the
library'. He realised that his new wife would not be happy with cramped
living quarters at one end of the hall, with only a screen separating them
from all the bookshelves. He rented a room for the two of them, away from
the library, in a wing on the right-hand side of the house's inner courtyard.
Lisbeth's eyes widened as she entered the room: it was the biggest she had
lived in since she had arrived in Shanghai. It had showers and toilets and

---

[*] 'Marriage change of name 1944/8/11 applied.'

there was even running water and a sink in the room. No one in the ghetto had the luxury of a refrigerator, but she considered herself lucky that she and Bruno owned an ice box. Space was tight but she became very good at arranging things: the ice box stood in the entrance; the hot plate sat on the ice box – this was her new kitchen! The couple had two couches: one to sit on and the other to sleep on. Finally, their table and chairs made the single room a dining room, bedroom, kitchen and hall. Lisbeth was delighted with this step up from the Czech Club. She described her new home as 'practically luxurious by Shanghai standards'. Her husband was also happy: their room in the wooden-carved Mandarin house had a window overlooking the garden and he could look out onto greenery.

Weeks passed, and the steamy Shanghai summer eased into a mild damp autumn. As Lisbeth's slight form expanded, she found the humidity even more oppressive than usual, and longed for the cooler days to come. Night-times offered little respite. I do not know how soon after the wedding Lisbeth was first jolted awake in the small hours by her husband's screaming. She sat bolt upright, still heavy from sleep but her heart pounding, and tried to gently shake him out of his terror. She soon learnt that Bruno's nights were rarely peaceful; the man was plagued by paralysing images of Buchenwald. But now, as she lay in bed in her new home, with the unfamiliar sensation of a man's body beside hers, she thought of their child and counted the days until winter, when she would at last meet the tiny person who was growing within her.

29

Autumn to Winter 1944:
Cake, Coffee and Air Raids

In the early days of living together, couples often discover that their partners have traits they never expected. Some are more easily adjusted to than others. Lisbeth had not foreseen having to calm her sweat-drenched husband from his terrors each night. But she learnt to manage her broken sleep, and was glad to feel needed. Other changes were less distressing; she soon adapted to the change of her first hot drink of the day from her customary black tea to the strong coffee on which her husband depended. But she would never get used to Bruno's timekeeping. Lisbeth was not a 'morning person', but she would at least arrive somewhere close to the arranged hour. But for Bruno, she soon discovered, this proved impossible. Perhaps as a result of his constantly shattered nights, he never emerged from bed before late morning, or even lunchtime at weekends.

I feel sure that Bruno truly loved his new wife. Lisbeth was soon welcomed by his many friends, and she enjoyed watching him shine at the hub of his social circle, a sun surrounded by planets. She was content to remain in his shadow. His outgoing nature rubbed off on his new wife. The couple enjoyed going out in the evenings, and often met friends for card games. Lisbeth learnt to play poker, at which she quickly excelled. Her facility with numbers and her inscrutable expression gave her an immediate edge; her poker face only faltered when a slight smile appeared as she scooped up her winnings. And Bruno brought her economic security – or at least as much as the ghetto allowed. The couple often went to the cinema. Despite the war, Shanghai continued to screen recent Hollywood films, since a stack of unreleased movies were among the many goods stockpiled in the city. Even downmarket Hongkew had three movie houses.[1]

Bruno and Lisbeth shared a deep love of music, especially the European classical composers. Listening to these almost made them feel as if they were back home. They were not alone in finding music a source of solace at such a difficult time. One of their neighbours owned a record player, and Lisbeth and Bruno joined their fellow tenants in taking records to the neighbour's room for weekly musical evenings, where they relaxed to Mozart and Bach. Lisbeth and Bruno had a good record collection, and kept buying more. Lisbeth would bring coffee and cake to the soirées, while her husband brought their treasured discs. As well as Brahms, Stravinsky and Bach, Bruno found a new favourite. Three months after their marriage, Aaron Copland's ballet orchestration, *Appalachian Spring*, was premiered in America. The ballet's theme was the wedding celebration of two American pioneers, and the challenges the newlyweds faced in their uncertain future. Copland's suite would become one of the pieces of music Bruno played most often.

During my second visit to Shanghai in 2017, I visited the 'Wall of Names' – a vast copper plaque etched with the names of 13,732 of Shanghai's Jewish refugees, which stands in the paved courtyard outside the Shanghai Jewish Refugees Museum. The museum was founded by the local government in 2007 to commemorate the 20,000 refugees who fled Hitler and made a new life in the city; it is housed within the former Ohel Moishe synagogue, set up by Shanghai's Russian Jews in 1907.[2] I was shown around by a young man, James Yang, who had become fascinated with this aspect of his city's history.

I walked the length of the plaque, looking closely at the list of thousands of names. And then I found what I was searching for: Edith Epestein and Elisabeth Epestein. This proof of my relatives' existence in wartime Shanghai brought unexpected tears to my eyes. I asked my guide why my grandmother and aunt's names had been spelled incorrectly. He explained that much of the list had come from a census, compiled on Japanese orders in 1944. The authorities had hired three teenage Jewish girls to gather the names of all the Jews in the city. Some had then been clearly mistyped by the Japanese secretaries, reflecting the sounds that the Japanese heard.

Further along the wall, I found Bruno Loewenberg. And then, to my surprise, my aunt's name appeared again, this time as Lisbeth Loewenberg. The list must have come from multiple sources, with my aunt counted twice. Although this resulted in an overestimate, the number of names listed was an underestimate of the total number of Jews in Shanghai. At least 5,000 European Jews who lived in the city during the 1940s had been left off the wall. In some cases, the omission was the result of self-preservation. Many Jews, still marked by their experiences in Europe, and frightened by rumours of Meisinger's plans, understandably refused to give their names to the Japanese, known allies of Hitler.

The list of almost 14,000 names was overwhelming. I was starting to piece together my relatives' past; yet behind every other name on that wall was someone else's story, of their displacement, loss of homeland, and hopes for a future in a freer world.

The author looking at the wall of names, Shanghai 2017.

Lisbeth was working harder than ever at the Lion Bookshop. She now had a vested interest in Bruno's business, which continued to flourish. New libraries sprung up within the Designated Area, but the competition did not hurt the Loewenbergs: the demand for books was endless. Bruno found locations for two more branches inside the ghetto: the Lion Bookshop now advertised sites at 605 Tongshan Road and 52 Chusan Road. The new libraries generated enough income for the pair to live relatively well. Although they didn't have much, they were still better off than most. This helped ease the anxiety Lisbeth felt about her pregnancy, and she began to relax into happiness.

Over the months leading up to the birth, the couple developed a daily routine. They could still afford Bruno's coffee, and the eggs Lisbeth loved to eat for breakfast. They still had 'French' bread for lunch, while each afternoon her mother came over from the Czech Club to prepare an evening meal for them all. Edith's presence offered more than just practical help: Lisbeth admired her talented mother's cooking, and this continued daily contact kept them close.

As no new supplies were being imported, people had to make do with what foodstuffs remained in the city. Some warehouses still held stores of cocoa butter and raw chocolate, so Café Louis were able to carry on selling fancy chocolates, which now cost more than ever. When sugar became scarce, and unaffordable even for Lisbeth and Bruno, the couple simply stopped using it. Imaginative cottage industries created ersatz versions of foods. Edith became used to cooking with butter made from sesame seeds, and 'strange-tasting' margarine manufactured in some rooms in Hongkew. Although there was no butter or cheese, there was no shortage of condensed milk. Cheap millet could be found in Chusan Road market, tainted with mould; some people made a stew from a cow's spleen, the taste of which they disguised with thick onion gravy.

Despite being restricted to the square mile in Hongkew, in the months leading up to the birth Lisbeth was happier than she had been since she was a little girl. She realised that 'happiness has nothing to do with possessions'. 'If you have things, it's very good, but you always have to know that you can also do without. To come together [for] an evening with coffee and cake and listen to classical recorded music; that was the epitome of luxury. You can be very happy doing just that. You can be just as happy in one room as you can be in a [whole] house.'[3]

But happiness is as fragile as a nest of spun sugar. Just as Lisbeth's small world was growing calmer, Shanghai was starting to feel the dangers of war. The Japanese had made air raid drills mandatory for the ghetto inhabitants in 1943, but as the refugees had seen little more than the occasional flyover of an American plane, no one took the enforced practices seriously. By the beginning of 1944, Lisbeth and Bruno were quite used to the drills. But the conflict in the Pacific was getting closer and, with the start of the year, the tide of war was shifting in the Allies' favour. Both the Nazi forces in Europe and the Japanese in the Pacific were in retreat. American planes were spotted more frequently over the skies of Shanghai. A lone US raider appeared nightly, between midnight and the early hours of the morning, flying in from the west.[4] The ghetto inmates looked up with hope as the American pilot aimed his bombs at the Japanese vessels in the harbour, or the waterfront warehouses and docks near the Japanese consulate beside Garden Bridge. And by the summer of 1944, the air raids began.

Lisbeth was entering her second trimester of pregnancy – that phase when the condition's 'bloom' can really kick in – when the first major raid hit the city. It was the night of 9 June 1944. The next came on 5 July, then another four days later.[5] By the autumn, rumours hinted at a possible Nazi defeat. Hongkew's residents, who were still deprived of any news from Europe, dared to hope. The Japanese-controlled radio broadcast only pro-Axis propaganda, glorifying the victories of their pilots and denying any Allied success.[6] But few in the ghetto believed the vituperative speeches or the gloating reports of Japan's daily triumphs.[7] The courageous (or foolhardy) among them tuned in to BBC broadcasts, glued to their sets every night as they listened in the dark.

Towards the end of 1944, the Americans had reached the Philippines, and stepped up their bombing of China. In November, another raid hit Shanghai. The city's resources and industrial production were now so crippled that electricity was rationed to a few hours' use in the evenings; Lisbeth and Bruno turned to oil and kerosene lamps instead.[8] The Japanese ordered blackouts, and curfews in restaurants, whose doors shut as night fell. Emergency first-aid centres were set up, and air raid drills began to be taken more seriously.[9] American bombers were now seen in daylight as well as at night. Their presence reassured – even inspired – some of the younger refugees. They at last felt a connection with the outside world, and that someone cared about their plight. But for Lisbeth, she prayed that nothing would stop her carrying her baby to term. Like other women in the final weeks of their pregnancy, her emotions were in turmoil: excitement at the approaching birth of her son or daughter, alternating with terror at the inevitability of hours of labour in the ghetto's overstretched hospital.

30

December 1944: A Cruel Winter

On 2 December, 1944, one of the bitterest nights of the winter, Lisbeth felt her contractions begin. I imagine Edith rushing to the Mandarin house to be by her daughter's side. I picture her fussing around to make sure everything was ready for Lisbeth's stay in hospital, including a warm blanket for the baby. And if Lisbeth was anything like most first-time mothers, her excitement at the thought of meeting her newborn infant must have been mixed with fear: how much pain would the birth bring? Especially for a delivery in the ghetto's Emigrant Hospital attached to the *Heim* on Ward Road, the only one they could use. Although the staff were compassionate German-speakers, they were desperately short of equipment and medicines. Since Pearl Harbor, imported German drugs and chemicals were unable to get through to Shanghai.[1] And many of the doctors were as undernourished as the patients.

Worst of all, Lisbeth and her mother were about to return to the medical centre where, almost three years before, they had watched Arnold succumb to his cancer.

But they had no choice. The Shanghai General Hospital, in which Lisbeth had been treated for typhoid, lay outside the Designated Area, and was out of bounds to the stateless Jews. So the women set off, arm in arm, from the Mandarin house to the maternity ward a little further down Ward Road. Lisbeth, bundled up in the woollen coat that barely stretched round her, was shivering, partly with nerves, but mainly because the weather was so icy cold.

I do not know what my aunt's labour was like; she never spoke of it to me, or my sister. What I know is that on that icy evening, Lisbeth was delivered of a little boy. She and Bruno chose the name Michael.[2]

I imagine that Lisbeth's elation at the safe arrival of a healthy baby was soon replaced by overwhelming exhaustion. She gratefully handed over the infant to the staff as she tried to sleep for an hour or two, until she was woken to feed him. For four days and nights, she was in a daze of exhaustion and love as she watched her baby gain strength. She closed her eyes as she inhaled the scent of his head, with its soft covering of dark hair. As her milk started to flow, so did the wave of emotion – the wonder at this little face cradled close to her breast, the pain at the unaccustomed suckling, and the joy at this perfect new person she and Bruno had created.

The head nurse present on the ward on 7 December 1944, Doris Grey, was well accustomed to the Ward Road hospital's 'dirt and lice and straw'.[3] But the German refugee never forgot the extreme cold of that December night. She and the other maternity nurses did their best to keep the newborn babies warm. They placed them under heating lamps, which another refugee doctor described as 'electric suns'. He did not work at the hospital, but later heard that on that night, despite the lamps, a number of babies delivered in the primitive maternity ward 'died from exposure to cold'.[4] But Doris was there, and she knew that what the doctor heard was not true.

> Six babies, newborn, died in one night. And of course at that time we didn't know any better and thought [it was] because it was not heated. We couldn't heat, we couldn't use any electricity. But we kept them [warm] with hot water bottles and blankets and everything ... people were saying they died of frost cold, you know. They didn't.[5]

Grey and her team later discovered – it is not recorded how – that the babies had not succumbed to the cold, as many thought, but to one of Shanghai's deadly viruses.

A record of refugee deaths shows that on 7 December, one of the six tiny victims had been born just five days earlier. The baby's name was Michael Loewenberg.

I found myself weeping when I saw this name coldly recorded on an official list, and read the dates of birth and death with so few days between them. Here was a first cousin of mine, whom I would never meet, and of whom my aunt never spoke. If just seeing this evidence of my cousin's short life set out on a spreadsheet could make me cry so long after the event, how must my aunt have reacted in reality? The woman who lost her twin at birth was again separated from an infant boy who should have stayed by her side. I can only guess how she reeled from the tragedy. Losing an infant so soon after its birth must be like having one's soul ripped from one's body. What emptiness she must have been left with, after carrying so much hope along with the child for those nine months. And how cruel a blow to a woman who had already lost her homeland, the stability of her childhood, her ability to dance and her much-adored father.

Is it any wonder that something inside Lisbeth died with her baby that night? And that when no more tears were left to be shed, she dried her eyes and withdrew into herself, to become the cool, impassive woman whom I knew and found myself unable to love?

31

Spring 1945: 'Mein Bruder, Mein Bruder*!*'

Over the coming days and weeks, like her mother before her, Lisbeth had to cope with the loss of a child. Her breasts hardened with the milk that no baby would suckle. She would still have been bleeding, a small hardship one can forget if distracted by the delight at holding one's child. Lisbeth was left with only the physical signs of a recent delivery, but no baby. She would never again smell his head, or caress his hair, or see his first smile.

Who knows what conversations took place between Edith and her daughter at this time. Since my grandmother had gone through both a stillbirth and the loss of her own first baby, I hope she may have whispered Lisbeth words of sympathy and understanding. But this, like so much else about my family, remains a mystery. Just as I shall never know the cousin I lost, whose name was never spoken, and whose tiny remains may still lie buried somewhere beneath Shanghai's new roads.

After 7 December, Lisbeth's emotional armour redoubled to shield her from further grief. With the war building to its peak, Shanghai's skies were filled with more Allied planes. Lisbeth watched them with detachment. The threat of air fire did not scare her; she had already been dealt the worst hand life could offer. She stayed put, unlike others who, at the first sound of an alarm, rushed to the reinforced gaol on Ward Road for protection. As a distraction, she learnt to tell one type of plane from another. The first she recognised were the P-51s – Mustangs, long-range single-seat fighters. Later, as the raids grew more frequent, she watched the huge B-29 Superfortresses gleam silver overhead.[1] She could soon distinguish the aircraft – the B-29s, B-24s and P-51s – from the timbre of their engine sounds alone. And the massive B-29s, in neat formation, cruised much higher in the sky than any Japanese planes, far out of reach of enemy guns.[2]

As 1945 came, so did more rumours of Allied victory. The ghetto buzzed with *Bonkes* – every two hours a new tale arrived of events happening in Europe, of what the Americans were doing, and of Japanese plans to restrict the lives of Shanghai's Jews even further. Word even went round of a concentration camp being set up in the city.[3] Until early May came, and with it the most glorious news: Hitler was dead, and the Germans had surrendered in Europe! Lisbeth and Bruno read the reports in the *Shanghai Jewish Chronicle* at their kitchen table, unable to suppress their smiles; the author of the evil from which they had fled had shot himself in the mouth, and the war in Europe was over! For the first time in months their hearts lightened. But their joy – and that of the whole refugee community – was short-lived, when the next news arrived.

The Japanese authorities did not censor the city's Russian media in the way they censored that of the Jews. The previous autumn, appalling news of unimaginable happenings in Europe began filtering through from Russian newspapers and radio stations. The reports – surely too terrifying to be credible – were now being corroborated, and published in the *Shanghai Jewish Chronicle*.[4] A series entitled 'Treblinka' reported what Russian soldiers had found when they discovered the Nazi death camp inside occupied Poland. Then the city's Russian community screened newsreels of the camp's liberation. Hundreds of refugees defied the ghetto's 'pass' laws to go to see these in the former French Concession.

The films proved more shocking than anyone could have ever imagined. The audience gasped at the sight of heaps of twisted, starved bodies, skin-covered skeletons; of gas chambers and crematoria filled with ashes and half-burned corpses. During one of the films, a refugee leapt to his feet, white as a sheet. He screamed *'Mein Bruder, mein Bruder!'* as he watched a pale, emaciated man guiding Russian soldiers, the camp saviours, through his former hell-on-earth. He had to be calmed down at the sight of his brother, and led out of the theatre by other refugees.[5]

If Lisbeth and Bruno saw these images they must have dared not imagine what had befallen their families, left behind in Europe. In fact no one in Shanghai yet had any idea of the scale and effectiveness of the Nazis' extermination campaign. Lisbeth never spoke to me of any relatives – her aunts or uncles, such as Arnold's sister in Prague, or her photographer grandfather, Julius, or grandmother Paula, or the hop-trading grandfather on her father's side, still living in Austria; I have to assume they all perished. I know for certain that Bruno never again saw any of his large family, including his much-loved sister and her son, all his cousins, uncles and aunts, after the war.

Just as my mother Ilse escaped death by leaving France in 1939, I later learnt how fortunate Lisbeth and Edith had been to emigrate to Shanghai when they did. When I discovered that they had moved to 4/13 Schwertgasse, the much smaller flat close to the Stadttempel, I searched the internet for information about the address. I was directed straight to an entry on a Czech database, headed 'Elisabeth Mann'. The result came so fast I had no time to prepare myself for its contents, which made me catch my breath.

Elisabeth Mann
Born 24.12.1880 in Friedek*
Born name: Huppert
Last residence before deportation: Vídeň† 1, Schwertgasse 4/13
Transport IV/10, no. 772 (10.09.1942, Vienna → Terezín)
Transport Ea, no. 868 (16.05.1944, Terezín → Auschwitz)
Murdered.[6]

The woman who would occupy my relatives' flat had been taken from that address and deported to Terezín. The outside world had been led to believe that this Czechoslovakian 'spa town' was a transit camp for Jews awaiting 'resettlement'. Its residents were forced to send cheerful postcards home to relatives, perpetuating one of Nazi propaganda's greatest deceits.

---

* Friedek (Frýdek) was in Silesia, now a part of the Czech Republic.
† Vídeň is the Czech name for Vienna.

On 16 May 1944, Elisabeth Mann was moved on from Terezín, via Transport Ea, no. 868. The same database showed that her husband, Julius Mann, was taken with her, no. 867 on the same list. That day, 2,500 people were transported from Terezín. Of these, 2,460 were murdered at their destination. Only 40 survived. Elisabeth and Julius were not among them; they both died in Auschwitz.

Had Edith and Lisbeth still lived in Schwertgasse in September 1942, they would have shared the same fate as the Manns.

The refugees' horror at the fate of Europe's Jews was compounded with guilt at their comparative safety. But by now their 'haven' felt more and more exposed. The Japanese had scattered communications equipment and military installations throughout the streets of Hongkew, even storing munitions in a wing of the gaol on Ward Road.[7] They had placed anti-aircraft batteries on the flat roof of Broadway Mansions, making the apartment block a near daily target of P-51s. Thousands of Chinese moved out to the countryside, and Japanese civilians exchanged their homes for ones in Frenchtown, which they thought would be safer. Lisbeth and Bruno, and the other stateless Jews, had no choice but to stay. Confined to the ghetto, in houses built on soil so swampy that digging cellars was impossible, they had nowhere else to hide.

32

17 July 1945: The Animals Sensed it First

In late June 1945, Shanghai learnt that US forces had captured a tiny Japanese island in the East China Sea. The battle for Okinawa was one of the war's bloodiest, with tens of thousands of lives lost on both sides. But the costly victory gave the Americans control of an air base within striking distance of the Japanese mainland. A base that was also merely 500 miles from Shanghai. When the refugees first heard the news of this victory in the Pacific, they were elated. Within weeks, their joy turned to anguish.

It happened just after noon, on a hot sticky Tuesday; the date was 17 July 1945, a day that Lisbeth and everyone else in the ghetto would remember for the rest of their lives.

The animals sensed it first, before the sound of any alarms. The stray cats and mangy dogs who survived deep in the lanes pricked up their ears. The cats darted about, looking for places to hide; the dogs began barking incessantly. Then even human ears heard it. First came a faint humming, then the drone of approaching Allied aircraft. A noise now so familiar that few people peered up at the cloud-filled sky. Seconds later they heard the deep roar of planes, too close for the air raid sirens' screaming to be any use. The warnings came too late. Twenty-five new Superfortress aircraft were racing towards them from the US airfield on Okinawa.[1] Then their bombs were whistling down on the ghetto.

A total of 263 American bombs rained down on Shanghai.[2] The Allies discharged their deadly cargo at 12.13pm. The hazy clouds were low, obscuring the sun, so people heard, rather than saw, the bombers above. Fleeing birds increased the confusion, their flocks cloaking the planes from everyone's view. Flimsy buildings shook and collapsed, some from the pressure of the blasts alone. Others burst into flame after impact. Minutes later, as the smoke cleared, the air was filled with the reek of blood and dust from shattered concrete.

The refugees who rushed outside looked on in shock at the chaos.

Within minutes of the deafening explosions, they saw hundreds of victims – Chinese, Japanese and European – lying injured or dying in the streets; almost worse were the body parts scattered around. People wandered the streets of Little Vienna, disorientated and covered with grey debris, some with blood pouring from their noses and ears. Corpses had been flung by the blasts to the top of the fish and fruit stalls of Chusan Road market, and severed limbs lay on the corner of Ward Road. The sickly stench of burning flesh and the tang of metal drifted through the air, powdery from fallen masonry. The eerie silence was broken by the cries of the wounded, and shortly after by Japanese vehicles racing up and down carrying piles of mutilated bodies. One woman saw 'a large truck with the dead, [and her] blood turned to jelly. Hanging hands and feet of the people who had lived a moment ago reminded [her] of [the bombing of] Warsaw.'[3]

Later reports would disagree about the true target of the attack. Some said it was the radio station that the Japanese had placed on Point Road, and which members of the Shanghai resistance knew was vital for their naval manoeuvres. Others thought the bombs had been dropped short of their intended targets, a plane factory in the Eastern district where Japanese aircraft were repaired and refitted, or the Chiangwan Aerodrome north of the city.[4] Whatever the truth, the attack devastated the ghetto.

Inside the Mandarin house on Ward Road, Lisbeth tried to stay calm. She looked out of the window and watched the bombs flying around her, covering her ears from the deafening noise. She and Bruno followed the advice to stand under the door frames. Bruno was not afraid; he had survived worse. But Lisbeth 'was sure the house was going to collapse: that all its walls were going to come down'. The villa's two glass walls rattled as they were shaken by the missiles falling all around. But although the bombs landed close by, none fell on the house. It was completely unharmed: not one glass window or panel of carved wood was damaged.

Her next thoughts must have turned to blind panic as she thought of her mother. Could she possibly bear losing another family member? She must have raced over to the Czech Club, where Edith was living; it had also been spared. Lisbeth was filled with indescribable relief knowing that her mother was unharmed.

She later said that the bombing that day was the only time during the war when she was truly afraid. 'There was one corner in the Designated Area that was an intersection, that was completely destroyed... the day after the bombing, there were hundreds of corpses lying around, because it had hit right smack there and all four corner houses were hit.' The piles of bodies were mostly Chinese, but Lisbeth recognised some of the refugees among the hundreds of dead. Passing one corpse, she stopped in her tracks. She felt nauseous as she realised the remains were those of a customer of the bookshop, someone she had liked very much. The cold statistics of war suddenly hit home.

The ruined corner Lisbeth was standing at was the junction of Tongshan, Kung Ping and East Yuhang Roads. The bombing of all those buildings caused hundreds of deaths, as ten or so Chinese often lived in one room. Close to the junction was the SACRA apartments compound, part of which housed a kindergarten for the immigrants' children. The building took a direct hit, and was almost completely destroyed. Twelve refugees inside were killed instantly, and forty injured; all of its residents were made homeless.[5] The news travelled fast as thought, sending sobbing mothers flying to the rubble, fearing the worst for their infants. Miraculously, their teacher had let the children out early; everyone had left minutes before the building was hit. Other lives were also saved, if indirectly. Yards away, on Muirhead Road, the Salvation Army compound was completely destroyed. This was the building to which the rebellious yeshiva students had refused to be moved – a resistance that had saved their lives.[6]

The reaction of the refugee community was extraordinary – swift and effective, with no sign of panic. The Jews rushed to help both Chinese and Europeans, ignoring the danger from shrapnel and debris still falling around them.[7] Their doctors operated on the injured in the street, some resorting to penknives, or ran to hastily set up medical centres to treat whomever they could. Others scrabbled to dig survivors out of the rubble. Non-medics and the elderly did their bit: when dressings and bandages ran out, women fetched shirts and bed linen to be torn into strips. Older stateless refugees made tea or coffee and gave up pillows and blankets for the wounded. Men stood outside homes in the lanes to guard against looting.

Many of the victims pulled out of the debris were Chinese. Unused to being helped by strangers, as soon as their heads were cleared from the rubble they would ask, 'How much?' One man asked this question, and pulled out his wallet, while his leg was being amputated.[8] Hundreds of wounded people, their bodies shredded by shrapnel, were taken to the yard inside Ward Road gaol, as the attached hospital was already full of patients. Prison guards opened the gates and turned the yard into a makeshift operating theatre. Refugee doctors carried out major procedures with no pain relief – neither morphine nor anaesthesia – on stoical Chinese.

By sunset, all the injured had been treated. Members of the Chevra Kadisha – the sacred burial society – performed their service of love by collecting as many body parts as they could find. They laid out the remains of their dead, with honour and dignity, in rows in the ceremonial hall of Chaoufoong Road's *Heim*. Among the corpses was that of the *Pao Chia*'s chief officer, a doctor named Bader. At the coffin of another, the *Kadisha* authorities lingered a little longer, their heads bowed in respect. They were remembering the popular president of the Juedische Gemeinde, Felix Kardegg.[9]

The next morning, Chinese residents of Hongkew came to the refugees with rickshaws loaded with food and offers of money for the *Heime*. When the cash was politely refused, they brought fruit and cakes instead. The ghetto bombing marked a change in the attitude of many Chinese to the Jews: from being neutral, even occasionally hostile, they now warmed to their uninvited neighbours.[10] The Japanese were also impressed with the refugees' response to the crisis, and their willingness to help others regardless of social standing or race. Encouraged by this, the Jews approached the head of Stateless Refugees Affairs with a hopeful appeal.

But Tsutomu Kubota's admiration did not stretch that far. No, he said, he would not now throw open the ghetto.

The American air raid on 17 July 1945 killed 32 Jewish refugees, 300 Japanese and 4,000 Chinese; the true number of Chinese deaths was never confirmed, and may have been much higher. Over 500 people were wounded, and 700 refugees and thousands of Chinese found themselves homeless yet again.

Lisbeth never breathed a word of this to me. But, years after the bombing, she calmly stated a fact: 'They say that any bomb you can see does not hit you, because the one that hits you is directly above you, obviously.'

How vividly that little word 'obviously' – pronounced 'ahbviously' – brings back my aunt's Californian drawl. I can see her right there before me – the rational, unemotional woman whose reaction to that day first struck me as cold and unfeeling. But now I understand better. By July 1945, the death of one tiny being had sapped all Lisbeth's grief. The death of others, however physically near her, could not move Lisbeth Loewenberg. All her tears had been shed.

33

August 1945: 'Hiroshima Melted'

Only a week after the bombing of Hongkew, the US Fifth Air Force began another wave of air raids. The refugees were now better prepared, finding makeshift helmets. One even used a quilted tea cosy over a discarded, damaged steel helmet for extra protection – a defence so pathetic as to seem laughable, had its use not been in earnest.[1] With each detonation, Lisbeth felt the walls of the Mandarin house shake, but no more bombs fell directly on Hongkew.

Rumours raced through the ghetto. Some were exhilarating – bearing hints of the end of the war; others – of the gas chambers in Europe, with their 'sound machines' to drown out the noise of human screams – were unbelievably shocking. The refugees' reactions teetered from anxiety to jubilation, then back to despair.

On 27 July, city papers reported that America, Britain and China had offered Japan an ultimatum: surrender or face their country's destruction. Shortwave radio broadcast news that the Americans had airdropped thousands of leaflets over eleven cities in Japan, which clearly stated that the US would use 'unprecedented bombardment' unless Hirohito accepted the Allied terms of surrender. Japanese propagandists tried to cover up the threat. They warned civilians not to handle the pamphlets, for they would 'rot the hands of those who touch them and blind the eyes of those who read them!' Many women in the countryside were terrified of the fluttering paper landing around them.[2]

The women's fear of the leaflets was misplaced; far worse was to come. Their emperor ignored the ultimatum.

Ten days later the US Air Force took world-changing action. It was 6 August, the day of Lisbeth and Bruno's first wedding anniversary. But they and the rest of Shanghai only learnt of the strike a day later. In the library on Ward Road Lisbeth heard rumours of a 'horrifying new weapon', and that 'Hiroshima melted'.[3] The hall echoed with anxious chatter. Would Shanghai be next? Or would this new bomb end the war?

On Tuesday 7 August, the newspapers' conflicting reports confirmed the rumours. One Shanghai paper carried a brief notice from Dōmei, the official Japanese news agency. It read:

A new type of bomb was dropped over Hiroshima. Little damage resulted.[4]

The *Shanghai Times* then printed two short articles from America's Central Press Service. The first, from Osaka, read:

Hiroshima Hit: A small force of B-29s at 8.20 o'clock yesterday morning, August 6, raided the city of Hiroshima with high explosives and incendiaries.

The second, from Tokyo, was headlined 'Atomic Bomb', the first time the words had been used in the press. These words were repeated in the text:

President Truman and Prime Minister Attlee announced simultaneously yesterday, Monday, that American aircraft … dropped an 'atomic bomb' on Hiroshima.

No one understood this new missile's true nature. On 9 August, a day so hot and sticky that Shanghai's residents cursed the power cuts that brought their fans to a standstill, Lisbeth read more contradictory reports from Japan. A reprinting of a Tokyo newspaper article included the following words:

A small number of enemy B-29s penetrated into Hiroshima on August 6 shortly after 8am and dropped a number of explosive bombs ... It seems the enemy dropped new-type bombs attached to parachutes which exploded in the air. Although details are still under investigation, their explosive power cannot be made light of.[5]

While confirming that 'a considerable number of houses were destroyed and fire broke out at various places', a second statement from Japan's war minister estimated the damage as only 'fairly great'. Lisbeth and Bruno saw through the understatement. They heard that the Japanese now called the unprecedented weapon *pika-don*: *pika* describing its blinding light, and *don* the booming noise of the blast.

The next day, a Shanghai radio station broadcast news of a second *pika-don*, dropped the previous day on Nagasaki. It was apparently 'not as serious' as the one over Hiroshima.[6] By now all believed Japan had no choice but to surrender. Fuelling this hope was news of Russia's declaration of war on Japan, on 8 August, breaking the two nations' longstanding pact of neutrality. Within days, Stalin's troops liberated the puppet state of Manchukuo from the remains of Japan's Imperial army.

Lisbeth and her husband at last dared to believe that Allied victory was near. At 10.30pm on 10 August, they were woken by the noise of someone in the usually deserted street outside. A woman with dishevelled hair was rushing through the ghetto, shouting at the top of her voice: 'The war is over! The war is over!' They recognised her – a normally well-behaved, quiet person – and looked on, astonished. It was true, she insisted, the Czech Club had confirmed it in a telephone call to the Swiss consulate. Half an hour later, a Russian doctor also heard from the Swiss embassy that peace was possible in a matter of days.[7]

Lisbeth and Bruno rushed outside. The ghetto was packed with people, shouting and laughing, singing songs in German, Yiddish, Polish and Russian. Total strangers – refugees, Russians, Chinese – hugged and kissed one another. Suddenly no one bothered about the curfew, or the blackout, or hushing their voices. Lisbeth joined others brazenly lighting up and smoking in the street, the glowing tips moving like fireflies. Everywhere she looked Lisbeth saw lights blazing, and curtains ripped down; she and Bruno did the same as soon as they returned to Ward Road. They flung open their windows in 'a symbolic show of freedom from the complete darkness of blackout'.

The jubilation continued the next day. Lisbeth and Bruno went out again at 8am to join in the celebrations, and watched in amazement as a crowd gathered round Wayside Police Station. Members of the refugees' camp police, the Ordnungsdienst, and the Zionist organisation Betar, in their respective blue and brown uniforms, announced they were taking over the station. The Japanese inside offered no resistance, packing up and leaving silently as the Jewish nationalists hoisted their blue and white flag up the flagpole.[8]

This victorious gesture proved premature: just two and a half hours later, a group of Japanese officers returned to the Muirhead Road station. 'Very politely they thanked the Blues and Browns for their readiness to assist them', but explained that the war was not over, and they could manage 'nicely for themselves'. As calmly as before, and without hostility on either side, the men exchanged places, and Betar lowered their flag. Other authorities were less tolerant. Later that morning, twenty Japanese gendarmes – the military police from Bridge House – stormed the Soochow Road hospital where a Stars and Stripes and a Soviet flag had been raised. They waved their pistols, shouting and screaming as they rushed to the roof where they ripped down both Old Glory and the Hammer and Sickle, and threw them to the garden below. Other hastily erected Union Jack flags over British-owned buildings soon vanished as well.

Tsutomu Kubota, the director general of the Stateless Refugees Office, was furious. On 13 August, he summoned senior members of the *Pao Chia* for a severe dressing-down, with Ghoya acting as interpreter. As impressed as he had been with the refugees' behaviour in response to the 17 July bombing, he was now 'sorely disappointed'. 'You have dropped the mask and we have seen your true face. You were mistaken. You have been listening to rumours. The war is going on.'[9] He ordered the rebels to stand in the glare of the sun for a day; some were thrown into the Wayside Police Station bunker overnight. Lisbeth and Bruno reluctantly rehung their blackout curtains. The rebellious Europeans were punished. The Japanese tightened their patrols on the ghetto, their gendarmes scrutinising everyone's passes. The war was not over, and the refugees were still prisoners.

But not for much longer.

The end came quietly, two days later. Just after midday on 15 August,* Lisbeth and Bruno were glued to their wireless. Like everyone else in the city, they were listening to a broadcast of the announcement Hirohito was making to his people. Although they could not understand a single word of the speech, they knew what it meant. The emperor was telling Japan that he was accepting the terms of the Potsdam Declaration, and had agreed to surrender. The couple clung to each other – war was finally over! Confirmation in English came a few hours later, and V-J Day – victory over Japan – was declared.

Shanghai's residents living outside the Designated Area began rejoicing at once, hoisting bamboo victory banners and setting off fire crackers by the thousand. But in Hongkew, the celebrations were strangely muted. It was as if the excitement of five days earlier had drained all their energy. One refugee wrote of the community's reaction: 'To-day, hardly a loud word is to be heard. Just quiet congratulating and handshaking.' It was hard for them to show total joy. The war might have ended, and enemy flags been ripped from the buildings on the Bund, but the ghetto and its rules still stood. The new Chinese chief of police, ousting the defeated Japanese, declared: 'the regulations pertaiting [sic] to the District have not been cancelled and are to be strictly obeyed.'[10]

It was over a week before Lisbeth and the other refugees heard the long-awaited news: the ghetto was ending at last! On 22 August 1945, the authorities announced that from the following day, the notification concerning special passes for stateless refugees would be 'hereby withdrawn'. Despite their huge relief at this announcement, Lisbeth and Bruno had to wait two more weeks before seeing any real change. It was only from 3 September, when the first American Goodwill Mission toured the *Heime* and the Designated Area, that the ghetto's signs were removed, and its inmates were freed at last.

Compared to the instant regime change Lisbeth had seen the day after Pearl Harbor, this change in control over the city was barely visible. No Allied troops had arrived, nor any Chinese, so the Japanese army stayed

---

* 14 August in the United States.

on, in the absence of any other force to maintain law and order.[11] But only their foot soldiers remained patrolling the streets. The Japanese high command vanished, along with their secret police. The gendarmes spent days burning documents in huge bonfires outside Bridge House, ensuring no evidence remained that could be later used against them. Then, after stripping the insignia from their khaki uniforms, they silently slipped away in their trucks.[12]

Among the officials who disappeared from the city was Kanoh Ghoya. But before he left, he wandered back into his old domain in the ghetto, saluting and bowing to the crowd gathered round him. The 'King of the Jews' genuinely hoped 'to be friends again' with his former subjects. He was soon cornered by a group of refugee teenagers, who responded by thrashing him soundly.[13] During the beating, the astonished Ghoya protested his innocence, crying, 'So sorry, so sorry,' while insisting 'I never killed anyone! I never killed anyone!'[14] The Jews never saw him again after that.

As one conflict ended, another was beginning. Two Chinese groups were struggling for power, with civil war breaking out between Chiang Kai-shek's Nationalist government and Mao Tse-tung's Communists. The Red Army was already reported to be dangerously close to Shanghai.[15] Lisbeth listened to reports of this new violence with growing unease. Her elation at peace was tempered with realism; she could not ignore the politics around her. Which of China's two forces would win Shanghai, and what might this mean for her family? Who would treat them less badly: the Nationalists who hated all foreigners, or the Communists, who would soon crush private businesses like that owned by her husband?

Throughout the war, the city's Japanese rulers had tolerated those who had fled Hitler, perhaps protected them, even. Although Lisbeth and Bruno had been forced to live in a ghetto, they had never been harmed, but left alone to make the best of their lot. The devil they knew – Kubota and his office for stateless refugees – was no more. What would the devil they did *not* know have in store for European Jews like themselves?

34

September 1945: A New World Order

The Americans arrived in their thousands, a month after V-J day. They would turn the city on its head. And Lisbeth Loewenberg was not impressed.

On 19 September, she and Bruno went down to the Bund to watch the US Marines sail into port. American minesweepers cleared the way for the arrival of around 100 ships. Admiral Kinkaid, commander-in-chief of the US Seventh Fleet, led the convoy in the USS *Rocky Mount*.[1] He and his men had come to take control of the leaderless city, to the delight of the crowd standing by: the Marines disembarked to cheering and tremendous applause. The US Army Air Corps arrived shortly after, acquainting Shanghai's astonished residents with their first jeeps and GIs.[2] The Americans were there at Chiang Kai-shek's invitation; when hostilities ended after Hirohito's surrender, his Nationalist forces were still hundreds of miles from Shanghai. Chiang Kai-shek feared the Communists would get to the city before his army, and was forced to seek help from the Americans.

The 'crazy Yanks' immediately changed the mood of Shanghai. Loud and ebullient, their pockets were stuffed with the dollars they had been unable to spend in Okinawa. They soon replaced the grim austerity of the Japanese occupation with boisterous bonhomie, handing out Hershey Bars, Milky Ways and chewing gum to the city's street children. In those early weeks after V-J day, US and Japanese forces overlapped in the city, a situation that bemused the residents. Arch Carey, a British man who had only recently been released from a Japanese camp, said it was 'almost beyond belief, to see unarmed American GIs and sailors on shore leave step off the pavements to allow Japanese armed guards on patrol to pass'.[3]

Lisbeth watched the US forces, now all over the city, and found their behaviour outlandish. She would never forget seeing them tell the rickshaw men to get out of their vehicles so that they, the GIs, could take their place and pull the pullers instead. It seemed to upset the old colonial world order that she had grown used to after five and a half years in the city.

But many in Shanghai cheered the arrival of the GIs. They boosted the city's flagging economy by spending several million US greenbacks during the first week or so after their arrival.[4] And with them came their food. Surplus CARE packages (from the new Cooperative for American Remittances to Europe) held luxuries that Lisbeth had quite forgotten: beef in broth; bacon and lard; fruit preserves, honey and sugar; even coffee and milk powder. The Americans had prepared these rations for their invasion of Japan, an act the atom bombs had made redundant. The United Nations Relief and Rehabilitation Administration (UNRRA) sent even more. Many of the goods – from tinned food to medical supplies such as blood plasma – ended up on the black market.[5]

Shanghai life was improving in other ways with the Americans. The mostly Russian and Chinese prostitutes, and the city's clubs and bars, welcomed their wealthy new clients. Chinese shopkeepers brought out the silks and fine lingerie that, in leaner times, they had kept hidden, which the GIs sent to their women back home. Café Louis and other restaurants were revitalised by US cash. The arrival of the US military post exchange stores gave work to hundreds of refugees, as well as Chinese labourers. The Americans employed many of the immigrants, training them up as mechanics, or hiring them to create signs and posters for display in the post exchange. The salaries for such work were astronomical by wartime standards. In October 1945, Horst Eisfelder found work at the US Signal Corps Stores, supervising Chinese manual labourers, which paid $70 a month; his first job in 1940 had earned him a monthly wage of only $1–2.[6]

Free to move around the city again, the refugees began to recover. America's Joint Distribution Committee was sending funds to the *Heime* once more, and a branch of their office reopened its doors. Some Europeans found the energy to revive theatrical and other artistic shows. In April 1946, *Die Masken Fallen* – banned five years earlier for being anti-Nazi – was restaged. Its characters depicted Austrian Nazis at the time of the *Anschluss*, 'in all their mendacity and despicableness, their brutality and cynicism, their hypocrisy and violence.' Its 'highpoint' was a concentration camp scene.[7]

In late December, YIVO, a global Jewish cultural organisation, organised an exhibition of paintings and photography in the Shanghai Jewish School with the aim of 'creating a better understanding between Jews and non-Jews'.* Among the pieces displayed were artworks by David Bloch, Fred Schiff, Fritz Melchior and the commercial artist Hans Less.

After the catalogue's title page came a full-page advertisement for one of the show's major sponsors: the Lion Bookshop. Bruno was not an outwardly religious man; he didn't observe the Sabbath, saying that he was the same Jew on Friday as he was on Saturday, that is, a Jew seven days of the week. Despite this, he was a strong believer in the work done by YIVO. Their committee must have recognised his passion for Jewish culture, for that year – 1946 – they appointed him their branch's first president.

The couple's bookshops continued to thrive. The whole community was feeling more optimistic; and the number of pregnancies rose. Just 50 babies had been born in 1945, rising to 114 the following year.[8] But Lisbeth and Bruno were not among the new parents. Who can say why? Maybe Lisbeth could not face another loss. Or perhaps the pair were simply unable to conceive; the mental stress of their past experiences and the uncertainty of what lay ahead for them in China would surely have had a profound impact on them.

---

* YIVO is the Yiddish Scientific Institute, founded in Poland in 1925 for the purpose of archiving Jewish history worldwide.

Above left and above right: Page of the YIVO art exhibition catalogue showing the Lion Bookshop advertisement, December 1946; Lisbeth and Bruno in one of their libraries.

Shanghai's prosperity was starting to crumble. The city was now ruled by a Chinese Nationalist government, which dampened the refugees' elevated mood. Corruption and black-market dealing were back with fresh vigour, and the inflation that had begun at the end of the war was galloping out of control. The government made the Americans pay their staff in Chinese currency, but its value decreased by the hour. People converted their wages back into US dollars as fast as they could. Those who were paid before lunch had a great advantage over those paid in the afternoon, when the exchange rate was already much worse.[9] Stolen army supplies were traded openly in places such as Blood Alley, with people buying goods just to be rid of their cash.

Then, as suddenly as they had come, the Americans were gone. It was May 1946; the US Army superiors had decided to move their headquarters to Nanking.

The Loewenbergs watched them leave with growing anxiety. They knew the city's newly arrived representatives of the Chinese Nationalist government had no interest in foreign-run businesses. How quickly they had forgotten the help they had received from the Americans![10] The mayor, Chien Ta-chun, was delighted to have the British and French Concession territory back in Chinese hands, but cared little for the foreigners who once worked there. When the surviving Westerners were released from the Japanese camps, Chien refused to give them back their jobs in the Municipal Council, throwing thousands out of work. The mayor then set the tone of his rule by hiring a new senior official: none other than the former gangster and opium king, 'Big Ears' Du Yue-sheng. The appointment of this unashamed law-breaker to take over from the Japanese authorities did not augur well for honest foreign enterprise.

Conditions were ripening for a Communist coup. Mao Tse-tung – with whom the Nationalists refused to share power – was amassing his troops. Shanghai's Westerners saw the writing on the wall, and by 1947 their exodus from their adopted home began in earnest. Even Sir Victor Sassoon went, selling off his holdings in the city whose skyline he had shaped so dramatically. As the city's population rose to over 5 million, the chance of making a living looked bleak for the German-speaking refugees. Seven years after Lisbeth had arrived in Shanghai, she and Bruno felt their time was running out. As rumours of Mao's arrival in the port grew stronger, the couple's future in China seemed to be fading.

35

Winter 1947: A Ticket to Freedom

Hongkew's streets were crowded with carts filled with suitcases. It was 1947, and Shanghai's European refugees were leaving in droves. However, unlike their flight almost a decade before, this time they had no clear destination. No city had opened its doors or was willing to take them. Lisbeth and Bruno mulled over the options with friends. Very few would ever return to Austria or Germany. As they learnt more of what the Nazis had done to their friends and families, they vowed never to set foot there again. Many had nothing – or no one – to go back to. Everything they used to call home was now gone – not just the buildings they had once lived in, many of which had been demolished by Allied bombs, but more importantly, their Jewish culture and community, both wiped out by Hitler. What was the point of going back to a homeland with no vestige of 'home'? The refugees braced themselves to start again, to find a new life outside Europe. But where would they go?

A serious obstacle remained, one that brought back memories of their escape from the Reich: almost every country had strict immigration quotas, and visas were hard to come by. Palestine was the only exception. Some of the more idealistic Jews – including many of the young members of Betar, the Jewish nationalist youth movement – were excited by the prospect of a Zionist state to be created in the Holy Lands; at least there, although life would be physically hard, they were sure to be welcomed by their people.[1] But Lisbeth and Bruno dreamt of a country where they could use the English they had now mastered. Their first choice was America. Edith agreed to go along with their plan, although deep down she wanted to go to England. She longed to embrace Ilse, whom she'd not seen for over nine years, and who was now a mother herself. Ilse's first child – a daughter named Claudia – had been born that April: Edith was eager to meet her new granddaughter. For her, these surviving family members were what really meant 'home'.

Entering America was not simple. The annual US quota for immigrants was based on the number of each nationality's citizens who were already resident there, based on numbers from the 1910 census. As very few Austrians had made America their home at that date, the quota was tiny: only 1,413 Austrians were allowed in each year. Lisbeth knew how lucky she was to have married a German; America's German immigrant quota was almost 26,000 (and had hardly been used during the war). But Edith still came under Austria's meagre allotment.

As the humid summer of 1947 began to edge towards autumn, all three went to the American consulate, a neoclassical building on the corner of Peking Road and the Bund, to register for visas. They looked up at the Stars and Stripes fluttering on its sixth-storey tower, and crossed their fingers. Now that they had decided to leave China, they were impatient to go.

Lisbeth and Bruno did not have long to wait: by September their German quota numbers had come up. On 13 September, the couple returned to the consulate. The weather was still uncomfortably warm as they passed through the heavy carved doors to the vice consul's office. They had to supply a sworn affidavit that they would not become a financial burden on their new country. This they did, before the US vice consul, a young American named John Hale Stutesman, Jr.

The pair left the building elated, clutching the precious papers stamped with their immigration visas. The mundane, typewritten sheet was rendered significant by its seal, that of the consulate general, embossed across a photograph of the holder. The head and shoulders shot of Lisbeth, her new signature across the top, showed a serious and confident woman of 25, her dark hair piled high and her brows finely plucked into arches. She was wearing a pearl necklace – perhaps a gift from her husband – and a decorative Chinese jacket, with fashionable wide padded shoulders.

The US paperwork confirmed that Lisbeth Loewenberg was 'at present unable to obtain a valid passport or travel document issued by the country to which she owes allegiance as she is stateless', and that 'she makes this affidavit to serve in lieu of a passport to proceed to the United States'. On the reverse, stamped and signed by the consulate official, was her immigration visa, QIV 9547, under the German quota. Bruno's papers were the same, with the number QIV 9546.

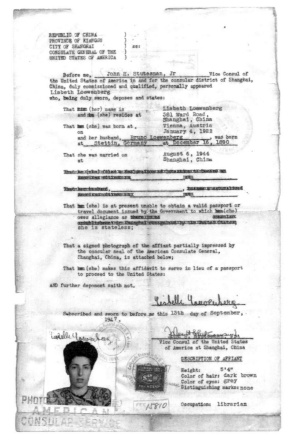

Visa and photograph of Lisbeth, with Stutesman's signature.

The couple returned home to Ward Road. For some time, they had been economising wherever they could, to save the money needed for their tickets to America. Eventually they had the cash, and some over. The reborn American Jewish JDC was offering aid to refugees who wanted to get to the States. For those without savings, the 'Joint' would help pay their passage; for those like the Loewenbergs, the charity processed their payments for travel.

On 24 December 1947, Lisbeth and Bruno went to the JDC offices on 320 Szechuan Road, just south of the creek, to buy their tickets. They left with a small receipt, less than half a foolscap page. Yet its significance was immeasurable: in block capitals it confirmed they were to sail 'FROM SHANGHAI TO SAN FRANCISCO' on a former American troopship, the USS *General MC Meigs*. The date of sailing from Shanghai was 4 January 1948, Lisbeth's 26th birthday.

The cost of the couple's two fares was just $416; the Loewenbergs had continued their thriftiness, opting to sail 'emergency class'.[*]

The USS *General Meigs*' 'List or Manifest of Alien Passengers' for the 4 January departure has many columns giving details of all 'aliens' the US immigration inspector was to expect at the port two weeks later. Column 3 lists 30 names: at places 3 and 4 are Bruno and Lisbeth Loewenberg.[2] Under Column 9, giving nationality, the entry is 'Stateless', as it is for all 30 'alien' passengers. Column 20 is headed 'By whom was passage paid?' Beside every alien's name are the initials AJJDC – the American Jewish Joint Distribution Committee, the charity that had processed all payments in Shanghai.

Column 10, headed 'Race or people', lists each person as 'Hebrew' – the euphemism now adopted to avoid the emotive word 'Jew'.

Edith's visa had still not arrived, but she was listed on the USS *Meigs* manifest as MO-IN-LAW and MO opposite the names of Bruno and Lisbeth, under the column 'nearest friend or relative in country whence alien came'.

Lisbeth and Bruno prepared to leave. Their few possessions made packing simpler; they had little luggage. Once Bruno had sold his stock of

---

[*] Emergency class is the same as third class, which may or may not be the same as steerage; at any rate, in this class passengers were accommodated below decks.

Ship's manifest for USS *General Meigs* with relatives' names, linking Edith to Bruno and Lisbeth, and showing 'Hebrew' given under 'Race or people', January 1948.

books, they owned few items of value. But in Bruno's jacket pocket was a precious letter, collected two days before sailing, from the Central Road office of the Far Eastern Jewish Central Information Bureau for Emigrants. The letter was headed: 'SUFFERERS OF WAR & OTHER CALAMITIES', and read:

Dear Sir,

The bearer of this letter, Mr. Bruno LOEWENBERG and wife are leaving Shanghai for U.S.A. via San Francisco by s/s 'GENERAL MEIGS' on January 3 [sic], 1948.

Mr./Mrs. Loewenberg are Jewish Refugees from Berlin and have been registered with us since their arrival in Shanghai on Sept. 12 39. Their particulars are:

Bruno Loewenberg, born 16.12.1890 at Stettin, book-seller

Wife: Liesbeth nee Epstein, born 4.1.1922 at Vienna

We shall be much obliged if, in case of necessity, you would kindly extend to them any moral and juridical assistance required.

Thanking you in anticipation for your kindness, we remain

Yours very sincerely

M. Birman, Manager

Fareastern Hias*

When she awoke on her birthday, Lisbeth could hardly believe she was leaving the city she had called home for almost eight years, and the mother from whom she had never been parted. With no visa, it was impossible for Edith to travel. Instead, she arrived early in the kitchen on Ward Road to prepare her daughter and son-in-law their final breakfast. After farewells and embraces and tears, Edith shooed the pair off to board their ship. She stayed on to clear away the remains of the meal. Any sorrow Edith felt at their departure was soon dispelled by what happened next. 'Within a second' of the pair going out of the house on Ward Road, 'hundreds of people were coming in'. It was the young Chinese beggars, to whom Bruno had given his coat, seizing their chance. Seeing their benefactor and

---

* Hebrew Sheltering and Immigrant Aid Society.

THE AMERICAN JEWISH JOINT DISTRIBUTION COMMITTEE, INC.
FAR EASTERN OFFICE
320 Szechuen Road, 5th Floor

CHARLES H. JORDAN
FAR EASTERN REPRESENTATIVE

SHANGHAI December, 24, 1947.

R E C E I P T

THIS IS TO CONFIRM THAT THE COST OF PASSAGE FROM SHANGHAI TO
SAN FRANCISCO BY ....emergency.... CLASS HAS BEEN PAID BY :

Mr. Bruno Loewenberg
Mrs. Lisbeth Loewenberg

equiv. of U.S.$ 416.-
(U.S.$ fourhundredsixteen)

The American Jewish Joint Distribution Committee Inc.
FAR EASTERN OFFICE

The Far Eastern Jewish Central Information Bureau For Emigrants

SUFFERERS OF WAR & OTHER CALAMITIES
FOUNDED IN 1917
AFFILIATED WITH HEBREW IMMIGRANT AID SOCIETY OF AMERICA

IN YOUR REPLY PLEASE REFER TO
No. 72274

"HIAS"
SHANGHAI
24. CENTRAL ROAD. ROOM 206

ADDRESS FOR LETTERS
P. O. BOX 1425
CABLE ADDRESS: "HIAS"
PHONE 19290

Mr.H.M. P I C A R D
Representative of "HIAS"
593 Market-Street
San-Francisco, Cal.

Shanghai, January 2, 1948.

Phone: YU kon 0601

Dear Sir,
      The bearer of this letter Mr. Bruno LOEWENBERG and wife
-is/are leaving Shanghai for U. S. A., via S a n – F r a n c i s c o
by s/s "GENERAL MEIGS" on January 3, 1948.

Mr./Mrs. Loewenberg   -is/are Jewish Refugee(s) from Berlin
and -has/have been registered with us since -his/her/their arrival in
Shanghai on Sept.12, 39 -his/her/their particulars are:

      Bruno Loewenberg, born 16.12.1890 at Stettin   book-seller

      wife: Liesbeth nee Epstein, born 4.1.1922 at Vienna

      We shall be much obliged if, in case of necessity, you would
kindly extend to them any moral and juridical assistance required.
Thanking you in anticipation for your kindness, we remain
                              Yours very sincerely

                              M. Birman, Manager.

Receipt for cost of passage from Shanghai to San Francisco, December 1947, and
letter from HIAS, January 1948.

[263   ]

his wife leave with their suitcases, they rushed in from the courtyard, sat down at the table, and ate every scrap of food that was left. They then went through the wardrobe, grabbing whatever Lisbeth and Bruno had left in the closet, stripping it bare 'within one minute'.

On the Bund, Lisbeth looked across at the USS *General Meigs* awaiting her and Bruno. Although similar in size to the *Conte Rosso*, the American troopship bore little resemblance to the Italian liner. And if she expected the two-week voyage ahead to be as luxurious as the one that had brought her to China, she could not have been more wrong.

The sea was terribly rough for the whole fourteen days, and Lisbeth was sick the entire time. She and Bruno soon realised their error in choosing to sail 'emergency class'. They were sharing a dormitory with 100 others, and, even worse for my fastidious aunt, a communal toilet block. She hated using these facilities, where the doors would swing open with each lurch of the ship. At first the nauseous Lisbeth climbed down from her upper bunk bed, to limp across to the row of nightmarish toilets. Eventually even this proved too much, and she stayed in her bunk, throwing up where she lay.

Lisbeth's husband, unaffected by the ship's rolling, remained annoyingly cheerful. He kept encouraging his wife to come up on deck, to look at the sea and the sky. But she refused to move, even for meals. They were not worth the effort. She loathed the cheap, 'barely edible', American food, 'with the same brown gravy over everything'. Far from being served at a cloth-covered table, diners had to line up in messes for cafeteria food – a new experience for Lisbeth, and one she deplored. All she could face eating was jello, also new to her, and a food which she would be unable to look at for decades afterwards. She bitterly regretted not having travelled second class 'in style'.

Back in Chusan Road, Edith had to wait two more months for her visa. But when it finally came, she did not go to America. Now that Lisbeth had left, her thoughts turned to her elder daughter. Edith and Ilse had last been together in Vienna in the summer of 1938. So much had happened since then. She must have longed to compare what they both had gone through. Her daughter had no idea of the Epsteins' wartime experiences during their Shanghai years. How they had survived, among others like them, in a 'Little Vienna', avoiding trouble with the Japanese; how the shared morale of the Jewish community had helped so many overcome hunger, poverty and disease. Most of all, Edith had to tell her daughter about Arnold's life, and premature death.

Edith Epstein chose to make her home in London. In the spring of 1948, she sailed from Shanghai to the port of Southampton in England, her journey again assisted by 'the Joint'. She hoped that Lisbeth would understand the separation, which she knew would disappoint her younger daughter. But Edith had a son-in-law to meet in London, and an eight-month-old grand-daughter to embrace. In five years' time, a second granddaughter would be born, who decades later would reconstruct all these events.

After a turbulent and enervating fortnight at sea, Lisbeth arrived at the Port of San Francisco with her husband on 17 January 1948. As Pier 22 came into view, once again her first sight was an imposing waterside clock tower, this time bearing the American flag.

As the couple disembarked, they were met by members of a Jewish welcoming committee waiting to greet all the 'Hebrews' off the ship. When answering the representative's questions, Bruno admitted that they were not destitute, but had brought the maximum amount of cash allowed out of Shanghai – US$500.

Neither he nor Lisbeth had considered the consequences of their candour. From that moment, they were refused all financial aid. The Jewish representative told them to take a cab downtown to a small residential hotel where the committee had rented some rooms. They had to pay for the cab and the hotel themselves. Lisbeth's ordeal was not over. With the land still swaying under her feet, she felt her dizziness heightened by ruefulness. Had they spent all their savings on better tickets, not only would the journey have been tolerable, but the committee would have offered more than welcoming words. They 'would have been far better off'.

Lisbeth awoke the next day after her first good night's sleep since leaving China. There was no noise from the ship's engines, or the sound of other passengers retching, to disturb her. But that in itself felt unsettling.

When she looked down from her hotel room window, she was as shocked as she had been by her first sight of China. The streets were deserted, and eerily silent – as disconcerting to her as Shanghai's teeming crowds and hubbub had been. A hot wave of anxiety shot through her.

Where were all the people? Had someone declared 'martial law', with a curfew, she wondered? She was 'afraid of the nothingness'.

It was only later that she remembered what day of the week it was: 18 January 1948 was a Sunday. In those days no one walked in downtown San Francisco on the city's day of rest. This shift in her way of thinking marked the first of many adjustments my aunt would have to make in her new American life.

36

1948 to 1956: San Francisco and London: The New Lion Bookshop

During that first night in San Francisco, nothing had been able to disturb Lisbeth's slumber, the sea voyage had so drained her. But after that she tossed and turned on their lumpy mattress as the unfamiliarity of her new city sent her mind racing: the smells and sounds, the shops everywhere, and the well-built, American-accented people – all so different from Shanghai. The Jewish Committee had found a room for her and Bruno in 'a tiny residential hotel on Geary, practically at the corner of Jones', not far from Union Square. For the next few nights, she was barely able to sleep, with the constant noise of the cable car that 'rattled and rattled and rattled' its path up Jones Street.

The couple spent their first week getting the feel of the city. Each day, they explored the neighbourhood on foot, with its trams and steep, leafy streets, returning exhausted each evening. How quickly they became accustomed to this new-found freedom to roam – such a relief after their time cramped within the square mile of the ghetto! But their elation was mixed with trepidation: would they be able to find jobs that paid enough to find a real home of their own? When the hotel owner found out that the Jewish Committee was not paying the couple's rent – which they did for most people – he lowered it. But their one room was just a stopgap.

After her second week in the city, Lisbeth decided her vacation had gone on long enough. She scoured the newspapers for any opportunities for work, finally setting off from the hotel to search directly. Shanghai had instilled in her a strong sense of enterprise, and the power of self-reliance. No 'family connections or rich friends' could help you in China, she knew. She expected no favours; one's success or failure depends on 'your true ability ... or survival instincts ... or enterprise, whatever you want to call it'. If you were unhappy, it was wrong to blame conditions around you; you had to blame yourself. My aunt also made no secret of the arrogant side of her nature – her view that her brain was sharper than most people's. She thought it was Shanghai that made her arrogant; however, she also mused that she might have been this way wherever she had lived.

On her very first day of walking downtown, Lisbeth's self-confidence proved justified. She found a 'fantastic job as a typist and file clerk' in a publisher's office. She was taken on by *Collier's* magazine – an American weekly famous for publishing short stories by writers like Ray Bradbury and Roald Dahl (perhaps fortunately for Lisbeth, decades before the latter's antisemitism first came to light). Her pay was $30 a week.

The office employed representatives to find new subscribers – not only to *Collier's*, but to *Cosmopolitan* and *Good Housekeeping*. Lisbeth's job was to process the orders the salesmen brought back. This led to her second shock in the bizarre world of America. As she filed the subscribers' information, she could not believe what she was reading. People were giving the address at which they expected to live in one or even two years' time. This was a certainty that she might have possessed in her early childhood, but was now utterly unfamiliar. She asked her colleagues: 'How do people know that after one year they will still be at that address?' If Lisbeth had ever had any sense of permanence, Shanghai had erased it. Now she could barely believe in what might happen tomorrow, let alone two years ahead. Decades later, she confessed that she never overcame this feeling. 'It's all just transitory,' she said.

Within a few weeks of their arrival, Bruno also found work. On 5 April 1948 he signed a contract with an M. Romiginese, the owner of a small bookshop at IIII Polk Street, just south of San Francisco's Nob Hill. The

French Bookstore was on the ground floor of a three-storey Victorian redbrick. Bruno was to lease the 'northern one-half of [the] bookstore premises', agreeing to buy 'all books written in the English Language, of not less than 400 volumes, now on said premises, for the sum of One Hundred (100.00$) Dollars.' The lease was for up to one year, at a monthly rent of $75. Rominginese would continue selling the store's French, Spanish and Italian language stock, leaving his new business partner the rest.

After reading Lisbeth's interviews, and then studying the contents of her wooden box, I was sometimes surprised at which documents appeared to have been lost or discarded. I could not find her highly decorated wedding certificate inside the box with the sunflower clasp. It turned out that she had donated it, along with the document Ghoya had signed granting her permission for her name change, to 'some kind of a museum'. Yet I did find the typed contract for my uncle's first San Francisco venture. On the back Bruno had scribbled some notes for its publicity. He was never able to see a blank corner of a page without adorning it with one of his doodles. Under the heading 'LION BOOKSHOP' are the words: 'Rendezvous with books'; 'Books for Hobby and Gifts – for Study and Success'. Above, in his distinctive spidery handwriting:

> Books are <u>Textbooks</u>
> more: are <u>Hobby</u>
> more are <u>Friends</u>
> more are <u>Life</u>

This could have been Bruno's epitaph.

Friends were central to his happiness, and he would continue to make new ones throughout his long life.

Within months of arriving in England in 1948, Edith – still charming and good looking at the age of 54 – had found a new husband. Egon Fuchs was a Jewish widower, a 60-year-old former doctor of law from Czechoslovakia, with a penchant for Churchillian cigars.[1] According to their marriage certificate, the two likely met as neighbours; he lived at 34 Clarendon

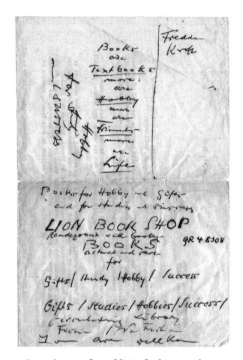

Bruno's notes for publicity for his new shop.

Road, Notting Hill, and she was at number 85. The wedding took place at Kensington Registry Office on 30 October 1948. My father Josef was a witness.

Back in California in late 1952, Lisbeth was soon to turn 31 and her husband had just celebrated his 62nd birthday. The pair were still childless. But around the same time, in London, her sister Ilse was pregnant again.

I think back on this time, and wonder how my aunt could have stayed so far away from Ilse despite all they had both been through. She never once visited the sister she had not seen since the age of sixteen. True, Lisbeth was generous with gifts. She sent packages of smart clothes to London, and she kept all Ilse's letters in the box with the sunflower clasp. Ilse wrote in one that she and Josef had 'decided on Julian for a boy or Rachel for a girl', and thanked Lisbeth for the gift for little Claudia – 'a lovely suit ... very elegant' – and two coats for herself. She went on: 'I wish you could come here some time – it would be nice to have a sister here!' How those words press on my heart.

By not coming to London during her first years in America, whatever her reasons, my aunt never saw her sister again. In 1953, Ilse took her own life.

Being a mother was something Ilse took unbelievably seriously, and which she never felt she could do well enough. At some point in my twenties, my father gave me a notepad with a green and red art deco cover. It had belonged to Ilse, and was crammed with her notes in green ballpoint, from 1951 until a few months before her death. I kept it, unread, in my desk for years. It felt wonderful to know that I possessed this single object that she had touched, and written in with passion. But I hardly dared open it, or scour its pages for clues to understanding her nature.

It always felt too painful to go through the notepad that held my mother's thoughts. Only now, as I am piecing together her story, have I plucked up the courage. The green writing shows that in 1951 Ilse began attending evening classes on child psychology. Claudia must have been about to start school that autumn. Ilse's first entry, on 12 February 1951, read: 'Let ch[ild] decide which school! Don't be ambitious for child!' As I flipped through the pages towards the end, my heart beat faster and my mouth went dry. What would be her final entry?

It came – this time in pencil – on 21 May 1953. Three days after she wrote her last letter to Lisbeth. She was seven months pregnant, and her evening classes had changed from child psychology to philosophy. I did not learn anything more of her state of mind from this notebook. Then very recently I was given something else that did exactly that. A document that contained more than I ever wished to know. Just typing that sentence has made my throat close up and my stomach churn.

I know you cannot save a person who is determined to end their life. Ilse made her decision around two weeks before she died, according to the date on a letter she left for Josef. I remember being told once that those final days were some of the calmest of her adult life. I knew that the letter existed, but had never seen it or knew its fate. Until August 2022, when Claudia – suffering from cancer and wishing to put things in order – unexpectedly handed it over to me. It took me a week to dare open the small envelope that clearly held many pages. My younger son was by my side.

I know that Ilse was suffering from an acute mental illness, but the words in that familiar writing still proved unbearable. Her thirteen-page letter repeated over and over her regret at her decision to have a second child. How she wished she could have put the clock back, and been dissuaded from her desire to avoid Claudia being an only child. 'I felt she should have a sibling – but now – too late – I see she would have been much better off alone.' I had often wondered how much support Edith offered my mother at this time. Ilse's words – I hope she will forgive me for including them here for all to see – gave the answer. In reference to her decision to end her life, she told Josef: 'My mother will say it "runs in the family" – don't be too hard on her. I am sorry to hurt her, but I do wish she had dissuaded me – but then … she was as flippant about it as about most things – I wish she had talked to me seriously.'

The envelope had 'J. 3.10' on the front in my mother's hand. Then in pencil, she had added – 19.10: the day she must have chosen to carry out her decision. My father only received this 'evidence' back from the coroner's office six months later, on 14 April 1954, in response to his request for the letter's return.

Before Ilse's death, my grandmother may have felt pulled in two directions with her two daughters living so far apart. Two years later, after the loss of a third child – albeit this one an adult – she was still unsure where to spend the rest of her life. On 1 November 1955, Edith wrote to Lisbeth, who was still begging her to come and live in the United States: 'The doubts about coming have nothing to do with my great love for you. Please do write soon.'

In 1956, Edith's new husband, the cigar-smoking doctor of law, died from a heart attack.

Two granddaughters, aged three and nine, who had lost their birth mother, were no longer enough to keep *Ohe* in London. She agreed to go out to California to join Lisbeth. I am sure she could see that, with my father's marriage to Ruth, Claudia and I were in the good hands of a caring new mother. Yet with two young granddaughters and a grandson now myself, I find it hard to understand how our grandmother could have left us. With her departure, the fragile threads connecting us to our birth mother's family were weakened further still.

37

Love, Art and Family:
Here, There, Then and Now

Edith would never become a grandmother again. After the baby they lost in Shanghai, Lisbeth and Bruno never had another child.

But my aunt had others to love. She had Bruno, as well as her mother, who now lived nearby. And by the mid-1960s Lisbeth finally started travelling to Europe. She often came to see us, her two nieces. She even mentioned us in her last interview with another Holocaust historian, Patricia Kalman: 'My sister stayed in England, she married there and had two children but unfortunately, she has passed away. I go every year to England because her two daughters, my nieces, they are the only relatives I have. They are lovely girls.' This revelation took me my surprise, and brought tears to my eyes.

Bruno usually accompanied her on her visits to England. The couple never spoke of their past, and Lisbeth's impassive nature made her unfathomable to us. But over the years I came to understand my uncle's bittersweet humour, and to appreciate his unique character, especially his warmth and sociability.

In San Francisco, Bruno's charisma continued to be as powerful as ever. Over the next 30 years, he would carry on with the work that he loved, opening a series of book stores in the city. His last – Bruno's Bookshop – was on 1347 Polk Street, not far from his first. I remember visiting it: a treasure trove crammed with antiquarian books, maps and prints. The walls of their house were vibrant with lithographs by Miró, Chagall and Buffet – even some prints by Picasso – as well as other artists I could not name. Antiquarian maps hung on the walls or were propped against bookshelves packed with hard- and paper-backed volumes; weighty art books covered most of their coffee table's surface. On the mantelpiece sat ornaments: carved jade birds, gilt table decorations, bronze ducks and a heavy-branched candelabrum. And there, in a corner of the room, stood the one piece of furniture I had always admired – the lacquered Chinese-style cabinet.

Bruno surrounded by an attentive crowd of friends in Lands End park, San Francisco.

Everyone in the couple's neighbourhood and downtown near his shop knew the old man with the thick silver hair and strong German accent. Bruno continued to attract attention wherever he went. Lisbeth, meanwhile, remained 'in his shadow, her virtues unseen', in the words of Richard Feldman. As a young drama student from New York in the late 1970s, Richard was the couple's lodger, almost their surrogate son. In the evenings, after studying or performing in a show, he would join my aunt and uncle for a drink and snacks. He and Bruno would talk philosophy over shots of vodka in the living room, or he would chat with Lisbeth in the kitchen, eating chocolate and drinking tea.

In 2017, I met with Richard in New York City. Now a faculty member at the Juilliard, he was happy to reminisce about Lisbeth and Bruno. As we compared memories of my aunt, Richard's words were kinder than mine.[1] Although he agreed with my description of her as 'cool', 'aloof' and 'complex', he used 'discerning' over my 'haughty'. He did agree that she was more 'intellectual' than 'feeling', and acknowledged her sharp intelligence. According to him, my aunt's clear lack of interest, and skill, in cooking, never changed. Apart from lightly boiled eggs, the only dishes she ever made were an oil-drenched avocado salad and a rather idiosyncratic – and not entirely tasty – beef and parsnip roulade. I was also interested to learn more about her and Bruno's relationship. Having lived with the couple for so long, he understood it better than I could. He was certain there was real love between them: 'Their closeness – as different as they were in their personalities – was palpable. They called each other by their pet name of *Äffchen*, which means "little monkey".' Once he mentioned that word, the memory of hearing them say it to one another flooded back.

I believe Richard was one of the very few people in whom my aunt truly confided. When I asked him about her tragic fall as a teenager in Vienna, he said she had told him that her disappointment was so intense that if she could not dance that night, she would rather die. It made me wonder whether she was more like Ilse than either of the sisters realised, since Ilse later made the same choice when she, too, found life unbearable.

Richard also gave me unexpected insights into my uncle's almost overpowering nature. He mentioned Bruno's 'shadow' a number of times, the man whose 'sun shone so brightly' he made his wife seem 'invisible'. He described my uncle as 'a glorious, magnificent human being'. Whether in a gallery downtown or at a restaurant sipping his soup, he always drew people's glances. They were sure this distinguished looking character, who in his late eighties still had a 'great head of hair', was someone famous, he looked so special. Richard told me how strangers would approach Bruno as he sat at his usual seat in his favourite diner as if he were some sort of omniscient guru who understood the true meaning of life; they would say things like, 'you know the answer, don't you?'

Richard mentioned something that explained the longevity of his own relationship with my aunt. As he and she cleared away the supper, they would 'retire back to the kitchen'. There they would confide their shared feelings, of being 'two "shadow people" who formed a friendship', living with Bruno, the man who cast such a bright light.

Meanwhile, Richard continued, Lisbeth stood by, often silent, efficiently keeping the couple's life running smoothly. By now proficient with bookkeeping and accounts, my aunt ran the couple's finances, taking control of their joint funds and always ready to top up her husband's bank balance to fund his latest impulse buy of artwork or books. The frugality Shanghai imposed on them seemed to affect them differently, although they might have had these opposing traits anyway. While Bruno never counted the cents, Lisbeth was always careful with money. Throughout her life, she felt reassured knowing she had money in the bank, even if she was reluctant to actually spend it. She was never extravagant, and in later years, when comfortably off, rarely treated herself.

The only exception I recall was Lisbeth's generosity to my sisters and me on our birthdays. These were always marked – if a week or more late – with gifts mailed from America. Magical parcels would arrive, containing nylon dresses frothing with flounces and frills, sparkling with metallic thread and velvet bows. One year, when a Disney film had revived interest in the American folk hero, Davy Crockett, we were thrilled to find a child-sized fringed waistcoat, along with a fur hat complete with stripy racoon tail. A photo shows my bemused baby half-sister with the hat on askance, beside me in the waistcoat (and is that a gun in my hand?). In later years, the clothes were replaced with cheques for significant sums of dollars.

Richard also related the story of how the couple once made a trip back to Germany. In the 1960s, Bruno had returned to Berlin, Lisbeth by his side. It was a difficult journey. He was collecting reparations from the government for the loss of his German home and business. In a Kafkaesque building, down many hallways and corridors, Bruno eventually found a man at a desk. The man said: 'Ah yes, we have been waiting for you.' And so, 25 years after being persecuted by the Nazis, Bruno was awarded compensation for his losses. He used this, Richard told me, to improve his latest Californian bookshop.

The three Meller sisters in the Davy Crockett outfit and frothy
dresses from the US, 1956 and 1957.

Bruno's light shone until the end. He sold his last business in April 1970,
his eighty-first year, for the sum of $3,500. He continued making friends
until the very end of his life. One of the last of these was an art dealer
named Doniphan Blair, who owned San Francisco's Ancient Currents
Gallery. In his retirement, my uncle had begun painting in oils, inspired by
the Land's End scenery that lay just beyond his door. His home soon filled
with vibrant, primitive landscapes and portraits of tortured, fear-haunted

Lisbeth at home.

souls. Some now decorate the walls of our Cambridge home. Doniphan was among the first to exhibit Bruno Loewenberg's work. The gallery owner was fascinated by this energetically creative man, nearing 90, whom he described as 'very hip'. The two would meet in the afternoon for shots of vodka or schnapps – 'three, even more sometimes'. Blair was amazed that Bruno could 'drink [him] under the table'.[2]

Doniphan Blair went on to interview Bruno, in 1982 publishing an in-depth article in the *Clinton St Quarterly* about the refugee's life. My uncle proudly sent me the piece, entitled 'Bruno Loewenberg: Artist and Survivor'. Its tagline read: 'In the end art is freedom.' During the interview, Bruno described his time in Buchenwald, recalling detailed memories of starvation and Nazi cruelty that were almost too painful to read.

Not long before, in 1977, Edith died in America.

I have little memory of spending time with our grandmother, Ohe. Of course we met, when I was a small child, and later in America. I still treasure a little trinket box that she gave me. Decorated with a Chinese dragon and mythical winged creature in painted coral on ebony-coloured wood, it sits beside my photograph of Ilse smiling. But I have no recollection at all of her departure from London. I was only three, while Claudia was nine. My sister felt the loss of *Ohe* much more keenly than I did. She was close to her grandmother, who made her feel special, as all first grandchildren are. Once again my elder sister had been abandoned. How hard it must have been to face yet another bereavement, coming just three years after our mother's death.

Our social butterfly grandmother found her third husband, Fred S., soon after arriving in San Francisco. Previously married and with a family of his own, he was a man to whom neither my sister nor I ever warmed; we did not trust him. The couple came to see us at least once, but I have little memory of their visits, apart from the time when their relaxed attitude in the lounge at San Francisco airport made them miss the flight to London. They arrived at our home much later than expected, to my father's great annoyance. I sense that Josef never felt close to his mother-in-law – in his eyes, a frivolous, unintellectual woman. He certainly never warmed to her last spouse.

On Edith's death after a short but severe bout of flu, our misgivings about Fred were confirmed. Edith's will bequeathed all her money and possessions to him, for sharing out between himself and the couple's grand-children. But Fred kept everything for his own family. He passed nothing of Edith's personal belongings or money on to us, not a single black-and-white photograph from Vienna, no letters from Arnold, nor a single bracelet or ring. It is the loss of any family photo albums that makes me saddest. I have jewellery of my own, but I would exchange it in a moment for something

Edith Epstein, date unknown.

personal from my grandmother's past. The loss of these last threads of inheritance, like my aunt's silence and my mother's death, robbed me of another link to my family's roots.

My uncle Bruno was blessed with a longer life than Edith. Despite all the hardships he had lived through, his health endured, as did his positive outlook. He seemed content with life, and never lost his faith in humanity. He stayed grateful for life's simplest pleasures: the beauty of a gnarled and windswept tree; a good cup of coffee or a bowl of clam chowder; listening to classical music with those he loved. And when he reached his ninetieth birthday, in December 1980, he decided to mark the occasion with a party.

At the end of the celebrations, the man who still radiated charisma sat surrounded by admirers. Bruno rose to make a speech I shall never forget. At that time I knew so little about what he had been through. So when he raised a glass to acknowledge those present, I was shocked to hear his usually strong voice start to falter, and to see his dark eyes overflowing with tears. Bruno began his speech with the words: 'Dear friends – including those who are only in spirit here with us.' I had no idea then that his entire family – among them the adored sister whose actions had released him from Buchenwald, and doubtless saved his life – had been killed at Auschwitz. Nor did I know, as Bruno then confessed, that he had felt guilty his whole life for being the family's only survivor.

My uncle then quoted a maxim that had hung in a framed panel on his parents' living-room wall. The words had been crafted in pokerwork by his sister in 1905. They read: *'Sorg, aber sorge nicht zu viel, es geht doch wie Gott es haben will!'* Which he translated as: 'Worry, but worry not too much, everything goes the way God wants it to go, after all.' He then told a story about apologising to a friend for his slow walking, due to his bad left leg. The friend – his 'Jewish guru' – had responded with a Hebrew phrase that meant 'Well, you still have a good right one.' My uncle smiled as he ended the speech: 'That is the way to look at the world! Let us enjoy what we have, our time together, this evening and the future to come.'

On 29 October 1986, after a brief stay in hospital, and a few weeks short of his 96th birthday, Bruno died. He attributed his lifelong youthful attitude and creativity to his 'basic naïvety and spontaneity' – traits he believed essential for continuing to make art, 'independent of old age'. These qualities are

Bruno and the author at his 90th birthday party,
San Francisco, December 1980.

ones 'born into you: you can't acquire them later.' His love for art, he added,
contributed to his long life, and his survival of so many horrors, 'because the
reality of things doesn't touch you, at least not as much as your own fantasies'.

Eleven years after Bruno's death, another nonagenarian died in San
Francisco. It was Ho Feng-Shan, the man who had saved my family and
countless other Viennese Jews in the late 1930s. In 2001, Yad Vashem, the Israeli
organisation dedicated to remembering the Holocaust, awarded the 'Chinese
Schindler' the title of Righteous Among the Nations. I'm sure Bruno would
have approved of this accolade, but as far as I know the two never met. How
they would have talked: so much to say about what I imagine was a shared
philosophy of life, and so many reminiscences gathered from their ten decades.

Bruno had his art for protection. Lisbeth had her armour of detachment.
With the death of her husband of more than 40 years, she was left alone in
her third and final homeland. She stayed on in Seal Rock Drive, surrounded
by their books and paintings. She encouraged me to visit, which I did. On
one such trip, she amazed me by raising the subject of our family. This was
when Lisbeth told me of her aunt Lidzie, whose early death had led to her
uncle Herbert's suicide. Then, out of the blue, she went on to say what a
'wonderful job' my stepmother Ruth had done in raising Claudia and me.
I agreed, almost speechless. These words, from a woman who had barely
experienced motherhood herself, touched me deeply. But then she fell silent,
and yet again I could not summon up the courage to ask her about Ilse.

Bruno.

Lisbeth's health began to fail soon after Bruno's death. Although she did have friends, most had come through her husband. Her lodestone was gone: the much older man in whose orbit she had revolved for so long. She developed various ailments, including cancer and a haematological disorder that required regular trips to a clinic. By my last visit, in the autumn of 1995, she was shockingly frail. Neither the intranasal oxygen delivered from a cylinder she dragged around on a trolley, nor her monthly visits to the clinic for red blood cell transfusions, could imbue her with colour or life. Eventually she had to be cared for at home, and hired a young Russian nurse and her boyfriend.

And so, ten years after Bruno, on 7 September 1996, Lisbeth too was gone, bequeathing me the cabinet and her Chinese box. Was her gift to me as deliberate as her other actions? Did she know the documents and photographs inside would lead to my discovery of her story? If so, I hope she would approve of these efforts to bring her voice to life, as well as that of Ilse's. It is my gift back to her, the aunt I always found so difficult to love. Yet how much I had wanted to be able to, in the absence of her sister!

I'll never truly understand how my aunt and mother could go as far as to carry out their self-destructive acts. Or what kept Lisbeth so apart from Ilse, in both body and soul. The two sisters never saw each other again after 1938, when they said their goodbyes in Vienna. But I hope I have at last helped to reunite them, here in the pages of this book.

Epilogue: Shedding
Tears in Shanghai

When I first undid the sunflower clasp on the gift my aunt left me, I had no idea how far the box's contents would take me. It took my sister Claudia and me thousands of miles from home, but brought us closer than we had been for many years.

It happened one evening after a day's sightseeing in Shanghai. We had been awestruck by the city's famous landmarks, starting with the Bund and a visit to Sassoon's old Cathay Hotel.* From its roof garden, over ten storeys above the Bund, we looked down upon the sweeping promenade by the Huangpu.† Its unmistakeable skyline had barely changed since our aunt had stepped off the *Conte Rosso* almost 65 years before. Claudia and I were as impressed as Lisbeth had been by the row of stately banks, hotels and offices. But the view on the opposite side of the river, in Pudong, had dramatically changed. Gone were the industrial *godowns* and factories that our aunt had seen. In their place blossomed the space-age skyline of 21st-century Shanghai. The two rose-pink spheres of the Oriental Pearl Tower gleamed seductively, its needle-sharp antenna at the top thrusting higher than any other structure in China. The city was looking firmly ahead,

---

* Now the Fairmont Peace Hotel.
† The new name for the Whangpoo.

not back. As we discovered on our search for our family's old addresses, little now remained of the 1940s streets that Lisbeth had known.

The novelty of being in China – its utter foreignness – and the need to cram so much into this short visit overwhelmed us. One evening, as my sister and I lay collapsed on a bed with large cocktails in our hands, Claudia began to speak about our mother. For the first time in years we properly talked about Ilse, and my sister shed the only tears I had ever seen her weep for the mother we both had lost. This unusual revealing of her feelings greatly endeared my sister to me, an unexpected outcome of our quest to find Lisbeth. I treasured that moment long after.

My second journey to Shanghai brought me face to face with my aunt, even though she had been dead for over twenty years. I visited the Refugee Museum, and was studying its collection of memorabilia. Stylish glass cabinets set out countless documents and photographs, as well as personal items: passports and spectacles, cutlery and battered luggage, wedding certificates. All were displayed in replica rooms of the homes of Jewish refugees.

As I walked around with my Chinese guides, James Yang and Yun Ye, gazing at historic images of life in Shanghai and reading about the immigrants' experiences, I was astonished to recognise one of the refugees on display. 'But this is my aunt!' I exclaimed, goosebumps along my arms. Under the heading 'Sleeping on the Sofa in the Sitting Room', was Lisbeth's name above some text.[*] I quickly recognised it as an extract from her interview with the Holocaust historian, Steve Hochstadt. But nothing had prepared me for the shock of seeing her life on show like this.

A few minutes later, something else shook me.

Just as we were about to leave, a group of schoolchildren, aged thirteen or fourteen, arrived in the museum courtyard. They were wearing identical jackets in two-tone navy and sky blue, scarlet bandanas around their necks. Their teacher, a young woman, approached me. She told me her class was studying wartime Hongkou, when the Jews and Chinese had lived together under Japanese rule. The museum's curator – a charming man, called Jian Chen, to whom I had explained my personal connection to the Shanghai

---

[*] In fact, it was misspelled as Lisheth.

refugees – must have told her about my relatives, for she asked if one or two of her students might interview me. They would love to practise their English, she added. How could I possibly refuse?

Only two boys dared approach me. I noticed that our chat was being videoed, and a microphone used, which made me as nervous as they were. The first boy must have been confused about my age, for he asked what it had been like living here during the war. I explained that it had been my aunt and grandmother who had been the refugees, not me. I thought back to what I knew, and did my best to answer him, putting myself in their shoes. Then the other youth picked up the microphone. He asked how my grandmother had felt when passing the Japanese guards. 'Was she frightened?' he said, dark eyes shining.

The boy's question took me by surprise. It was deceptively simple, and one whose answer I should so dearly have loved to know. But, like so much of my family's story, I had had to fill in its gaps with imagination and guesswork. I turned away for a moment, then described how I thought Edith would have reacted to such intimidating men: by keeping out of their way. That seemed to satisfy him, and he rejoined his classmates with a bounce in his step.

Chinese students at the Shanghai Jewish Refugees Museum, 2017.

I suddenly felt ashamed. Had I only now, at this moment, begun to truly understand my relatives' experience, and feel the first glimmer of real empathy for them? My reading and research over the previous two years had given me countless facts and statistics. But this boy had stripped the data clean away, and gone right to the heart of their story. He made me understand their lives as vulnerable refugees much more clearly.

I set out writing this book viewing my aunt as someone whose ability to 'feel' I had questioned. But the man to whom she had spoken in most depth knew her better. I met Steve Hochstadt on a visit to Berlin, to talk about Lisbeth. He first met her in April 1989, when he accompanied some Shanghai survivors on a tour of China, starting with Shanghai. He began interviewing her during the trip, and continued later that year at her home in San Francisco. The aim of the group's visit was 'to renew their ties with this city of refuge', and to celebrate a Seder* there. The Chinese government had granted access to sites normally closed to tourists, such as the Ohel Rachel synagogue. Several journalists and a cameraman were also on the tour, to record key events along the way.[1]

Steve had clearly enjoyed my aunt's company, not just in Shanghai but in Beijing and even at the Great Wall. It was there he had taken the photo of the 67-year-old Lisbeth that he included in his book.

One afternoon in Berlin, we enjoyed a meal together. Then Steve showed me a short letter he had written to my aunt following their tour of Hongkou.

A line in his letter to Lisbeth jumped out immediately. 'Did you tell me a secret which you wish me to keep, as I have kept it until now?' I skipped over other phrases – 'tragic memory' and 'you confided in me with some purpose' – to read what followed. 'After you spoke to me, I thought you had talked in a moment of weakness. Later I changed my mind: it took a moment of <u>strength</u> to bring the memory to words.' Before I had time to absorb any more, Steve explained what had happened.

As the former refugees were driven through the Hongkou streets, which they had not seen for over 40 years, different cries arose from the minibus: 'I

---

* A Passover dinner.

lived there, the second alley from the corner …' 'Over here on the left used to be markets …' 'That's the market where I used to go with my mother …' 'That's Bubbling Well Road …'

But Lisbeth stayed silent.

Then the group got out of the vehicle to walk through the streets in the light Shanghai drizzle. They came to the camp at the former Ward Road, where 'the rain and history darkened ordinary buildings'. While others began to move back to the bus, to get out of the rain, my aunt lingered in the courtyard, 'immobilised by her memories'. Steve asked if she had lived there. 'No.' 'Visited friends?' he asked. 'No,' was the answer again. Then my aunt 'paused and found strength'. 'There had been a hospital for Jews here in the compound,' she told him. She went on to explain that 'there her father and son both had died'. Steve knew that this revelation had been costly. As she spoke, Lisbeth's eyes filled with tears. The historian embraced her.

The cameraman who was accompanying the group noticed this, and came over to ask what had happened. He turned on his cine camera. Lisbeth explained that in that building her father had died of cancer. Then she added in a matter-of-fact tone, 'He would have died anywhere the same.' She would not repeat what she had said of her son. 'A few minutes later,' Steve related, 'the cameraman returned. The camera had not worked, he told her, and she had been so emotional, would she do it again?'

So my aunt did feel passionately, as I had glimpsed occasionally in San Francisco; she just kept her feelings well hidden. I should not be surprised by her uncommunicative nature. Lisbeth had lived through so much pain and upheaval, and loss. Nazi persecution uprooted her from her middle-class European home, tearing away all ties with her birthplace. And before that, a teacher's harshness had driven her to her desperate suicidal act. How could I have thought her unemotional?

People suppress horrific memories for their sanity's sake, avoiding the revival of such disturbing experiences. And so their history is lost; a generation hides its grief, and the next is too self-absorbed to enquire. Yet Lisbeth's gift, the box with the sunflower clasp, has done the talking for her. It offered me the ties to my heritage that were snatched away by Ilse's death and my aunt's silence. It has brought me a closer understanding of not just these two women's stories, but of those of the rest of my Jewish family, and the places they called home. It even spurred me on to claim my Austrian passport. I hope by uncovering this unspoken tale, I have strengthened the fragile threads of my family's history, bequeathing to my children and grandchildren a better understanding of their Viennese roots. And if this book has given one single reader an ounce more empathy with those who might seek to end their own lives, or refugees forced to flee their homeland, or those still targeted by the scourge of antisemitism, then my time writing it has been well spent.

Notes

CHAPTER 1: VIENNA, JUNE 1937: THWARTED AMBITION

1. According to Martin Gilbert's *The Dent Atlas of the Holocaust*, (London: Dent, 1993), p. 22, on the date of the *Anschluss*, 13 March 1938, Vienna was home to 176,034 of Austria's 183,000 Jews.

2. Matzo Island: https://www.upi.com/Archives/1985/01/13/Viennas-vanished-Jewish-quarter/4132474440400/.

3. *Sino-Judaica: Occasional Papers of the Sino-Judaic Institute* (Volume 3, 2000); Kalman, Patricia, *The Shanghai Ghetto: Two Accounts of Refugees in China*, p. 55.

4. Roth, Joseph, tr. Michael Hofmann, *The Radetzky March*, (London: Granta Publications, 2002), Kindle edition.

5. Kerstin Timmerman, of *Vienna Walks*, researched our family using various sources, including the Israelite Community Archive, the National Archives in the UK (https://www.nationalarchives.gov.uk/) and the LDS-Archive (Latter Day Saints who run www.familysearch.org), resulting in a 24-page document.

6. Elon, Amos, *The Pity of It All: A Portrait of Jews in Germany 1743–1933*, (London: Allen Lane, 2002), p. 224.

7. Hayes, Peter, ed., *How Was It Possible?: A Holocaust Reader* (Lincoln, Nebraska: The Jewish Foundation for the Righteous, 2015), p. 31.

8. Scheyer, Moriz, *Asylum* (New York: Little, Brown and Company, 2016), p. 263.

CHAPTER 2: VIENNA, MARCH 1938: A WORLD FALLS APART

1. Scheyer, *Asylum*, p. 5.

2. Mercer, Derrik, *Chronicle of the Twentieth Century* (Paris: Jacques Legrand, 1988), p. 494 and Scheyer, *Asylum*, pp. 5–6.

3. Scheyer, *Asylum*, p. 7.

4. Kalman, Patricia, interview with Lisbeth in *Sino-Judaica: Occasional Papers of the Sino-Judaic Institute* (Volume 3, 2000), *The Shanghai Ghetto*, p. 56.

5. Holocaust Encyclopedia: https://encyclopedia.ushmm.org/content/en/article/the-nuremberg-race-laws.

6. Scheyer, *Asylum*, p. 9.

7. Scheyer, *Asylum*, p. 10.

CHAPTER 3: VIENNA AND PRAGUE, MAY TO AUGUST 1938:

A FLIPPANT REMARK

1. *Jewish Telegraphic Agency News*, Vol. IV, No. 47, 25 May 1938: http://pdfs.jta.org/1938/1938-05-25_047.pdf?_ga=2.30067967.1745450759.1627993199–942038819.1627993199, p. 3.

2. *History of the Austrian Jewish Community*, Conference on Jewish Material Claims Against Germany (Claims Conference) http://www.claimscon.org/our-work/negotiations/austria/history-of-the-austrian-jewish-community/#section_2.

3. 'ERRICHTECT UNTER DER REGIERUNG DES KAISERS FRANZ JOSEPH I IM JAHRE 1910'.

4. Paldiel, Mordecai, *Saving One's Own: Jewish Rescuers During the Holocaust*, (Philadelphia: Jewish Publication Society, 2017), p. 454.

5. Heppner, *Shanghai Refuge: A Memoir of the World War II Jewish Ghetto*, (Lincoln: University of Nebraska Press, 1993) p. 19, citing Mashberg, Michael, 'American Diplomacy and the Jewish Refugee, 1938–1939', *YIVO Annual of Jewish Social Science* 15 (1944), pp. 339–54.

6. Hochstadt, Steve, *Exodus to Shanghai: Stories of Escape from the Third Reich*, (New York: Palgrave Macmillan, 2012), pp. 47–8.

7. Eber, Irene, *Voices from Shanghai*: Jewish exiles in wartime China (Chicago: University of Chicago Press, 2008), p. 9.

CHAPTER 4: BERLIN, JUNE 1938: AN UNHEEDED WARNING

1. Anspach, Emma, and Almog, Hilah, 'Hitler, Nazi Philosophy and Sport', online article published by Duke University in 2009 and updated 2013: https://sites.duke.edu/wcwp/research-projects/football-and-politics-in-europe-1930s-1950s/hitler-and-nazi-philosophy/.

2. Bruno's interview with Doniphan Blair, 'Bruno Loewenberg: Artist and Survivor', *Clinton St Quarterly*, 1982, with the author's permission.

3. Hochstadt, *Exodus*, p. 249, footnote 7.

4. On 14 June 1938, Jewish businesses were defined in the third regulation to the Citizenship Law passed in Nuremberg. From then on, if an owner or partner in a business was defined as a Jew, the company was considered Jewish and had to be registered as such, paving the way for compulsory Aryanisation. On 6 July 1938, many businesses were ordered to cease operation by 30 December 1938 if they were 'Jewish' consistent with the decree of 14 June 1938. http://www.u.arizona.edu/~shaked/Holocaust/lectures/lec8b.html.

CHAPTER 5: VIENNA, NOVEMBER 1938 TO MAY 1939:

FIRE AND COMPASSION

1. Joseph Goebbels; the speech is cited in Friedländer, Saul, *Nazi Germany and the Jews, Volume 1: The Years of Persecution 1933–1939*, (London: Phoenix, 1997), p. 113.

2. Mercer, Derrik, editor-in-chief, *Chronicle of the 20th Century*, (London: Chronicle, 1989), p. 503.

3.   Thirty thousand Jewish men were arrested across the Reich and sent to Dachau, Buchenwald or Sachsenhausen camps, among them many whose families were made to pay high ransoms for their release. Hochstadt, *Exodus*, p. 14; Kranzler, David, *Japanese, Nazis & Jews: The Jewish Refugee Community of Shanghai, 1938-1945*, (Hoboken, New Jersey: KTAV Publishing House, 1976), p. 29 and footnote 14 on p. 36.

4.   Hochstadt, *Exodus*, p. 48.

5.   Bonelli, Charlotte, and Bodemann, Natascha, *Exit Berlin: How One Woman Saved Her Family from Nazi Germany*, (New Haven: Yale University Press, 2014), p. 153.

6.   'On seeing the Jews so doomed, it was only natural to feel deep compassion, and from a humanitarian standpoint, to be impelled to help them,' Ho said years later. https://edition.cnn.com/2015/07/19/asia/china-jews-schindler-ho-feng-shan/index.html; http://usa.chinadaily.com.cn/epaper/2015-04/24/content_20529513.htm.

CHAPTER 6: BUCHENWALD, JUNE 1938 TO JULY 1939:

'ONLY THE BIRDS ARE SINGING'

1.   Bruno's interview with Doniphan Blair, *Clinton St Quarterly*.

2.   Heppner, *Shanghai Refuge*, p. 24.

3.   Mercer, *Chronicle*, p. 519.

4.   US Holocaust Memorial Museum: https://encyclopedia.ushmm.org/content/en/question/how-did-the-nazis-and-their-collaborators-implement-the-holocaust

5.   All details from Bruno Loewenberg's passport.

CHAPTER 7: VIENNA, JULY 1939 TO JANUARY 1940:

A MIRACULOUS PHONE CALL

1.   From Lisbeth's unpublished interview with James R. Ross, author of *Escape to Shanghai: A Jewish Community in China*, (New York: The Free Press, 1994), personal communication.

2.   Bonelli and Bodemann's *Exit Berlin* states that letters took four weeks to get from New York City to Shanghai in June 1939, p. 116.

3.   This rate of European entry to Shanghai had brought the Jewish immigrant community to around 16,000 by mid-1939 and, with 2,000 refugees arriving each month, was projected to result in more than 30,000 European Jews in the city by the end of the year. Competition for jobs, housing and food was becoming intense, and the Japanese were pressured to take preventative action in August 1939; Kranzler, *Japanese, Nazis and Jews*, p. 268 onwards.

4.   Hochstadt, *Exodus*, p. 48.

5.   *While you are in England. Helpful Information and Guidance for Every Refugee*, German Jewish Aid Committee, p. 12.

6. The three categories were: A – Considered a threat to national security requiring immediate internment; B – Considered suspect and subject to certain restrictions; C – Considered to be a genuine refugee from Nazi oppression.

https://www.gale.com/intl/essays/rachel-pistol-refugees-national-socialism-great-britain-1933–1945.

7. Hochstadt, *Exodus*, p. 48.

8. Kalman, *Sino-Judaica*, p. 56.

9. Hochstadt, *Exodus*, p. 69, for all Lisbeth's following uncited quotations.

CHAPTER 8: BRUNO THE 'BOOKMAN'

1. Kalman, *Sino-Judaica*, p. 60.

2. The Treaty of Tientsin also had a clause forbidding the Chinese from continuing to use the character signifying 'barbarian' when referring to the British.

3. White residents of British or North American descent referred to themselves as 'Shanghailanders', 'probably for its suggestion of islanders, surrounded by a vast sea of humanity', while they described the city's Chinese residents as 'Shanghainese'. Dong, Stella, *Shanghai: The Rise and Fall of a Decadent City, 1842–1949*, (New York: HarperCollins, 2000), p. 19; Grescoe, Taras, *Shanghai Grand : Forbidden Love and International Intrigue in a Doomed World*, (London: Macmillan, 2016), footnote p. 9.

4. Eisfelder, Horst 'Peter', *Chinese Exile: My Years in Shanghai and Nanking*, (New Haven, CT: Ayotaynu Foundation, 2004), p. 40.

5. Krasno, Rena, *Strangers Always: A Jewish Family in Wartime Shanghai*, (Berkeley, California: Pacific View Press, 1992), p. 156.

6. Eisfelder, *Chinese Exile*, p. 39.

7. Ibid., p. 39.

8. Heppner, *Shanghai Refuge*, p. 62.

9. Eisfelder, *Chinese Exile*, pp. 165–6.

10. Kranzler, *Japanese, Nazis and Jews*, pp. 395–7 for adult teaching of English by committees; Hochstadt, *Exodus*, p. 156.

11. Shanghai Municipal Police Report dated 11 November 1941, courtesy Professor Robert Bickers.

CHAPTER 9: FEBRUARY 1940: EXOTIC HARBOURS AND FLYING FISH

1. Quotes and content concerning Lisbeth's trip to Shanghai are all taken from her interviews with Steve Hochstadt, *Exodus*, and Patricia Kalman, *Sino-Judaica*.

2. Eber, Irene, ed., 'Jewish Refugees in Shanghai 1933–1947 A Selection of Documents', *Archive of Jewish History and Culture*, ed. D. Diner, Vol. 3. (Gottingen: Vandenhoeck & Ruprecht, 2018), Introduction, p. 13.

3. Ibid., on Lisbeth's voyage having maybe 150 refugees, document 43, p. 195.

4. Kranzler, *Japanese, Nazis and Jews* p. 89.

5. Heppner, *Shanghai Refuge*, p. 28.

6. Kranzler, *Japanese, Nazis and Jews*, p. 87.

7. Heppner, *Shanghai Refuge* p. 32.

8. Kranzler, *Japanese, Nazis and Jews*, p. 88.

9. Gérard Kohbieter, interviewed in Hochstadt, *Exodus*, p. 64.

10. Ilse Greening, interviewed in Hochstadt, *Exodus*, p. 66.

11. Kranzler, *Japanese, Nazis and Jews*, p. 88.

12. Gérard Kohbieter, in Hochstadt, *Exodus*, p. 64.

13. *A Place to Save Your Life: The Shanghai Jews*, produced by Karen Shopsowitz; Filmmakers Library, 1994. (A film about European refugees travelling to China.)

14. Kranzler, *Japanese, Nazis and Jews*, p. 285.

15. 'The Shanghai Boom', in *Fortune*, (New York: Time Inc., 1935).

16. Wakeman Jr, Frederic, *The Shanghai Badlands: Wartime Terrorism and Urban Crime, 1937–1941* (Cambridge: Cambridge University Press, 2002), p. 109.

17. Hochstadt, Steve, 'Shanghai: a Last Resort for Desperate Jews', in Frank Caestecker and Bob Moore, eds., *Refugees from Nazi Germany and the Liberal European States* (New York, Oxford: Berghahn Books, 2009), p. 109.

18. Lotte Schwarz, interviewed in Hochstadt, *Exodus*, p. 61.

19. Heppner, *Shanghai Refuge*, p. 31.

CHAPTER 10: 8 MARCH 1940: A SHOCKING REUNION

1. Wakeman, *Shanghai Badlands*, p. 6; Wasserstein, Bernard, *Secret War in Shanghai*, (London: Profile, 1999), p. 16.

2. Montalto de Jesus, Carlos A., *Historic Shanghai*, (Shanghai: Shanghai Mercury Limited, 1909), pp. 40–41.

3. Kranzler, *Japanese, Nazis and Jews*, pp. 271 onwards.

4. Eber, 'Jewish Refugees', pp. 193–5.

5. Angus, Fay, *The White Pagoda*, (Wheaton: Tyndale, 1978), p. 70.

6. Lisbeth and other Westerners in Shanghai used the term 'coolie' for these underpaid, almost slave, labourers. However these days the term is considered offensive, and so I have chosen to avoid using it here.

CHAPTER 11: THE MID-1930s: SHANGHAI MILLIONAIRE

1. Ernest Culman, interviewed in Hochstadt, *Exodus*, pp. 133–4.

2. Montalto de Jesus, *Historic Shanghai*, Introduction, pp. ix–x; Earnshaw, Graham, *Tales of Old Shanghai – The Glorious Past of China's Greatest City* (Hong Kong: Earnshaw Books, 2012), p. 40.

3. Dong, *Shanghai*, p. 220; Grescoe, *Shanghai Grand*, p. 22.

4. Oakes, Vanya, *White Man's Folly* (Boston: Houghton Mifflin Co., 1943), p. 18.

5. Messmer, Matthias, *Jewish Wayfarers in Modern China: Tragedy and Splendor* (Plymouth, UK: Lexington Books, 2012), p. 10.

6. *All About Shanghai: a Standard Guidebook*, (Hong Kong: Oxford University Press, 1983), p. 88.

7. Dong, *Shanghai*, p. 220.

8. Grescoe, *Shanghai Grand*, p. 234; Krasno, *Strangers Always*, pp. 11–13.

9. Krasno, *Strangers Always*, p. 48.

10. Sergeant, Harriet, *Shanghai*, (London: Cape, 1991), p. 78.

11. French, Paul, *The Old Shanghai A–Z*, (Hong Kong: Hong Kong University Press; 2010), p. 226.

12. Oakes, *White Man's Folly*, p. 46.

13. Auden, Wystan Hugh, and Isherwood, Christopher, *Journey to a War*, (New York: Octagon Books, 1972), p. 160.

14. Earnshaw, Graham, *Tales*, p. 57.

CHAPTER 12: 8 MARCH 1940: THE JOURNEY TO WEIHAIWEI ROAD

1. The east–west road that separated the two foreign concessions was Edward VII Avenue on its north side, while to the south it was Avenue Édouard VII. On this boundary road the traffic was governed by different regulations: those travelling east (closer to the Anglophone district, as Shanghai traffic drove on the left) were bound by British traffic rules, while those driving west, on the side closer to Frenchtown, came under French jurisdiction. The two police authorities patrolling the avenue were reported to work together 'in perfect harmony'. *All About Shanghai*, p. 55.

2. Bickers, Robert A., *Empire made me: an Englishman adrift in Shanghai*, (London: Allen Lane, 2003p. 45.

3. Ibid., pp. 163–5; Dong, *Shanghai*, pp. 165–8.

4. Wasserstein, *Secret War*, p. 18.

5. Ibid., pp. 15–18.

6. Cited as the words of 'an eminent American author', *All About Shanghai*, p. 48.

7. As shown in a contemporary street map of the block, courtesy Robert Bickers.

CHAPTER 13: SHANGHAI 1940:

THE BOOKSHOP ON BUBBLING WELL ROAD

1. In 1943, a British schoolboy in a Japanese internment camp on the city's outskirts knew this to be true. The young J. G. Ballard pounced on any copies – however ancient – he could find of the *Reader's Digest*, *Collier's* and *Life*. He later described how these magazines helped him survive the horror around him, becoming as essential nourishment for his desperate imagination as an extra sweet potato was for his hunger. See Ballard, J.G., *Empire of the Sun*, (Leicester: Charnwood, 1984).

2. Kranzler, *Japanese, Nazis and Jews*, p. 398.

3. French, *Old Shanghai A–Z*, p. 136, and Eber, 'Jewish Refugees', pp. 266, and 281; also Ross, *Escape*, p. 121.

4. In the mid-nineteenth century, Chinese ladies rode down Bubbling Well Road 'in splendid silks and satins, got up in the height of Chinese fashion', while Westerners adorned themselves with 'flowers, jade, and kingfishers' feathers'. Dong, *Shanghai*, pp. 36–7.

5. Kalman, *Sino-Judaica*, p. 61.

6. Kranzler, *Japanese, Nazis and Jews*, p. 398.

7. Eisfelder, *Chinese Exile*, p. 166.

8. Letter written by Paulick to E.D. Sassoon and co. Ltd, The Bund, explaining his national status and biography: http://kuenste-im-exil.de/KIE/Content/DE/Objekte/paulick-visitenkarte.html.

9. Hochstadt, *Exodus*, p. 156, and Eisfelder, *Chinese Exile*, p. 166.

CHAPTER 14: MARCH 1940: A COUCH FOR A BED

1. Some of the description of the house at Yang Terrace comes from a contemporary map, and some from Lisbeth's interview with Steve Hochstadt in *Exodus*, p. 93; I have imagined the rest.

2. Kalman, *Sino-Judaica*, p. 57.

3. Dong, *Shanghai*, p. 258; Eisfelder, *Chinese Exile*, p. 47.

4. Margolis, Laura, 'Race Against Time in Shanghai', Survey Graphic, 1944.33(3)1944. A member of one of the wealthy Sephardi families in the city said she 'had never met a poor Jew before'. (*Harbor from the Holocaust*, PBS production by WQED, available at: https://www.pbs.org/show/harbor-holocaust/

5. These basic shelters, the *Heime*, now housed two and a half thousand destitute European refugees, and fed another eight thousand unable to support themselves. Kranzler, *Japanese, Nazis and Jews*, pp. 287–8.

6. Margolis, 'Race Against Time', p. 168

7. Kalman, *Sino-Judaica*, p. 57.

8. The Epsteins' building had more than one bathroom, and may have been home to around half a dozen families. Lisbeth mentions 'bathrooms and showers'. (Unpublished interview with James Ross, personal communication.)

9. Agel, Jerome and Boe, Eugene, *Deliverance in Shanghai*, (New York: Dembner Books, 1983), pp. 205–6.

10. Bacon, U., *Shanghai Diary: A Young Girl's Journey from Hitler's Hate to War-Torn China* (Milwaukie, OR: M Press, 2002), pp. 45 and 160; also Greening interview with Hochstadt, *Exodus*, p. 108.

11. Eisfelder, *Chinese Exile*, pp. 191–2, and Kranzler, *Japanese, Nazis and Jews*, pp. 121–2.

12. Lewin, O. (ed.), *Almanac–Shanghai 1946/47*, (Shanghai: *Shanghai Echo* Publishing Co., 1947), p. 78.

CHAPTER 15: SPRING 1940: LINGERIE SHOPS AND CORPSES

1. French, *Old Shanghai A–Z*, p. 175; *All about Shanghai*, p. 93.

2. Shaw, R., *Sin City* (London: Futura, 1986), p. 80.

3. The Speelman Committee's formal name was the Committee for the Assistance of European Jewish Refugees in Shanghai, or the CFA. Kranzler, *Japanese, Nazis and Jews*, p. 94.

4. Ibid., p. 115, and Sergeant, *Shanghai*, p. 181.

5. *All About Shanghai*, p. 118.

6. Around 80 bodies were collected daily by this society. Eisfelder, *Chinese Exile*, p. 53. See also Angus, *White Pagoda*, p. 78.

7. These grisly warnings were to deter Chinese rebels. In 1938, the severed head of a prominent Chinese editor, Tsai Diao-tu, had been left on a Frenchtown police station lamp post. A message tied to it read: 'Look! Look! The result of anti-Japanese elements.' Dong, *Shanghai*, p. 260; Reissman interviewed by Steve Hochstadt in *Exodus*, pp. 80–81.

8. Henriot, C., 'Shanghai and the Experience of War: The Fate of Refugees', *European Journal of East Asian Studies*, 2006, pp. 238 onward, and 242.

9. *Foreigners Assail Japanese Red Tape; Tokyo Naval Officials Refuse Permits for Yangtzepoo and Hongkew Areas. New York Times*, 31 August 1937; Kranzler, *Japanese, Nazis and Jews*, p. 116.

10. Sergeant, *Shanghai*, p. 315.

11. Without loans from the American Jew, a financier named Jacob Schiff, the Japanese could not have defeated their enemy. Schiff was a partner in the investment company Kuhn, Loeb & Schiff. Hochstadt, *Exodus*, p. 103.

Of course, antisemitism was not completely unknown among the Japanese. In 1918 and 1922, their militia had joined forces with the White Russians in Siberia, in an attempt to drive back the Bolsheviks' Far East advances. This contact meant that some of the Russians' crude antisemitism rubbed off onto Japanese officers. Many became infected with their co-fighters' 'hatred of Bolsheviks and Jews, and made them synonymous to some Japanese.' Kranzler, *Japanese, Nazis and Jews*, p. 177; for a detailed discussion on Japanese attitudes to Jews, see Chapters 7 and 11.

Some believe that this Japanese antisemitism has been exaggerated. See Steve Hochstadt, *'Jews and Japanese in Shanghai: Japanese Acceptance of Jewish Refugees and Rejection of the Nazi Model'*, paper delivered at Glazer Institute of Jewish Studies, Nanjing University, Nanjing, China, April 16, 2010.

12. Kranzler, *Japanese, Nazis and Jews*, p. 136.

CHAPTER 16: LITTLE VIENNA'S INGENUITY:

SOAP, BRATWURST AND STRUDEL

1. Words of a representative of the International Committee for Granting Relief to European Refugees (the IC), Kranzler, ibid., p. 85, citing Eduard Kann in *Shanghai Jewish Chronicle*, April 1940.

2. Kranzler, *Japanese, Nazis and Jews*, p. 116.

3. Kranzler, *Japanese, Nazis and Jews*, p. 117; French, *Old Shanghai A–Z*, p. 98; Eisfelder, *Chinese Exile*, p. 197.

4. *Jewish Refugees in Shanghai, 26 Stories of Jewish Refugees in Shanghai during World War II*. Eds. Pu Zukang, Li Shan. (Shanghai: Jiao Tong University Press, 2016), p. 254 onwards.

5. The average age of the emigrants arriving in the late 1930s was around 40. Kranzler, *Japanese, Nazis and Jews*, p. 283; Steve Hochstadt, personal communication based on his analysis of 1944 census data.

6. Kranzler, *Japanese, Nazis and Jews*, p. 289.

7. Zunterstein in Eber, 'Jewish Refugees', p. 210. Much of this section based on Kranzler, *Japanese, Nazis and Jews*, p. 285 onwards.

8. *Jewish Refugees*, Zukang, Shan. Eds., p. 164.

9. Agel and Boe, *Deliverance in Shanghai*, p. 12.

CHAPTER 17: SUMMER 1940:
THE BLACK AND GOLD MARBLED LOBBY

1. In Hochstadt, *Exodus*, p. 93.

2. https://www.virtualshanghai.net/Texts/Articles?ID=59

3. Kranzler, *Japanese, Nazis and Jews*, p. 115; also Krasno, *Strangers Always*, p. 18, and Kranzler, *Japanese, Nazis and Jews*, footnote 14 p. 124.

4. Grescoe, *Shanghai Grand*, p. 232; 'The Shanghai Boom', in *Fortune*, (New York: Time Inc., 1935).

5. Dong, *Shanghai*, p. 133, 'voluptuous vampires' (there is a suggestion that this derogatory description of White Russian women originated from Comintern propaganda).

6. Ibid., p. 135.

7. Ibid., p. 132.

8. 'The Shanghai Boom', in *Fortune*, (New York: Time Inc., 1935).

9. *All about Shanghai*, pp. 88–9.

10. " Hochstadt, Steve, *Rossetty, Henry oral history interview*, (Lewiston, Maine: Bates College Shanghai Jewish Oral History Collection), pp. 37-38 . http://scarab.bates.edu/shanghai_oh/13

11. Lisbeth's unpublished interview with James Ross, personal communication.

CHAPTER 18: AUTUMN 1940: LOOKING FOR APRICOTS

1. Heppner, *Shanghai Refuge*, p. 53.

2. Interview with Steve Hochstadt in *Exodus*, p. 94, for much of this chapter.

3. The source gives these temperatures as 100 and 104 degrees Fahrenheit respectively. *All about Shanghai*, p. 114.

4. Kranzler, *Japanese, Nazis and Jews*, p. 369.

5. Hochstadt, interview 'Rossetty', p. 43.

6. Eisfelder, *Chinese Exile*, p. 92, and Oakes, *White Man's Folly*, pp. 360–61.

CHAPTER 19: WINTER 1940: THE DESTROYER OF DREAMS

1. Kranzler, *Japanese, Nazis and Jews*, pp. 390–92.

2. Kranzler, *Japanese, Nazis and Jews*, p. 131 and footnote p. 145.

3. Ibid., p. 391, and Hochstadt, *Exodus*, e.g. pp. 106–7; also video https://www.pbslearningmedia.org/resource/lucie-hartwich-shanghai-refugee-video/harbor-from-the-holocaust/.

4. Kranzler, *Japanese, Nazis and Jews*, pp. 390–92; Hochstadt, Steve, *Lucie Hartwich and the Kadoorie School: Educating Refugee Children in Shanghai*. In Ostoyich, Kevin and Xia, Yun, eds., *The History of the Shanghai Jews: New Pathways of Research* (Palgrave Macmillan, Cham. Switzerland: Springer Nature, 2022), pp. 104–5.

5. Kranzler, *Japanese, Nazis and Jews*, pp. 392, and 396.

6. Ibid, p. 292.

CHAPTER 20: SPRING 1941: COFFEE AT YANG TERRACE

1. Eber, 'Jewish Refugees', p. 549; Kranzler, *Japanese, Nazis and Jews*, p. 368 onwards.

2. Lewin, *Almanac*, p. 64.

3. Often after a long day's work 'as delivery boys or waitresses, grocery agents and cartoonists' and usually with 'empty pockets and hungry stomachs', the players rehearsed in freezing, unheated rooms. They faced many obstacles: few proper stages on which to perform (and the high cost of renting any that were available), lack of money for costumes, and above all, the dearth of any scripts or librettos in German or English. Despite these challenges, the directors and performers worked wonders. Lewin, *Almanac* p. 64; Kranzler, *Japanese, Nazis and Jews*, p. 368; Eber, 'Jewish Refugees', pp. 549–50.

4. While the first refugee plays were staged inside the *Heime*, later performances were put on at cinemas, the city having more of these than theatres. However, the shallow cinema stages tended to cramp the sweeping gestures of the actors. A better stage was to be found at the Lyceum in the French Concession, beside Cathay Mansions. This cinema, built in 1931, was once home to the British Amateur Dramatic Society: it still stands today. French, *Old Shanghai A–Z*, pp. 182–3.

5. Eber, 'Jewish Refugees', p. 600. For a discussion of interactions between German Christians and Jews in Shanghai, see Hochstadt, *Exodus*, p. 238. Germans were in fact a minority among the white Westerners who controlled Shanghai until the Japanese took over in December 1941. Before that the city was run by English, French and Americans.

6. Even Michel Speelman, the prominent émigré committee member, advised that 'provocative topics in Shanghai must be avoided at this point'. Eber, 'Jewish Refugees', p. 551; French online article http://www.chinarhyming.com/2010/10/14/when-shanghais-nazis-threatened-to-kill-jews-over-a-play/.

CHAPTER 21: 8 DECEMBER 1941: THE WORLD SHIFTS OVERNIGHT

1. Hochstadt, ,'Lucie Hartwich', p. 8; Kranzler, *Japanese, Nazis and Jews*, pp. 390–91.

2. Hochstadt, ,'Lucie Hartwich', p. 8.

3. Eisfelder, *Chinese Exile*, p. 91.

4. Testimony from film *A Place to Save Your Life*, 17 minutes in.

5. On the spelling of this name – *Peterel* as opposed to *Petrel*, used by many – see Wasserstein, *Secret War*, footnote on p. 97.

6. Wasserstein, *Secret War*, pp. 73–5.

7. Ibid., p. 76.

8. Ibid., pp. 97–8.

9. Ballard, J.G., *Miracles of life: Shanghai to Shepperton: an autobiography*, (London: Fourth Estate, 2008), pp. 54-55.

10. Eisfelder, *Chinese Exile*, p. 92; Wasserstein, *Secret War*, p. 99.

11. Wasserstein, *Secret War*, p. 99.

12. Ibid., p. 100.

13. Ibid., p. 99; Dong, *Shanghai*, p. 269.

14. Eisfelder, *Chinese Exile*, p. 32; Wasserstein p. 97.

15. Wasserstein, *Secret War*, pp. 101–2 and 99–100; French, *Old Shanghai A–Z*, p. 109.

16. Eisfelder, *Chinese Exile*, pp. 92–3.

17. Oakes, *White Man's Folly*, p. 357; Wasserstein, *Secret War*, pp. 19–20. .

CHAPTER 22: 16 DECEMBER 1941: A BIRTHDAY IN DARKNESS

1. Ballard, *Miracles*, p. 3.

2. Ernest Culman, interviewed in Hochstadt, *Exodus*, p. 104; Eisfelder, *Chinese Exile*, p. 92.

3. Margolis, Laura, Report in Eber, 'Jewish Refugees', pp. 366–7.

4. Kranzler, *Japanese, Nazis and Jews*, p. 454, and Eisfelder, *Chinese Exile*, p. 93; *A Place to Save Your Life* film.

5. Josef Meisinger, later dubbed the Butcher of Warsaw, was the German attaché in Tokyo, and the Nazis' chief representative in the Far East. The so-called Meisinger Plans – never proven – involved the shipping of Zyklon B to Shanghai for use in gas chambers there, or starvation or overwork of the Jews, or sending them out on ships with no food. Fortunately, Meisinger's network of spies in Shanghai was ineffective. He was also very unpopular, and the Japanese were highly suspicious of him; he achieved little in the city. Wasserstein, *Secret War*, pp. 91-92; 222 and 256; Dong, *Shanghai*, p. 275.

6. Horst Eisfelder's family were among those not taking Meisinger seriously, recognising that neither Shanghai's Germans nor Japanese had any respect for him. See also Wasserstein, *Secret War*, pp. 220-3.

7. Kranzler, *Japanese, Nazis and Jews*, p. 454.

8. *Empire Made Me* is the story of an ex-SMC policeman in Shanghai in the 1930s, whose drinking unleashed violently colonialist attitudes and lost him his job. Robert Bickers' antihero had lived and worked at the Salvation Army Men's hostel at number 7 Yang Terrace around 1934. The thought of the drunken ex-copper living just doors from where, six years later, my relatives would rent a room was strangely unsettling.

9. Robert Bickers also showed me small ads from the 1938 editions of the *China Press* and the *North-China Daily Herald*, which mentioned Yang Terrace. These showed that number 1 housed the Shanghai Health Studio ('Medical Cosmetics and Herbal Treatment') in July, while by December it was home to the Shanghai Navigation School. Another document was a 1941 street directory, listing the residents of each house in the terrace at that time. I looked eagerly for my relatives' name but, to my disappointment, the Epsteins were not listed. I had to assume that they – as well as

their neighbour, Bruno Loewenberg – were subletting from the named occupants. These were, at number 2: a Mrs Dickson, Dr Goldstein and Fritz Eisner, while number 5 (Bruno's place) named Mr and Mrs S.P. Miller and E. Braun. At number 7 was the Salvation Army Men's Hostel, beside the name of C.F. Gram. Not one tenant of the row was Chinese.

10. Kindly supplied by Professor Robert Bickers, University of Bristol. The bulk of the SMP's Special Branch records are now held in the US National Archives, in Record Group 263; https://archive.org/details/DerKreis/page/n1/mode/2up.

11. SMP Special Branch file D8149–F161 from Robert Bickers; in response to a letter No. F. 20/5 dated 19 July 1940, signed by the secretary and commissioner general of the Shanghai Municipal Council regarding the publication of political manifestoes [sic]. Signed by (illegible) for editor of *Der Kreis* ('The Circle'); certificate and letter F.20/5 issued on 19 November 1941.

12. Fraenkel merited a footnote in Eber's volume on Shanghai's Jewish refugees. He studied music and law in Berlin. Until 1933 he was a judge at the local appeal court, and thereafter made his living as a musician. He became a member of the Shanghai Municipal Orchestra in 1940 and taught at the conservatory. In 1947 he emigrated to the US. Eber, 'Jewish Refugees', p. 301.

13. SMC file from Robert Bickers, registration form for *Der Kreis: Monatsschrift fuer Kunst* 1:1 (December 1941). A rare copy survives in the Leo Baeck Institute Library Periodical Collection and can be found via the Internet Archive: https://archive.org/details/DerKreis/

The first edition of *Der Kreis*, produced by the Lion Publishing Company, contained 'contributions by Friedrich Karp (confession to the language), Wolfgang Fraenkel (basic problems of the new music) and Fred Schiff (boundaries of the painting) as well as a quotation "Spiegel" with statements by Robert Musil, Kurt Hiller, Karl Kraus and others.' https://archive.org/details/DerKreis/page/n1/mode/2up.

CHAPTER 23: FEBRUARY 1942: BREAD WITH BURNT-SUGAR CARAMEL

1. Kranzler, *Japanese, Nazis and Jews*, p. 458; Eisfelder, *Chinese Exile*, p. 95.

2. Margolis, 'Race Against Time'; Eber, 'Jewish Refugees', p. 367.

3. Eisfelder, *Chinese Exile*, p. 87 and personal (email) communication.

4. Eisfelder, *Chinese Exile*, p. 94.

5. Kranzler, *Japanese, Nazis and Jews*, p. 366, 'high point'. The number of newspapers set up by the Europeans in Shanghai (the *Shanghai Jewish Chronicle*, the *Gelbe Post*, and the *Shanghaier Morgenpost*) was more than in any other community settling in new cities at this time. The original German-language (Nazi-backed) paper in Shanghai was *Der Ostasiatische Lloyd*. Kranzler, *Japanese, Nazis and Jews*, p. 364; Eisfelder, *Chinese Exile*, p. 52.

6. Eber, 'Jewish Refugees', note 11 p. 280, and p. 402; also Eisfelder, *Chinese Exile*, p. 52.

7. Eisfelder, *Chinese Exile*, p. 93; Hochstadt, interview 'Rossetty', p. 33.

8. Hochstadt, interview 'Rossetty', p. 33.

9. The importance of German-language speech and radio has been noted: 'the soothing effects of a yet pulsating musical life helped maintain the refugees' sanity ... under the most adverse conditions.' Kranzler, *Japanese, Nazis and Jews*, pp. 376 and 380.

10. Eber, 'Jewish Refugees', note 75 p. 251; Kranzler, *Japanese, Nazis and Jews*, p. 424.

11. Eber, 'Jewish Refugees', footnote 33 on p. 231, and p. 370.

12. Kranzler, *Japanese, Nazis and Jews*, pp. 153, 157. Eber, 'Jewish Refugees', pp. 369 and 398.

13. A few weeks after the interview, a teacher named Miss Hoshino arrived at the school. Hochstadt, 'Lucie Hartwich', p. 112.

14. Doris Gray interview in Hochstadt, *Exodus*, p. 151; Kranzler, *Japanese, Nazis and Jews*, p. 300.

15. An Israeli photojournalist, Dvir Bar-Gal, has spent almost 20 years tracking down the remnants of Shanghai's four Jewish cemeteries. Their 4,000 graves have disappeared, and he learnt that their headstones have been sold in antique shops across the city. Claudia and I went on one of his Jewish tours of Shanghai in 2004.

16. Kranzler, *Japanese, Nazis and Jews*, p. 495, Eisfelder personal communication (including photo of his resident's certificate).

CHAPTER 24: FEBRUARY 1943: THE GHETTO

1. Eskelund, Paula and Schiff, *Squeezing Through! Shanghai Sketches 1941–1945*, (Shanghai: Hwa Kuo Printing Co., 1945), p.25.

2. Eisfelder, *Chinese Exile*, p. 167 onwards.

3. https://encyclopedia.ushmm.org/content/en/document/proclamation-of-restricted-zone-in-shanghai-for-refugees; Kranzler, *Japanese, Nazis and Jews*, pp. 489 onwards; Eisfelder, *Chinese Exile*, p. 168; Eber, 'Jewish Refugees', p. 437.

4. Kranzler, *Japanese, Nazis and Jews*, p. 491; *Shanghai Herald*, front page, 18 February 1943.

5. Eber, 'Jewish Refugees', p. 400.

6. Eisfelder, *Chinese Exile*, p. 170; Eber, 'Jewish Refugees', pp. 98 and 438.

7. Years later, the true sympathies of Fritz Wiedemann were shown to have lain with the Allies. Kranzler, *Japanese, Nazis and Jews*, p. 488.

8. Krasno, *Strangers Always*, p. 55; Heppner, *Shanghai Refuge*, p. 105.

9. The contradictory and sometimes confused attitude of the Japanese to the 'Jewish question' is discussed elsewhere. In general it seems the Japanese were favourable to the Jews 'based on the hope that Jews would provide capital and expertise that might facilitate [Japanese] economic development'. See Wasserstein, *Secret War*, pp. 140 onwards, and Kranzler, *Japanese, Nazis and Jews*, for more detail.

10. Kranzler, *Japanese, Nazis and Jews*, p. 477.

11. Wasserstein, *Secret War*, p. 143; Ross, *Escape*, p. 145.

12. Eber, 'Jewish Refugees', p. 400, footnote 5; 'conspiracy', Ross, *Escape*, p. 178.

13. Kranzler, *Japanese, Nazis and Jews*, p. 522 and Margolis in Eber, 'Jewish Refugees', p. 392.

14. Kranzler, *Japanese, Nazis and Jews*, p. 491; '40 square blocks' from Krasno, *Strangers Always*, p. 135.

15. Ross, *Escape*, p. 177; also Kranzler, *Japanese, Nazis and Jews*, footnote 28, p. 510.

16. Eisfelder, *Chinese Exile*, p. 171.

17. As reported in a SACRA meeting on 1 April 1943, SACRA needed to speed up the transfer of properties. To this end 'several persons who could place evaluation on apartments, furniture etc.' would be appointed. The minutes stated: 'In this connection the decision of SACRA, with Mr Kubota's approval, will be final.' Eber, 'Jewish Refugees', pp. 101 and 445.

CHAPTER 25: SUMMER 1943: A BODY IN THE YANGTZE

1. Eisfelder, *Chinese Exile*, p. 185.

2. Zhou, Qingyang, *Interactions Between the Chinese and the Jewish Refugees in Shanghai During World War II*, (Penn History Review: Vol. 25 : Iss. 2 , Article 3 2018). Heppner, *Shanghai Refuge*, p. 113.

3. Around 150 couples went through such 'Nazi-inspired divorces'. 'The German consulate offered the Christian wives of Jewish refugees the opportunity to divorce their husbands in exchange for consular support and financial aid.' There is no record if this arrangement worked for Aryan husbands visiting ghetto-bound wives. Kranzler, *Japanese, Nazis and Jews*, pp. 495–6; also Heppner, *Shanghai Refuge*, p. 114.

4. Eisfelder, *Chinese Exile*, p. 185.

5. The terminology was used in Shanghai's printed census forms, which listed addresses according to 'No. of Pao' – a group of ten households – and 'No. of Chia', and included named 'guarantors' of residents registered in the census. Eber, 'Jewish Refugees', p. 535; Kranzler, *Japanese, Nazis and Jews*, footnote 34, p. 511; Lisbeth's census form.

6. Ross, *Escape*, pp. 207–8; Eisfelder, *Chinese Exile*, pp. 184–5.

7. Kranzler, *Japanese, Nazis and Jews*, p. 493; Eber, 'Jewish Refugees', pp. 534–6 (translated).

8. In its first month of keeping law and order, the Jewish *Pao Chia* was 'able to prevent crime or arrest perpetrators in 66 cases'. Eber, 'Jewish Refugees', pp. 535–6.

9. Eber, 'Jewish Refugees', footnote p. 295; Kranzler, *Japanese, Nazis and Jews*, p. 413; Ross, *Escape*, p. 208.

10. Ross, *Escape*, p. 208, and Kranzler, *Japanese, Nazis and Jews*, p. 494.

11. This story appears in many books, e.g. Kranzler, *Japanese, Nazis and Jews*, p. 494; Ross, *Escape*, p. 208; Hochstadt, *Exodus*, p. 133.

CHAPTER 26: 'THE KING OF THE JEWS'

1. Kranzler, *Japanese, Nazis and Jews*, p. 497; Ross, *Escape*, p. 206; Kranzler, *Japanese, Nazis and Jews*, p. 496.

2. Ibid., pp. 524–5.

3. Eber, 'Jewish Refugees', p. 632; Eisfelder, *Chinese Exile*, p. 183.

4. Ross, *Escape*, p. 205; Heppner, *Shanghai Refuge*; Okura was later described as a sadist by Poles demanding retribution against both him and Kanoh Ghoya: Eber, 'Jewish Refugees', pp. 641-643.

5. Kranzler, *Japanese, Nazis and Jews*, p. 527; Ross, *Escape*, p. 204; Eber, 'Jewish Refugees', p. 481.

6. Ross, *Escape*, p. 204; Kranzler, *Japanese, Nazis and Jews*, pp. 529–30; Also police file, in Eber, 'Jewish Refugees', p. 452.

7. Ross, *Escape*, p. 206. This is a direct quote translated from the original German.

8. Heppner, *Shanghai Refuge*, p. 114; Bacon, *Shanghai Diary*, p. 171.

9. Eisfelder, *Chinese Exile*, pp. 174–5; Bacon, *Shanghai Diary*, p. 171.

10. A psychiatrist among the refugees recognised Kanoh Ghoya's 'psychopathic personality full of pathological ambition', a man wanting 'to be feared and at the same time, to be popular'. Kranzler, *Japanese, Nazis and Jews*, p. 498.

11. Ross, *Escape*, p. 205; Fritz Melchior cartoons in Eber, *Voices*, appendix; Kranzler, *Japanese, Nazis and Jews*; 'Good-bye Mr Ghoya', September 1945: https://collections.ushmm.org/search/catalog/irn28238#?rsc=22044&cv=2&c=0&m=0&s=0&xywh=-438%2C-77%2C1865%2C1668.

12. Kranzler, *Japanese, Nazis and Jews*, p. 499; Ross, *Escape*, p. 85 and 207, Krasno, *Strangers Always*, p. 136.

13. Bacon, *Shanghai Diary*, pp. 170–71; Kranzler, *Japanese, Nazis and Jews*, p. 496, Ross, *Escape*, p. 206.

CHAPTER 27: SPRING 1944: A LIFELINE SPLIT TWICE

1. Krasno, *Strangers Always*, pp. 136–7.

2. Of almost 1,500 refugee deaths recorded between January 1939 and April 1945, only 36 were suicides, a rate not unusual for European countries; the overall death rate of 13 per 1,000 was not much higher than that of 1974 statistics for West Germany (11.8) or Austria (12.6). Kranzler, *Japanese, Nazis and Jews*, pp. 605–7; p. 303 for comparison.

3. Eisfelder, *Chinese Exile*, pp. 52 and 197 and Kranzler, *Japanese, Nazis and Jews*, p. 366.

4. Ralph Hirsch in Hochstadt, *Exodus*, p. 164.

5. Many musicians were very poor, being unable to play in their former venues: Kranzler, *Japanese, Nazis and Jews*, p. 374. The full quote about art is: 'In a world full of hate, and despite war and destruction, our small community of about 15,000 homeless, Jewish refugees, without the barest financial resources, has understood [sic] to survive all vicissitudes. They remained steadfast to their belief in the morale and inviolability of art.' Lewin, *Almanac*, pp. 64-5.

6. Years later the immigrants' artistic efforts would be noted for their remarkable breadth and quality: 'The composition of the refugee community resulted in a far above average cultural life of a community of this size. Twelve to fourteen thousand people represent the population of a small city, and you will hardly find a community of this size showing similar cultural achievements.' Kurt Redlich letter to Kranzler, *Japanese, Nazis and Jews*, p. 363.

7. Carey, Arch, *The War Years at Shanghai*, p. 146; Oakes, *White Man's Folly*, p. 351.

8. Kranzler, *Japanese, Nazis and Jews*, pp. 374 and 369.

9. Krasno, *Strangers Always*, p. 195, footnote. The Japanese supported ARTA, the Office of Stateless Refugee Affairs sponsoring its event. In a newspaper interview, chief Kubota declared: 'The prices for pictures are quite cheap, for anyway it is usually the richest men in the city who buy pictures, all the others merely come to admire them.' Eber, 'Jewish Refugees', p. 537. To attract potential patrons, ARTA offered new members a free piece of graphic art and reductions on future purchases. The Kadoorie School show even offered a portrait sketched by one of the artists 'on the spot' for any visitor with $100 to spare.

10. Hochstadt interview with 'Rossetty' in *Exodus*, pp. 13–15.

11. Horst Eisfelder noted the price of staple items in 1938: a pound of meat cost 18 to 30 cents; sugar 20 cents a pound; and a large sack of rice $11 (Shanghai currency). Three years later, Rena Krasno recorded the following costs: a single grape 30 cents; an egg 40 cents; sugar $8 per pound; a small chicken $200–$300; a pair of shoes $800–$900; and a short rickshaw ride $15 (all Shanghai currency). Butter bought on the black market was $140 a pound. By spring 1943, sugar cost $9 per pound (or $25 on the 'black'); a pound of margarine $32 (up to $60 on the 'black'); and a sack of rice $1,750. In April 1943, Eisfelder's salary of $350 could buy him 'a tin or two of cigarettes or perhaps a few kilos of sweets'. Kranzler, *Japanese, Nazis and Jews*, p. 457; Eisfelder, *Chinese Exile*, pp. 95–6; Krasno, *Strangers Always*, pp. 4 and 21.

12. The system of daily charges involved using a letter of the alphabet marked inside every book. A list of letters they posted on the library wall showed that day's borrowing rate. Ross, unpublished interview with Lisbeth, personal communication, and Ross, *Escape*, p. 200.

CHAPTER 28: AUGUST 1944:

BIRDS, FLOWERS AND GOOD LUCK SYMBOLS

1. The refugee in the ghetto was named Eva Kantorowsky. Twice fearing herself pregnant, the rabbi's daughter had turned to her doctor for help. Although married, she knew that her and her husband's living conditions – squeezed into the tiny concrete room housing their lane building's electricity meters – were unfit for raising a child. She was prescribed the regimen of vodka and quinine, which made her 'terribly sick and weak', but worked. Ross, *Escape*, pp. 94, and 172-173.

2. Lewin, 'Almanac', p. 109.

CHAPTER 29: AUTUMN TO WINTER 1944:

CAKE, COFFEE AND AIR RAIDS

1. Eisfelder, *Chinese Exile*, pp. 94 and 51 .

2. Kranzler, *Japanese, Nazis and Jews*, p. 60.

3. Hochstadt, *Exodus*, p. 231.

4. Arch Carey, a British internee of Pootung Camp, recalled 'one lone US night raider, probably a B-17, that came over Shanghai almost every night, flying in from the west. It appeared between midnight and 3 a.m.' Carey, *War Years*, p. 149 and p. 205; Ross, *Escape*, p. 218.

5. Eisfelder, *Chinese Exile*, p. 203; Wasserstein, *Secret War*, p. 256.

6. Carey, *War Years*, p. 207.

7. Krasno, *Strangers Always*, pp. 142–3.

8. Wasserstein, *Secret War*, p. 256.

9. Kranzler, *Japanese, Nazis and Jews*, p. 552.

CHAPTER 30: DECEMBER 1944: A CRUEL WINTER

1. Kranzler, *Japanese, Nazis and Jews*, p. 301.

2. Spreadsheet of lists of refugee births and deaths in Shanghai, supplied by Steve Hochstadt.

3. Doris Grey's testimony is described in Hochstadt, *Exodus*, pp. 152 and 237.

4. Herbert Greening interview in Hochstadt, *Exodus*, pp. 237 and 262.

5. Hochstadt, *Exodus*, p. 237.

CHAPTER 31: SPRING 1945: 'MEIN BRUDER, MEIN BRUDER!'

1. Eisfelder, *Chinese Exile*, p. 204, and others, e.g. Culman in Hochstadt, *Exodus*, p. 166.

2. Eisfelder, *Chinese Exile*, p. 204; Carey, *War Years*, p. 205; Culman in Hochstadt, *Exodus*, p. 166; Schnepp in Hochstadt, *Exodus*, p. 172.

3. Hochstadt, *Exodus*, p. 164.

4. Ross, *Escape*, p. 215 and p. 216; Heppner, *Shanghai Refuge*, p. 122.

5. Eisfelder, *Chinese Exile*, pp. 209–10; Ross, *Escape*, p. 216.

6. http://www.holocaust.cz/en/database-of-victims/victim/54986-elisabeth-mann/.

7. Heppner, *Shanghai Refuge*, p. 131; Ross, *Escape*, p. 218.

CHAPTER 32: 17 JULY 1945: THE ANIMALS SENSED IT FIRST

1. Kranzler, *Japanese, Nazis and Jews*, p. 553; Ross, *Escape*, p. 218

2. Ross, *Escape*, p. 218; Kranzler, *Japanese, Nazis and Jews*, p. 553.

3. The woman's name was Rose Shoshana Kahan. Eber, 'Jewish Refugees', pp. 612–13.

4. Carey, *War Years*, p. 208; Ross, *Escape*, p. 218.

5. Kranzler, *Japanese, Nazis and Jews*, p. 553.

6. Ibid., p. 530; Eber, 'Jewish Refugees', p. 452; French, *Old Shanghai A Z*, p. 139.

7. Heppner, *Shanghai Refuge*, p. 126.

8. Ibid., pp. 126–7.

9. Ross, *Escape*, p. 220; Eber, 'Jewish Refugees', p. 614.

10. Kranzler, *Japanese, Nazis and Jews*, p. 555 and footnote 44 p. 570.

CHAPTER 33: AUGUST 1945: 'HIROSHIMA MELTED'

1. Heppner, *Shanghai Refuge*, p. 130.
2. Krasno, *Strangers Always*, p. 190, and footnote on same page.
3. Ibid., p. 195.
4. Heppner, *Shanghai Refuge*, p. 132.
5. The paper was Tokyo's *Mainichi*; Krasno, *Strangers Always*, p. 194.
6. Krasno, *Strangers Always*, p. 197.
7. Diary record in Eber, 'Jewish Refugees', p. 621; Carey, *War Years*, p. 210.
8. Eber, 'Jewish Refugees', p. 622; also Ross, *Escape*, p. 221 and Heppner, *Shanghai Refuge*, pp. 132–3.
9. Eber, 'Jewish Refugees', p. 624.
10. Eber, 'Jewish Refugees', pp. 624 and 625 for this paragraph's quotes.
11. Eisfelder, *Chinese Exile*, p. 212; Kranzler, *Japanese, Nazis and Jews*, p. 566.
12. Krasno, *Strangers Always*, p. 200; Carey, *War Years*, pp. 216–17; Dong, *Shanghai*, p. 280.
13. Eber, 'Jewish Refugees', p. 606; Kranzler, *Japanese, Nazis and Jews*, p. 564; Hochstadt, *Exodus*, p. 173.
14. Krasno, *Strangers Always*, footnote, p. 183; Heppner, *Shanghai Refuge*, p. 133.
15. Carey, *War Years*, p. 217.

CHAPTER 34: SEPTEMBER 1945: A NEW WORLD ORDER

1. Dong, *Shanghai*, p. 280 and Carey, *War Years*, p. 217.
2. Army Air Corps, Dong, *Shanghai*, p. 281; Eisfelder, personal communication.
3. Carey, *War Years*, p. 222.
4. Ibid.
5. Dong, *Shanghai*, pp. 281–2; Carey, *War Years*, p. 274.
6. Horst Eisfelder's first job in July 1940 had earned him 20 Chinese dollars a month (around US$1–2). In July 1945, before the end of the war and still inside the ghetto, Eisfelder was doing two jobs for US$3 per month. Just three months later, on 1 October 1945, he got work in the US Signal Corps Stores supervising Chinese manual labourers for $70 per month. Eisfelder, *Chinese Exile*, pp. 77, 95, 205, 215–16. This was an unheard-of amount, as according to one refugee, one could feed a whole family on US$10 dollars a month. Hans Less, unpublished memoir, supplied by his son, Steven Less.
7. Eber, 'Jewish Refugees', p. 599, review of performance in 1946 written by Pollack, 1946.
8. With the improvement of refugees' lives, more babies were born: 36 were born in the ghetto (Ward Road hospital) in 1942; 27 in 1943; 48 in 1944; 50 in 1945; and 114 in 1946. *Jewish Refugees*, Zukang, Shan. Eds., p. 66.
9. Eisfelder, *Chinese Exile*, pp. 232–3.
10. Arch Carey describes how 'the Chinese government … had been put back into the seat of government in China by the foreign Allied Powers and not by their own effort'. *War Years*, p. 219. Carey was amazed at how quickly the Chinese then forgot

the extent that they had relied on help from the Anglo-Americans (especially the Americans), immediately after the end of the war. Carey, *War Years*, pp. 224–5.

CHAPTER 35: WINTER 1947: A TICKET TO FREEDOM

1. Hochstadt, *Exodus*, pp. 187–8.
2. Ship's manifest for USS *Meigs* sailing on 4 January 1948 supplied by Professor Robert Bickers.

CHAPTER 36: 1948 TO 1956: SAN FRANCISCO AND LONDON:
THE NEW LION BOOKSHOP

1. The memory of the cigar-smoking Egon Fuchs came from my elder sister, Claudia.

CHAPTER 37: LOVE, ART AND FAMILY:
HERE, THERE, THEN AND NOW

1. Author's interview with Richard Feldman, New York 2017.
2. Personal communication from Doniphan Blair, 2016.

EPILOGUE: SHEDDING TEARS IN SHANGHAI

1. Hochstadt, Steve, 'One faraway city offered hope: Shanghai', *Miami Herald*, 4 June 1989.

Bibliography

Agel, Jerome and Boe, Eugene, *Deliverance in Shanghai*, (New York: Dembner Books, 1983).

All about Shanghai : a standard guidebook, (Hongkong, Oxford: Oxford University Press, 1983).

Allingham, Philip V., *England and China: The Opium Wars, 1839-60*. The Victorian Web 2006; Available from: http://www.victorianweb.org/history/empire/opiumwars/opiumwars1.html.

Angus, Fay, *The white pagoda*, (Wheaton: Tyndale, 1978).

Anti-Jewish decrees. Learning: Voices of the holocaust; Available from: http://www.bl.uk/learning/histcitizen/voices/info/decrees/decrees.html.

Bacon, Ursula, *Shanghai Diary: A Young Girl's Journey from Hitler's Hate to War-Torn China*, (Milwaukie: M Press, 2004).

Ballard, J.G., *Empire of the sun*, (Leicester: Charnwood, 1984).

Ballard, J.G., *Miracles of life : Shanghai to Shepperton : an autobiography*, (London: Fourth Estate, 2008).

Bickers, Robert A., *Empire made me: an Englishman adrift in Shanghai*, (London: Allen Lane, 2003).

Bradley, James, *The imperial cruise : a secret history of empire and war*. 1st ed., (New York: Little, Brown and Co., 2009).

Caestecker, Frank. and Bob Moore, eds., *Refugees from Nazi Germany and the liberal European states*. (New York: Berghahn Books, 2010).

Carey, Arch, *The War Years at Shanghai 1941-45-48*, (New York: Vantage Press, 1967).

Convention of Peking [Beijing] (1860). 2010; Full version of the Treaty signed by Lord Elgin and Kincardine with China]. Available from: Convention of Peking - "The World and Japan" Database (grips.ac.jp).

De Waal, Edmund, *The Hare with Amber Eyes : A Hidden Inheritance*, (London: Chatto & Windus, 2011).

Dong, Stella, *Shanghai: The Rise and Fall of a Decadent City, 1842-1949*. 2000, (New York: HarperCollins, 2000).

Earnshaw, Graham, *Tales of Old Shanghai – The Glorious Past of China's Greatest City*, (Hong Kong: Earnshaw Books, 2012).

Eber, Irene, *Voices from Shanghai : Jewish exiles in wartime China*, (Chicago: University of Chicago Press, 2008).

Eber, Irene, ed. *Jewish Refugees in Shanghai 1933-1947 A Selection of Documents*, Archive of Jewish History and Culture, ed. D. Diner. Vol. 3. (Gottingen: Vandenhoeck & Ruprecht, 2018).

Eisfelder, Horst 'Peter', *Chinese Exile: My Years in Shanghai and Nanking*, (New Haven, CT: Ayotaynu Foundation, 2004).

Emigranten Adressbuch fuer Shanghai 1939: mit einem Anhang Branchen-Register, (Shanghai: The New Star Co., 1995).

French, Paul, *The Old Shanghai A-Z*, (Hong Kong: Hong Kong University Press; 2010).

Grescoe, Taras, *Shanghai Grand : Forbidden Love and International Intrigue in a Doomed World*, (London: Macmillan, 2016).

Harmsen, Peter, *Shanghai 1937: Stalingrad on the Yangtze*. (Havertown, Pennsylvania: Casemate Publishers, 2013).

Heppner, Ernest G., *Shanghai refuge: A Memoir of the World War II Jewish Ghetto*, (Lincoln: University of Nebraska Press, 1993).

Hochstadt, Steve, *Exodus to Shanghai: Stories of Escape from the Third Reich*, (New York: Palgrave Macmillan, 2012).

Kaufman, Jonathan, *Kings of Shanghai*, (London: Little, Brown, 2020).

Kranzler, David, *Japanese, Nazis & Jews: The Jewish Refugee Community of Shanghai, 1938-1945*, (Hoboken, New Jersey: KTAV Publishing House, 1976).

Krasno, Rena, *Strangers Always: A Jewish family in Wartime Shanghai*, (Berkeley, California: Pacific View Press, 1992).

Leung, Yuen-sang, *The Shanghai Taotai: Linkage Man in a Changing Society, 1843-90* (Asian studies at Hawaii), (Honolulu: University of Hawaii Press, 1990).

Lewin, Ossi, Ed., *Almanac - Shanghai 1946/47*, (Shanghai: *The Shanghai Echo*, 1947).

Lindsay, Hugh Hamilton, *Report of proceedings on a voyage to the northern ports of China in the ship Lord Amherst*. 2nd ed., (London: B. Fellowes, 1834).

Margolies, Laura, *Race against time*. Survey Graphic, 1944. 33(3).

Montalto de Jesus, Carlos A., *Historic Shanghai*, (Shanghai: The Shanghai Mercury, Limited, 1909).

Nash, Peter, *Escape from Berlin*, (Edgecliff, NSW: Impact Press, 2017).

Oakes, Vanya, *White Man's Folly*, (Boston: Houghton Mifflin Co., 1943).

Pan Guang, *Eternal Memories: The Jews in Shanghai*, (Shanghai: Shanghai Brilliant Publishing House, 2015).

Pan Guang, *The Jews in China*, (Beijing: China Intercontinental Press, 2005).

Ross, James R., *Escape to Shanghai: A Jewish Community in China*, (New York: The Free Press, 1994).

Scheyer, Moriz, *Asylum: A Survivor's Flight from Nazi-Occupied Vienna through Wartime France*, (New York: Little, Brown and Company, 2016).

Sergeant, Harriet, *Shanghai*, (London: Cape, 1991).

The Shanghai Boom, in *Fortune*, (New York: Time Inc., 1935).

Shaw, Ralph, *Sin city*, (London: Futura, 1986).

Strobin, Deborah and Wacs, Ilie, with Hodges, S.J., *An Uncommon Journey*, (Fort Lee, New Jersey: Barricade Books, 2011).

Treaty of Nanking (Nanking), 1842. 2004 [cited 2016 June 8]; Full version of the Treaty signed by Victoria R]. Available from: www.international.ucla.edu/asia/article/18421.

Wakeman Jr, Frederic, *The Shanghai Badlands: Wartime Terrorism and Urban Crime, 1937-1941*, (Cambridge: Cambridge University Press, 2002).

Wasserstein, Bernard, *Secret war in Shanghai*, (London: Profile, 1999).

Wood, Frances, *No dogs and Not Many Chinese: Treaty Port Life in China, 1843-1943*, (London: John Murray, 1998).

Acknowledgements

I am often amazed at the extent of authors' acknowledgements. Now that I'm writing my own, I understand why. So many people helped me get to this point: I could have added more, had space allowed.

Heartfelt thanks go to readers of my earliest drafts. Their kind and constructive comments encouraged me when I had little idea of what I was doing. In Cambridge, these were my dear friends Martin Hyland, Judith Lennox, Chris and Roger Mann, Antoinette Mitchell, and Ralph Rickards, as well as Debbie Ganz who spotted the limitation of my original title.*

My writing group offered criticism since 2017, both perceptive and brutally honest. When their opinions conflicted, I learnt that you can't please every reader, but must stay true to your instincts. Thanks to Côte, Cambridge, for our regular room.

In London, Geoff Stevens' meticulous analysis picked up inaccuracies I'd glossed over, such as details of Nazi uniforms, and highlighted where my writing 'came to life' (or did not).

In Norwich, Keiron Pim gave me the benefit of his great skill as a mentor in narrative non-fiction. It was at his book launch in January 2016 that I first dared utter the words: 'I am writing a book.' Keiron happens to be my nephew, with a shared interest in our family story. Ian Thomson, like Keiron a mentor at Norwich's National Centre for Writing, gave an inspiring talk on creative non-fiction that taught me a lot.

An early boost came from a phone call from the late Felicity Bryan, who, despite my very premature draft, saw potential in the book. Her advice to put more of 'me' in the story was later repeated by many others. The common mantra was indeed 'fewer facts, more emotion', invaluable advice that went against my previous training as a business writer. Thanks go to my ex-colleagues at Acteon for their continued interest in the project that triggered my slightly early retirement.

Two historians provided essential help in my research: Steve Hochstadt (Emeritus Professor at Illinois College) and Robert Bickers (Professor of History at Bristol). Both have generously given their time and expertise over the years, responding to my continued questions with patience and warmth. Thanks to Doniphan Blair for full use of his interview

---

* *The Bookshop on Bubbling Well Road.*

with Bruno; and to the friendly staff at Cambridge's University Library – I doubt I could have written this book without the UL's incredible resources available to me as an alumna.

Further afield, Horst Eisfelder welcomed me into his Melbourne home to share his experiences as a German refugee in wartime Shanghai. In New York, Richard Feldman reminisced about my aunt and uncle. In Shanghai, Yun Ye guided me around her city and provided many books on China's Jews; Curator Chen Jian of the Shanghai Jewish Refugees Museum greeted me warmly, gifting me a fascinating anthology of refugees' stories.

And now to the literary professionals who turned my dream into reality.

Invaluable editorial advice came from Kitty Walker, and then Christian Livermore at Blue Pencil Agency. Both believed in the book, giving me the confidence to submit it to yet another round of agents.

Which leads me to the person who changed my life, the agent who in November 2021 memorably said: 'It's a yes from me!' Eternal thanks to Tom Drake-Lee at DHH Literary Agency, who 'got' the book (and said such nice things about my writing!). His insightful and diplomatic suggestions re-shaped the draft, and delivered another 'yes' – this time from Clare Bullock, Senior Commissioning Editor at Icon Books. Clare has since provided enormous encouragement and yet more tactful advice. Her sensitive and meticulous editing of the book has transformed my over-referenced story to one with, I hope, wider emotional appeal.

Excellent copy-editing was provided by Seán Costello, and Duncan Heath's thorough proof-reading and Jessica Gailey's excellent indexing completed the work. The images benefited from the scanning skills of Nick Halliday, and Saxon Digital Services (especially Lucy and Graham) performed a vital last-minute rescue.

I must mention a strange coincidence. Clare and I had apparently met, unknowingly, at Keiron's launch event back in January 2016: she had edited his book. Clare had no idea of this family connection when she commissioned mine six years later.

Which brings me to the last group of people to thank.

My family have provided unfailing support. Dan Meller, my elder son and a screenwriter, offered professional-level criticism that contributed to many re-workings of the drafts. My other son, Olly Meller-Herbert, and his wife Diane – as well as Dan's wife Lily – have continued to show enthusiastic interest in my time-consuming obsession. Above all, my husband, Joe Herbert, has read more versions of the book than anyone. He never stopped encouraging me, urging me to keep going despite numerous setbacks. I occasionally even took his advice on my writing.

And finally, thanks to Lisbeth, for bequeathing me her precious box of mementos.

Rachel Meller
Cambridge, November 2022

Index